Toward a Pentecostal Theology of Worship

TOWARD A
PENTECOSTAL THEOLOGY OF
WORSHIP

EDITED BY

LEE ROY MARTIN

CPT Press
Cleveland, Tennessee

Toward a Pentecostal Theology of Worship

Published by CPT Press
900 Walker ST NE
Cleveland, TN 37311
USA
email: cptpress@pentecostaltheology.org
website: www.cptpress.com

Library of Congress Control Number: 2015910591

ISBN-10: 1935931520
ISBN-13: 9781935931522

Dedicated to
Karen Luke Martin
My wife of 40 years, who is always eager to worship God

CONTENTS

INTRODUCTION TO PENTECOSTAL WORSHIP

Lee Roy Martin*

I would argue that worship is the highest occupation of the Church and that worship fulfills the ultimate purpose for which the people of God are redeemed. Not everyone, however, holds such a high view of worship. A few years ago, a young man in his mid-thirties visited the church where I served as pastor. He had recently resigned from a pastorate and had relocated in order to pursue another profession. I called him on the phone that afternoon to invite him back to church, but he informed me that he would not be returning. Disappointed, I asked him if our church had failed in some way. His reply was, 'No, I enjoyed the service as much as anywhere else, but my wife and I have decided that the Church is irrelevant'. This former pastor had come to the conclusion that the Church had become ineffective, without any significant impact upon society; and attendance to worship was, therefore, useless. I encouraged him to help the Church rather than abandon it, but my pleas were unconvincing to this discouraged minister.

While I realize that not all churches are as effective as they could be, many churches *are* vibrant centers of healing and transformation that engage culture and reach out to the community. However, even in the less-engaged churches, is the weekly worship of Almighty God irrelevant? Are the prayers of the saints irrelevant? Are the songs of Zion irrelevant? Is passing on the faith to the children irrelevant? Is reflection on the death and resurrection of Christ irrele-

---

* Lee Roy Martin (DTh, University of South Africa) is Professor of Old Testament and Biblical Languages at the Pentecostal Theological Seminary in Cleveland, TN, USA.

vant? Is the Lord's Supper irrelevant? Is continuing 'steadfastly in the apostles' teaching and fellowship, and in breaking of bread, and in prayers' (Acts 2.42) irrelevant?[1] How should we evaluate the effectiveness of the New Testament character Anna? She was 'a widow, about eighty-four years old, who never departed from the temple, but worshiped (λατρεύω) God with fastings and prayers night and day' (Lk. 2.37). Was her ministry irrelevant? I think of an elderly woman in Wynne, Arkansas, confined to a wheelchair and crippled by a stroke. Whenever I would conduct worship services in the nursing home where she lived, I would ask the people to share a testimony of God's goodness. This precious sister would lift her right hand (the left was paralyzed), and she would attempt to utter praises to God as tears flowed down her cheeks. The stroke made her praises unintelligible, but was her worship irrelevant? I would insist that worship is never irrelevant, in fact, it may be the most relevant thing that we ever do!

Scripture teaches us that genuine worship both glorifies God and witnesses to the world. The Lord declares, 'This people that I have formed for myself shall recount my praise' (Isa. 43.21). The New Testament states a similar sentiment: 'But you are a chosen generation, a royal priesthood, a holy nation, a people for God's possession; that ye should show forth the praises of him who called you out of darkness into his marvelous light' (1 Pet. 2.9). The writer of Hebrews insists that we must 'offer the sacrifice of praise to God continually, that is, the fruit of our lips giving thanks to his name' (Heb. 13.15). In his vision of God's throne, John the Revelator sees the great multitude of those who had been redeemed by the 'blood of the Lamb', and their constant activity is to be 'before the throne of God, and worship (λατρεύω) him day and night in his temple' (Rev. 7.14-15). Worship is relevant; and, therefore, our theology of worship is worthy of consideration and scholarly formulation.

The Pentecostal movement has radically transformed Christianity in the last 100 years. Walter Hollenweger has argued that Pentecostalism's 'most important contribution' to the larger Christian tradition has been in the 'sphere of liturgy and preaching', that is, in

---

[1] In this chapter, quotations from Scripture are the author's translation unless noted otherwise.

the practice of worship.[2] Explaining the phenomenal growth of Pentecostalism, Donald E. Miller and Tetsunao Yamamori write, 'The engine of Pentecostalism is its worship'.[3] It is unfortunate, however, that although Pentecostals have influenced Christian worship practices, we have been slow to take full advantage of our influential position in that arena. It is important to study recent trends in worship, the diversity of styles in worship, changes in musical tastes, and the pragmatics of adopting various liturgical practices. However, we must make the effort to approach these and other aspects of worship from biblical and theological perspectives. The scholarly study of worship is a vital theological task that affects our understanding of the nature and attributes of God, anthropology, soteriology, pneumatology, and eschatology.

Pentecostals have described their movement as a restoration that continues the work of the Reformation, the Wesleyan revival, and the healing movement. Luther restored the doctrine of justification by faith; Wesley restored the doctrine of sanctification; and the healing movement restored the doctrine of healing in the atonement. Then, the Pentecostal revival restored the doctrine of Spirit baptism and spiritual gifts. Pentecostal scholars, therefore, have expended considerable energy in articulating our theology of the full gospel, or fivefold gospel: that Jesus is savior, sanctifier, Spirit baptizer, healer, and soon coming king. However, our theologians, have focused upon the doctrines themselves while, for the most part, taking for granted the context of Pentecostal theology, which is worship. It is in the context of worship that people are saved, sanctified, baptized in the Spirit, healed, and filled with the hope of Christ's coming. Holding to our doctrines on paper is not enough – we must put them into practice if our movement is to have a future.[4]

---

[2] Walter J. Hollenweger, *The Pentecostals: The Charismatic Movement in the Churches* (Minneapolis, MN: Augsburg Pub. House, 1st U.S. edn, 1972), p. 466. Cf. Harvey G. Cox, *Fire from Heaven: The Rise of Pentecostal Spirituality and the Reshaping of Religion in the 21st Century* (London: Cassell, 1996), pp. 139-57.

[3] Donald E. Miller and Tetsunao Yamamori, *Global Pentecostalism: The New Face of Christian Social Engagement* (Berkeley, CA: University of California Press, 2007), p. 23.

[4] Regarding Pentecostalism's inclusion of the charismata in worship, see French L. Arrington, 'Spiritual Gifts as Normative for Public Worship', in R. Keith Whitt and French L. Arrington (eds.), *Issues in Contemporary Pentecostalism* (Cleveland, TN: Pathway Press, 2012), pp. 211-22.

A well-developed theology of worship is needed in Pentecostalism. Pentecostal pastors and evangelists have produced a number of popular level tracts, pamphlets, and books on the subject of worship; and although Pentecostal scholars have addressed the topic of worship in a number of publications, they have yet to develop a Pentecostal theology of worship.[5] The emphasis in Pentecostal worship has been on spontaneity and liberty rather than on liturgy and uniformity. Pentecostalism has no central authority, no official liturgy, no standard prayer book, and no church calendar. These characteristics are not likely to change because we each value our own cultural preferences for certain worship styles and practices. However, with the maturation of the Pentecostal–Charismatic movement comes a need for dialogue that is deeper than discussions of style. Our movement requires extended dialogue regarding a Pentecostal theology of worship.

As the reader has likely discerned, I care deeply about Pentecostal worship. It is that commitment and concern that gave birth to this volume, and while this brief study does not fulfill the need for a fully formed Pentecostal theology of worship, I hope that it makes a useful contribution to the discussion. Contributors to this work include biblical scholars, systematicians, and practical theologians; and I greatly appreciate each contribution. The strength of a multi-authored work is its diversity, but that is also its weakness. The diversity of voices insures creativity of approaches and freshness of ideas. These multiple authors, however, do not speak from a single context, and they do not display an artificial uniformity. It will be left up to the reader, therefore, to put together this Pentecostal theological choir and discern the areas of common thought and commitment.

> *… the true worshipers shall worship the Father in Spirit and in Truth: for the Father seeks such ones to worship him* (Jn 4.23).

---

[5] Cf. Martin Lindhardt, *Practicing the Faith: The Ritual Life of Pentecostal-Charismatic Christians* (New York: Berghahn Books, 2011), p. 1. Many of the Pentecostal published works on worship can be found in the footnotes in the pages that follow.

1

WORSHIP AND THE TORAH

Jerome Boone*

Worship is the vital connection between God and humankind for any significant relationship. Worship is like breath and blood to the human body, absolutely essential to sustaining life. Worship is an event and an experience that draws God and humankind into a real engagement, an engagement that is both transformative and restorative. Worship reshapes and empowers humankind towards God's creational design. God works redemptively through worship to transform God's people and the world in the direction of the consummation of the coming Kingdom. The resulting reality is the parallel existence of the Kingdom of God alongside of and in tension with many socially constructed cultures.[1]

---

* Jerome Boone (DMin, Columbia Theological Seminary) is Chair of the Department of Christian Ministries and Professor of Old Testament and Christian Formation at Lee University, Cleveland, TN, USA.

[1] I approach the topic of worship and the Torah from a lifetime of nurture in the Pentecostal faith tradition. My core discipleship formation was in a traditional Pentecostal community of faith. It radicalized my openness to God and taught me about the transformational power of experiencing the presence of God's Spirit. My college degree was earned in a Pentecostal school. As I continued my theological education, I encountered the evangelical community of faith. It was there that I learned the transforming power of practicing the spiritual disciplines. Lastly, I engaged with the spiritual life of a Reformed community of faith. In this community, I came to a greater appreciation for liturgy in worship and the power of the providential work of God in the world around me. This diverse experience within the Christian community has shaped how I understand worship. I believe worship is the single most important privilege and responsibility for our Christian

James K.A. Smith[2] has described in poignant detail the tensions that exist between the worldview of North American culture and that of the coming Kingdom of God for which God's people are striving. The worldview of culture is centered on humankind, with an emphasis on power and control over others. The worldview of Christ's Kingdom is rooted in the glory of God and service to humankind. All things are done to the end of bringing glory to God. All human interactions are reflective of Martin Buber's concept of I-Thou relationships in which relationships always seek to enable and empower the other while caring for the self as well.[3]

Walter Brueggemann has called attention to the power of religion as revealed in the Hebrew Bible to offer images of a world that counters the realities of the 'presumed' world in which we live. The 'alternative' world is a world intended by God that envisions a different reality than the present one controlled by the power of the empire (i.e. the dominant forces of culture).[4] The people of God, in worship, remember and are shaped by the vision of the alternative world given by God's revelation. In this sense, worship is a 'rite of passage', powered by the liminality of ritual and the work of the Spirit, to transform lives into the lived reality of a world to come. The people of God become a counter culture to the empire to the degree that their values and actions are transformed into the reality that God has imagined for the world. This transformed life enables the people of God to image their God in this present world.

The Torah, or Pentateuch, is a complex composition of the Hebrew Bible. It preserves some of the oldest revelations and traditions of ancient Israel. It also shows evidence of the development of Israel's religious faith over time.[5] There is no scholarly consensus

---

lives individually and corporately. I am grateful for the opportunity to share this study.

[2] James K.A. Smith, *Imagining the Kingdom: How Worship Works* (Grand Rapids: Baker Academic, 2013).

[3] Jack O. Balswick, Pamela E. King, and Kevin Reimer, *The Reciprocating Self: Human Development in Theological Perspective* (Downers Grove, IL: IVP Academic, 2005), pp. 40-49.

[4] Walter Brueggemann, *Creative Word: Canon as a Model for Biblical Education* (Philadelphia: Fortress Press, 1982), pp. 25-32.

[5] John Van Seters, 'Comparing Scripture with Scripture: Some Observations on the Sinai Pericope of Exodus 19–24', in Gene Tucker and Robert Wilson (eds.), *Canon, Theology and Old Testament Interpretation* (Philadelphia: Fortress Press, 1988), p. 111.

on the historical development of Torah.[6] Yet, there is strong consensus on the role of Torah in the life of Israel as a community of faith.[7] The Torah describes the essential formation of Israel's relationship and life with Yahweh, their God. Walter Brueggemann characterizes the role of Torah well – it is '*nomos*' (law), not in a legalistic sense, but more in the sense that sociologists suggest: 'as an articulation of world coherence, as a shaping of reliable order, as a barrier against chaos …'[8] It is in this sense that Torah within the Israelite community of faith 'engages in the construction of a world, the formation of a system of values and symbols, of oughts and mays, of requirements and permissions, of power configurations'.[9] Torah's role is authoritative and constructs a social reality in which Yahweh's people must live. Torah is polemical in that it is 'concerned to build a counter community … counter to every cultural alternative and every imperial pretense'.[10] It is from this canonical and authoritative perspective of Torah that the theme of worship must be explored.

Worship Defined

The discussion of worship in the Torah raises an important issue: what exactly constitutes worship? A biblical definition of worship in both testaments focuses on two activities: (1) 'to bow down' as an expression of respect/submission and/or (2) 'to serve' as an expression of commitment/obligation.[11] David Firth, drawing on key verbs related to worship in Deuteronomy, gives a well-documented advocacy for these two elements of worship.[12] He goes on to argue

---

[6] Samuel E. Balentine, *The Torah's Vision of Worship* (Minneapolis: Fortress Press, 1999), pp. 5-22.

[7] Balentine, *The Torah's Vision of Worship*, pp. 63-70; David G. Firth, 'Worship as Community Creation: Deuteronomy's Vision of Worship', in D.J. Cohen and M. Parsons (eds.), *In Praise of Worship: An Exploration of Text and Practice* (Eugene, OR: Wipf and Stock, Publishers, 2010), p. 7; Brueggemann, *The Creative Word*, pp. 14-39.

[8] Brueggemann, *The Creative Word*, p. 19.

[9] Brueggemann, *The Creative Word*, p. 20.

[10] Brueggemann, *The Creative Word*, p. 27.

[11] William D. Mounce, 'Worship', in William D. Mounce (ed.), *Mounce's Complete Expository Dictionary of Old and New Testament Words* (Grand Rapids: Zondervan, 2006), pp. 810-11.

[12] Firth, 'Worship as Community Creation', pp. 5-6.

that worship 'finds expression in both specific events and lifestyle commitments'.[13] Van Seters calls attention to the emphasis on exclusivity of service in the worship of God.[14] In the context of the book of Exodus, the tension is between serving Pharaoh and serving Yahweh. In the broader context of Torah, the tension is between serving Yahweh as opposed to serving other gods (Exod. 20.3-6).

David Peterson contends that an understanding of worship as restricted to the cultic gathering of God's people for rite and proclamation will not do. Consequently, he offers a broader perspective on worship. Peterson proposes 'worship of the true and living God is essentially *an engagement with Him on the terms that He proposes and in a way that He alone makes possible*'.[15] Peterson's perspective on worship is very appropriate for dealing with Torah. Allen Ross offers a definition of worship that complements that of Peterson but adds more specificity about worship activities in the Torah. He constructs a complex definition of worship based on his extensive exploration of the topic in the Bible. He contends:

> True worship is the celebration of being in covenant fellowship with the sovereign and holy triune God, by means of the reverent adoration and spontaneous praise of God's nature and works, the expressed commitment of trust and obedience to the covenant responsibilities and the memorial reenactment of entering into covenant through ritual acts, all with confident anticipation of the fulfillment of the covenantal promises in glory.[16]

Many key aspects of worship can be seen in Ross' definition. First and foremost, the nature of worship is a transitive verb. It denotes an action directed toward someone. The 'someone' in the Torah is the one, true, living God. As D.A. Carson points out, what is most important about worship is its direct object.[17] Second, worship presupposes relationship between God and the worshiper. Third,

---

[13] Firth, 'Worship as Community Creation', p. 4.
[14] Van Seters, 'Comparing Scripture with Scripture', p. 30.
[15] David Peterson, *Engaging with God: A Biblical Theology of Worship* (Downers Grove, IL: InterVarsity Press, 2002), pp. 19-20 (emphasis original).
[16] Allen Ross, *Recalling the Hope of Glory: Biblical Worship from the Garden to the New Creation* (Grand Rapids, MI: Kregel Publications, 2006), pp. 67-68.
[17] D.A. Carson (ed.), *Worship: Adoration and Action* (Eugene, OR: Wipf and Stock Publishers, 1993), p. 15.

the content of worship is 'celebration' of both the personal relationship and God's nature and works. Fourth, worship anticipates an on-going relationship with God in the context of divine blessing. In this sense, worship fulfills the goal of both creation and redemption of humankind. Ross' definition exceeds the realization of blessing expected in the Torah. Divine blessing from the Torah's perspective is understood much more in the context of this lifetime rather than the second advent of Christ Jesus. Nevertheless, Peterson and Ross define worship in complementary ways that provide a comprehensive description of worship depicted in the Torah.

More recently, Daniel Block has engaged in the task of constructing a biblical theology of worship.[18] He offers this concise definition: '*True worship involves reverential human acts of submission and homage before the divine Sovereign in response to his gracious revelation of himself and in accord with his will*.'[19] Block's definition is more general than that of Ross but is sufficiently detailed to get at the essentials of authentic worship.

Worship cannot occur in a vacuum. It must take place within the context of a worldview or metanarrative. The Torah articulates that worldview. In a reciprocal manner, worship perpetuates that worldview. Samuel Balentine[20] offers an attractive structure for discussing the worldview articulated in the Torah in relation to the theme of worship. He understands Exodus 19–Numbers 10 as the core narrative about worship. The key focus is the Sinai covenant (Exodus 19–24) and Israel's engagement with Yahweh on God's terms and in ways that He alone makes possible. The covenant relationship solidified in liturgy and ritual at Mt. Sinai led to the construction of the Tabernacle as a means for Yahweh to dwell among the people (Exodus 25–40). The maintenance of the covenant relationship required ongoing rituals, many of which are described in Leviticus 1–Numbers 10. An important context for understanding the core narrative of the Torah is given as a prelude in Genesis 1–Exodus 18. The prelude defines God's sovereignty over all that exists in heaven and earth and the role of humankind in the created world. It also emphasizes God's demand for righteousness and hu-

---

[18] Daniel I. Block, *For the Glory of God: Recovering a Biblical Theology of Worship* (Grand Rapids, MI: Baker Academic, 2014).

[19] Block, *For the Glory of God*, p. 29.

[20] Balentine, *The Torah's Vision of Worship*, pp. 59-77.

mankind's failure to be righteous. The divine selection of Abraham and his progeny reveals a plan for redeeming humankind. The exodus was God's rescue when the injustices of Egypt threatened to destroy the plan. On the other side of the core narrative is an important story about what happens when relationship with Yahweh is broken because of unfaithfulness (Numbers 11–Deuteronomy 34). The apex of this narrative is Deuteronomy, which calls for renewed commitment to covenant stipulations (chs. 29–30). Renewed commitment leads to renewed promises of life and blessings for the future.

Balentine's structure of the Torah presents a comprehensive and coherent worldview for Israel. Yahweh is the sovereign lord of all creation. Israel is Yahweh's chosen people to image God to a fallen world; thus, the vocational call to be a priestly kingdom and a holy nation (Exod. 19.6). Yet, when Israel fails in its vocational call, Yahweh is compassionate and forgiving; therefore, hope for the future renews life and blessings. This metanarrative is the appropriate context for exploring the theme of worship in the Torah.

The Christian community of faith – the Body of Christ – shares Israel's metanarrative in many ways. It too, believes that God created the world and all it contains. It embraces the truth that in God's creational design, humanity is to be God's partner in managing the creation. It realizes that the intrusion of sin into the creation frustrated God's creational design. Yet, it understands that God is working redemptively through God's people to counter the effects and consequences of sin and evil. The Christian community sees itself as heir to the role of God's people in the redemptive work of God. Therefore, almost all that is said about worship in the Torah is relevant to Christian worship. The book of Hebrews powerfully parallels the new covenant in Jesus Christ with the Torah covenant at Mt. Sinai. The book of 1 Peter clearly describes the Christian community as the people of God: 'But you are a chosen race, a royal priesthood, a holy nation, a people for God's own possession, so that you may proclaim the excellencies of Him who has called you out of darkness into His marvelous light'[21] (1 Pet. 2.9; compare Exod. 19.5-6). Worship is the response of God's people to who God is

---

[21] In this chapter, quotations from Scripture are from the New American Standard Bible unless noted otherwise.

and what God has done. Worship described in the Torah is instructive for worship in the Christian community today.

God: The Focus of Worship

Who is Israel's God? God for Israel is known by many names, the most important of which are Elohim and Yahweh. First of all, Elohim/Yahweh is the creator of the heavens and the earth and all that exists (Genesis 1–2). The poetic liturgy of creation in Gen. 1.1-2.4 gives the details. The liturgy begins with a description of the world in chaos: it is 'formless and void'; darkness and water covered the earth (1.2). God addressed the chaos and transformed it. Step by step, order emerged. Unexpectedly, the liturgy of creation reveals something extraordinary about humankind; they are made 'in the image of God' (Gen. 1.27). Humankind has a unique relationship with both God and the world. They are image-bearers of God and have the responsibility to partner with God in the management of creation (Gen. 1.27-28). They have divinely authorized responsibility to preserve wellbeing (*shalom*) in the creation. As Block points out, the faithful fulfillment of this task is 'worship'.[22]

The Torah testifies to the fact that God is not only creator of the heavens and the earth, but he is also creator of Israel. This is another essential aspect of the metanarrative that forms the context of Israel's worship in the Torah. God chose Abram (Abraham) and his descendants to be God's partners in preserving the true knowledge of God among humankind (Genesis 12–17). God as deliverer is the most revolutionary characterization of Yahweh in the Torah.[23] God is the deliverer and the exodus is the event. The story is the most decisive in all the Hebrew Bible for Israel's conceptualization of Yahweh. The story became paradigmatic in Israel's history. It was a paradigm of hope.

Yahweh the deliverer flows naturally into another epithet for God as the redeemer. Both concepts play an important role in Israel's worship. The two words are rooted in the reality of deliverance. The idea of redeemer may have a greater sense of relationship. Within the context of community, redeemer carried the sense of

---

[22] Block, *For the Glory of God*, p. 39.
[23] Walter Brueggemann, *Theology of the Old Testament: Testimony, Dispute and Advocacy* (Minneapolis: Fortress Press, 1997), pp. 173-81.

responsibility of a kinsman or a blood relative – see the concept of *goél* (גֹּאֵל), the kinsman redeemer.[24]

In the context of worship, both deliverance and redemption are powerful motivations of praise. The social reality constructed by the exodus affected all future generations of Israel. So, it was always appropriate in every generation to give thanks for the exodus. Remembering God's mighty acts is not only a celebration of the past; it is an anticipation of the future.[25] The God of Israel was defined by past events. Those acts of deliverance suggested future help in similar times of crisis. The prophecies during the Babylonian exile are clear evidence of this, especially Isaiah 40–55.[26]

The most essential characteristic of Yahweh is holiness. Yahweh is holy. As Pierce says, holiness is more than just an attribute, holiness is what makes God who He is and is also the result of His being God. It is the essence of His being and the element through which we must interpret all other attributes.[27] The concept of holy is so complex and used in such a variety of ways in the Torah that it is difficult to define. The basic idea of 'holy' is that of being unique, set apart or dedicated to a specific purpose.[28] From a moral and ethical perspective, holiness is related to purity and righteousness. As a descriptor of quality, holiness relates to perfection and sinlessness.

The most pervasive characteristic of God in the Torah, as well as throughout Scripture, is relationality. God is relational to the core of His being. Walther Eichrodt[29] developed his entire *Theology of the Old Testament* along the theme of covenant. The two-volume work was profoundly 'relational' in its perspective. More recently, Terence Fretheim has illuminated the relational nature of God in *God and World in the Old Testament: A Relational Theology of Creation.*[30] A signifi-

---

[24] R. Laird Harris, 'גאל' in R.L. Harris, G.L. Archer, and B.K. Waltke (eds.), *Theological Wordbook of the Old Testament* (Chicago: Moody Press, 1980), I, pp. 144-45. See Isa. 41.14; 43.14; 44.6, 24; 47.4; 48.17; 49.7, 26; 54.5, 8.

[25] Van Seters, 'Comparing Scripture with Scripture', pp. 28-31.

[26] Walter Brueggemann, 'Crisis Evoked, Crisis-Resolving Speech', in *Biblical Theology Bulletin* 24 (Fall 1994), pp. 95-105.

[27] Timothy M. Pierce, *Enthroned On Our Praise: An Old Testament Theology of Worship* (ed. E.R. Clendenen; Nashville, TN: B&H Academic, 2008), p. 45.

[28] Ross, *Recalling the Hope of Glory*, p. 43.

[29] Walther Eichrodt, *Theology of the Old Testament* (Philadelphia, PA: Westminster Press, 1961).

[30] Terence E. Fretheim, *God and World in the Old Testament: A Relational Theology of Creation* (Nashville, TN: Abingdon Press, 2005).

cant observation by Fretheim is that God–human relationships precede covenant relationships. Covenants do not typically establish relationships; instead, they 'seem designed to provide a firm grounding within which an already established relationship can appropriately develop'.[31]

The Pentecostal and holiness aspects of the Christian church offer a beneficial perspective on the holiness and relational nature of God. They emphasize that covenant with God through Jesus Christ is a 'beginning'. The salvation experience establishes a relationship with God in which believers strive for holiness (sanctification) and service. Christians in these faith traditions take seriously God's word: 'Speak to all the congregation of the sons of Israel and say to them, "You shall be holy, for I the Lord your God am holy"' (Lev. 19.2), and 'but like the Holy One who called you, be holy yourselves also in all your behavior; because it is written, "You shall be holy, for I am holy"' (1 Pet. 1.15-16). They strive to be holy in their lifestyles as a necessary pre-requisite to Holy Spirit baptism. Spirit baptism is seen as empowerment for witness to the good news of Jesus Christ. While holiness is understood as commuted by God through faith in Jesus Christ, it is also experienced in the work of the Spirit in an ongoing process of being holy.

Israel: The Worshiping Community

Worship and Mt. Sinai Covenant

Exodus 19.6 is a fundamental text for Israel's worship. The text is dense and loaded with implications about Israel's purpose, role in the world, relationship with God and destiny. The very issues that constitute a worldview or metanarrative are compressed into this text. The identity of Israel is stated succinctly: a priestly kingdom and a holy nation. The narrative that precedes it anticipates it. The narrative that follows it expands upon it. Covenant and worship are essential themes that support it. The bold statement is both prescriptive and descriptive. It prescribes what Israel will be going forward. It also describes the logical consequence of the Abrahamic covenant (Genesis 12–17). The descendants of Abraham, the people delivered from Egyptian bondage, the mass of humanity now

---

[31] Fretheim, *God and World in the Old Testament*, p. 15.

assembled at the base of Mt. Sinai (Mt. Horeb), have come to a watershed event. The event will define not only the present generation but all generations to come. Israel, the promised descendants of Abraham and Sarah, is drawn into a new covenant relationship with Yahweh.

The Christian community is likewise defined by the Christ event. It too, is drawn into a new covenant with God. The new covenant in Christ defines the identity, purpose, role in the world, and destiny of the Christian community. Peter's declaration is prescriptive for who the Church of Jesus Christ will be: a royal priesthood, a holy people, God's chosen possession, a people called to proclaim the excellencies of the God who calls humankind out of the darkness of sin to the marvelous light of God's righteousness. These are the people who rise up to worship the God of creation, deliverance, redemption, holiness, and covenant relationality. The motives for worship are abundant and, yet, new every day as God works redemptively in our lives and our world.

Exodus 19–24 focuses on the covenant ceremony for Yahweh and Israel. For years, scholars have illuminated the parallels between this pericope and components of typical ancient Near Eastern treaties.[32] The scholarly focus on covenant in this text has overshadowed another key reality found in this narrative: worship. Moses' demand of Pharaoh was that he let Israel go and 'worship' their God in the wilderness (Exod. 7.16). The narrative begins with a declaration about Yahweh's mighty acts and follows with stipulations for Israel's obedience. Israel responds with a pledge to be loyal to Yahweh and obey the demands. The Decalogue (Exodus 20) and Book of the Covenant (Exodus 21–23) follow as the content of the covenant stipulations. The covenant ceremony is ratified and concluded in Exodus 24.

The covenant narrative 'melds into a coherent whole the twin concerns of covenant and holiness'.[33] These two themes dominate the Torah's vision of worship. Authentic worship requires both covenant obedience and holiness; the two aspects of worship cannot be separated. It is the covenant that strengthens the relationship between God and God's people. The partnership reiterates the orig-

---

[32] George E. Mendenhall, 'Covenant Forms in Israelite Tradition', in *Biblical Archaeologist* 17.3 (1954), pp. 50-76.
[33] Balentine, *The Torah's Vision of Worship*, p. 122.

inal design of creation. God chose humankind to 'image' God in the world (Gen. 1.26-28). The partnership was broken as a consequence of sin and disobedience. The Sinai covenant restores that partnership with a portion of humankind – the descendants of Abraham and Sarah. It will be Israel's vocation as a priestly kingdom and a holy nation to image God to the world.[34] The new covenant in Christ Jesus extends that covenantal vocation to all humankind. Covenant obedience and holiness will be what shapes the 'imaging' of the true God. The prophets understood this destiny given to Israel (Isa. 42.6; 49.6). The vocation is a call to be counter-cultural. It is a call to preserve the knowledge of the true God among humankind.

The covenant ceremony initiated in Exod. 19.3-8 is finalized in chapter 24. The covenant is ratified in the context of worship. An altar is built at the base of Mt. Sinai. Burnt offerings and peace offerings are sacrificed symbolizing total devotion and fellowship with Yahweh. The covenant stipulations are declared to the people and they respond with an oath of obedience. God's word to Israel proclaimed through Moses defines what service Yahweh requires. Service is a key aspect of worship. The proclamation at Mt. Sinai clarifies how Israel will serve Yahweh. The declaration of the covenant stipulations reveals how Israel will participate in the restoration of God's creational design. Humankind was commissioned at creation (Gen. 1.26-28) to be God's partner in managing the creation. Sin destroyed that partnership. Israel will be God's covenant partner to re-order chaos in the social sphere.[35] The restoration of creational design whereby God's will is done on earth will bring glory to God. This is indeed, true worship.

In conjunction with the discussion of covenant and worship, it is important to emphasize that acceptable worship does not require a covenant relationship. Robert Webber discusses the covenantal nature of biblical worship.[36] He builds a composite definition of worship as a result of identifying and discussing specific components of

---

[34] Balentine, *The Torah's Vision of Worship*, p. 123; see also Block, *For the Glory of God*, p. 43.

[35] John Hilber, 'Theology of Worship in Exodus 24', *Journal of the Evangelical Theological Society* 39.2 (1996), pp. 177-89 (p. 186).

[36] Robert E. Webber, *Worship Old and New: A Biblical, Historical, and Practical Introduction* (Grand Rapids, MI: Zondervan, 1994), pp. 22-25.

biblical worship. He concludes, 'biblical worship that is rooted in an event, expressed as a covenant, characterized by a book, and ratified by sacrifice is to occur at specific times and places'.[37] While Webber's statement is biblically accurate, there is concern that it suggests that acceptable worship must occur in a covenantal context. Such is not the case. Abel (Genesis 4) offered proper sacrifice and worship apart from any covenant relationship. Clearly, Abel had a relationship with God, but it is not ever specified as covenantal. Cornelius (Acts 10–11) had a 'relationship' with God supported by a devout life, prayer, and reverence for God before he developed a covenantal relationship with God through Jesus Christ. Covenant is important in relationship with God because it intensifies the relationship and creates an environment in which the relationship can grow. The outcome is that worship matures, becoming even more faithful and a richer experience. What is clear is that covenant relationship is the *telos* (goal) towards which God draws humankind.

Allen Ross[38] and Michael Farley[39] are typical of those who find significance in the Mt. Sinai covenant worship event for Christian worship services. The key participants in the worship event are God, Moses, priests, elders, and the people of Israel. God is the focus of worship. Moses, the priests, and elders are leaders among the people who facilitate the worship event. The people of Israel are the primary worshipers (along with Moses, priests, and elders) at the event. It is God who summons Israel to the covenant relationship, calling the nation to be special people, a priestly people and a holy nation (Exod. 19.5-6). 'Today, as members of the new covenant, we are also a "chosen people, a royal priesthood, a holy nation, a people belonging to God"' (1 Pet. 2.9; Rev. 5.10).[40] The calling to be a priestly people for the rest of the world includes teaching the Word of God, intercessory prayer, and making provision for others to have access to God through atonement.[41] Obedience to this calling would make God's people a blessing to the rest of the world, a fulfillment of a key promise of the Abrahamic covenant.

---

[37] Webber, *Worship Old and New*, p. 25.

[38] Ross, *Recalling the Hope of Glory*, pp. 173-80.

[39] Michael A. Farley, 'What is Biblical Worship? Biblical Hermeneutics and Evangelical Theologies of Worship', *Journal of Evangelical Theological Society* 51.3 (Sept. 2008), pp. 591-613 (pp. 606-10).

[40] Ross, *Recalling the Hope of Glory*, p. 173.

[41] Ross, *Recalling the Hope of Glory*, p. 174.

The call to worship requires preparation. The people of God must prepare themselves through purification (Exod. 19.10-15). The holiness of God, God's essential attribute, is being emphasized. As Christians prepare for worship, they must have made preparation by way of repentance.[42] To repent is to abandon a life of habitual sin; it is to accept forgiveness of sin based on the atoning sacrifice of Jesus Christ. As Israel extended into covenant commitment at Mt. Sinai, burnt offerings and peace offerings were made to God (Exod. 24.5). The burnt offerings symbolized total dedication. The peace offerings indicated that the worshipers were at 'peace' with God. This is just what Paul had in mind when he writes in Rom. 5.1: 'Therefore, having been justified by faith, we have peace with God through our Lord Jesus Christ'. Acceptable worship comes from those who have dedicated themselves to God's character and mission and who are at peace with God.

A very important aspect of the Mt. Sinai event is the declaration of God's Word (Exod. 24.3-4, 7). The revelation of God was not only declared at Mt. Sinai, it was also recorded. The written record is referred to as the 'Book of the Covenant' (Exod. 24.7). The Book of the Covenant would be read and its message declared many times over the centuries of Israel's history. Portions of the book were taught to the people by the Levites on a regular basis. The entire book was to be read during the Feast of Tabernacles in every sabbatical year (Deut. 31.9-13). It is not difficult to see a parallel here to the declaration of the Word of God in the New Covenant in Jesus Christ. A primary activity of Jesus was revealing God's new covenant message in word and deed. The gospel writers preserved that revelation of God. Matthew, in particular, seems to have preserved large amounts of the teachings of Jesus. The revelation of God in Jesus Christ became the foundation of apostolic preaching and writing. When the church gathers today, 'God speaks to us in the reading and preaching of his word in Scripture, which transforms us and re-consecrates our lives …'[43]

The counterpart to the declaration of God's word at Mt. Sinai was the response of God's people: 'All that the Lord has spoken we will do, and we will be obedient!' (Exod. 24.7). Such a commitment,

---

[42] Block, *For the Glory of God*, pp. 55-80. Daniel Block discusses this issue more comprehensively than space will allow here.

[43] Farley, 'What is Biblical Worship?', p. 607.

led to the consecration of the people in a ritual ceremony (Exod. 24.8). After the commitment, representatives of the people participated in a covenant meal in the presence of God (Exod. 24.9-11). The obvious parallel to the covenant meal at Mt. Sinai is the Lord's Supper or Eucharist. Regarding this parallel, Ross says, 'Jesus in the upper room inaugurated the new covenant with people who were likewise committed to following him, saying similarly, "This is my blood of the [new] covenant"'.[44] The communion meal is a sacred event in which Jesus is both the host and the substance of the event.[45] The meal and the worship experience focus on both remembrance and promise. It remembers God's mighty acts. For Christians, the most significant act of history is the redemptive death of Jesus Christ. For Israel at Mt. Sinai, it was the exodus from Egyptian bondage. The promise aspect of worship and covenant centers on blessings. For Christians, it is the promise of Jesus' return (Acts 1.9-11), and the blessed hope of the Kingdom of God fully come. For Israel, it was the promise of peace in a land flowing with milk and honey.

Worship as Renewal

The book of Deuteronomy concludes the Torah with an openness to the future. Historically, it is the fortieth year after the exodus (Deut. 1.3). Much had happened during the interval between the covenant/worship event at Mt. Sinai (Exodus 19–24) and the opening narrative of Deuteronomy. Deuteronomy is about new beginnings. It is situated at the end of an era of wilderness wandering and divine judgment. It introduces an era of divine grace and covenant renewal. Deuteronomy is a powerful narrative about hope for the future in spite of human failure. It is perhaps, the single most important component of the worldview articulated by the Torah. It constitutes a core revelation about Yahweh that will give hope to Abraham's progeny time and time again. Deuteronomy and its message of hope is a vital part of the final form of the Torah which took shape hundreds of years after the Mt. Sinai covenant. It is a call to reclaim a vocation to be a priestly kingdom and a holy nation, a challenge that loomed large in the post-exilic era of Persian hegemony.

---

[44] Ross, *Recalling the Hope of Glory*, p. 179.
[45] Farley, 'What is Biblical Worship?', p. 607.

The literary form of an ancient Near Eastern covenant treaty in the overall structure of Deuteronomy has been recognized since the seminal work of George Mendenhall.[46] The book opens with a summary of Yahweh's relationship with Israel since Mt. Horeb (Deuteronomy 1–4). The narrative contrasts the faithfulness of Yahweh with the unfaithfulness of Israel. It tells of the beginning of the conquest of Canaan to the east of the Jordan River. The summary ends with strong warnings about the consequences of covenant violations. The bulk of the book of Deuteronomy (5–26) reiterates the revelation and covenant stipulations given at Mt. Horeb with a number of additional statutes and ordinances. A covenant ceremony is described and prescribed (27–28) for when Israel will occupy the core territory of Canaan. Yet, a covenant renewal is actualized in the land of Moab (29–32) before Moses dies. Deuteronomy ends with Moses' blessings for each of the tribes of Israel and the account of his death (33–34).

The Decalogue (Deuteronomy 5) is the key to understanding worship in Deuteronomy. The vision of Israel as a priestly kingdom and a holy nation is grounded in the commandments. First and foremost, worship demanded exclusive loyalty to God and God alone (Deut. 5.7). Balentine argues for the centrality of the Sabbath commandment in the Decalogue.[47] He contends that Sabbath is central to worship. It is, in his opinion, the critical intersection between God and humankind in the Decalogue, especially the Deuteronomic version.[48] On the one hand, Sabbath is a remembrance of creational design. God rested on the seventh day (Gen. 2.2-3). Sabbath is important for remembering and celebrating God as creator. On the other hand, Sabbath must be 'kept' (Deut. 5.15). This is a call to obedience. It reflects the redemption of the exodus and celebrates God as redeemer.[49] The people of God must image their redeemer by extending rest and freedom from labor to others on the Sabbath. Sabbath is a time for worship of God with implications for how God's people treat others. Commandments five through ten give substance to how God's people should treat others.

---

[46] Mendenhall, 'Covenant Forms in Israelite Tradition', pp. 50-76.
[47] Balentine, *The Torah's Vision of Worship*, pp. 186-98.
[48] Balentine, *The Torah's Vision of Worship*, p. 190.
[49] Balentine, *The Torah's Vision of Worship*, p. 189.

The ethical demands of the Decalogue for social justice underscore how significant the treatment of others is for worship. Worship of God and righteous living in community with humankind are inseparably connected. The demand for Sabbath has already foreshadowed this reality. The remaining six commandments address justice issues necessary for community: respect for parents as well as prohibitions against murder, adultery, theft, lying, and covetousness. The commandments are specific to key issues for the maintenance of community. They also set a trajectory for the stipulations that follow. Justice is complemented by benevolence in the goal of seeking wellbeing (*shalom*) for all. The tithe (Deut. 14.22-29) is God's portion and must be used to support both God's ministers – Levites – and the poor and marginalized. The sabbatical year (Deuteronomy 15) must be a year of release from mandatory labor and debt. There must be designated officials to ensure justice in the land: judges, priests, kings, and prophets (Deut. 16.18–18.8). There must be cities of refuge to provide a safe haven for the innocent (Deuteronomy 19). The spirit of the ethical demands of the Decalogue is captured in the admonition given to the officials charged with the responsibility of administering justice in Israel:

> You shall not distort justice; you shall not be partial, and you shall not take a bribe, for a bribe blinds the eyes of the wise and perverts the words of the righteous. Justice, and only justice, you shall pursue, that you may live and possess the land which the Lord your God is giving you (Deut. 16.19-20).

Deuteronomy draws to a close with a focus of covenant renewal (Deuteronomy 27–32). Balentine characterizes this section of Deuteronomy as the 'ever new, ever renewing summons …'[50] It is what Israel needed many times in their checkered relationship with Yahweh. Israel's future depended on Yahweh's willingness to continue a fragile relationship often marred by Israel's infidelity. Israel's hope is not to be found in anything humanly possible. Hope for Israel is found in God alone. Anticipated breaches in covenant faithfulness will be remedied by God's grace: 'Moreover the Lord your God will circumcise your heart and the heart of your descendants, to love the Lord your God with all your heart and with all your soul, so that

---

[50] Balentine, *The Torah's Vision of Worship*, p. 202.

you may live' (Deut. 29.14-15). Such a hope was not only rejuvenating to the second generation after the exodus; it was the hope of all future generations of Abraham's progeny.

Deuteronomy makes a special contribution to the theme of worship with its emphasis on loving and worshiping God wholeheartedly. The focus on heart (לֵב) is reflective of the Hebrew concept of heart as the core of a person's being. Bob Wetmore illustrates the complexity of the Bible's concept of heart.[51] The heart is the place of thinking, trusting, rejoicing, planning, and the exercising component of the will. The greatest commandment of the Bible, noting the significance of the heart, occurs among the admonitions in Deut. 6.4-5: 'Hear, O Israel! The Lord is our God, the Lord is one! You shall love the Lord your God with all your heart and with all your soul and with all your might.' All three of the Synoptic Gospels record Jesus' reference to it (Mt. 22.37; Mk 12.29; Lk. 10.27). The significance of the heart, from a biblical perspective, is quite evident in the contest with Pharaoh (Exodus 4–14). Many times the narrative describes Pharaoh's opposition to Moses and God as the work of a hardened heart (e.g. Exod. 4.21; 8.15, 19). Worship activities, apart from whole-hearted dedication to God is always unacceptable. The prophet Amos was outspoken about such false worship in his day:

> I hate, I reject your festivals, nor do I delight in your solemn assemblies. Even though you offer up to Me burnt offerings and your grain offerings, I will not accept them; And I will not even look at the peace offerings of your fatlings. Take away from Me the noise of your songs; I will not even listen to the sound of your harps. But let justice roll down like waters and righteousness like an ever-flowing stream (Amos 5.21-24).

Rituals and ceremonies never constitute worship in and of themselves. It is only in conjunction with whole-hearted commitment to God that the worship activities are meaningful.

Deuteronomy 10.12-13 is a key passage for understanding what God wants from God's people:

---

[51] Bob Wetmore, *Worship the Way It Was Meant To Be* (Eugene, OR: Wipf and Stock, 2003), pp. 56-61.

Now, Israel, what does the Lord your God require from you, but to fear the Lord your God, to walk in all His ways and love Him, and to serve the Lord your God with all your heart and with all your soul, and to keep the Lord's commandments and His statutes which I am commanding you today for your good?

Loving and serving God whole-heartedly is central to the answer. The text answers the important question using five verbs: (1) *fear* the Lord your God, (2) *walk* in all His ways, (3) *love* Him, (4) *serve* the Lord your God, and (5) *keep* the Lord's commandments and His statutes. This combination of demands encapsulates the message of Deuteronomy, especially as it relates to the worshipful human response to divine grace. Worship is more than ritualistic activity; it is more than sentimental feelings; it is more than good intentions. It is a whole-hearted commitment to love, reverence, obey, and serve God.[52] Worship requires exclusive relationship that orders all other commitments and priorities in a lesser way. In Jesus' words, 'seek first (in priority) God's Kingdom and God's righteousness ...' (Mt. 6.33). Only a resolve rooted and grounded in the heart will be able to support such a relationship.

Transformation: the Outcome of Worship

The Torah's perspective is that 'worship enables both a linguistic and a gestural construal of God's creational design'.[53] The linguistic element is expressed most prominently in the statutes and ordinances of the Sinai and Moab covenants. The covenant liturgy involves rhetoric, conveyed through speech, which 'has the capacity to speak new worlds into existence'.[54] The covenant speech works to create standards of justice which protect the poor and powerless. Shalom for all is the goal. The gestural aspect of worship reinforces the creation of an alternative world through symbolic acts. It is the rituals that create liminality that sponsors transformation. Liminality is the realm of the Spirit's work. It is described as that place in the change process that is between the reality of the presumed world

---

[52] Block, *For the Glory of God*, pp. 102-105.
[53] Balentine, *The Torah's Vision of Worship*, p. 238.
[54] Balentine, *The Torah's Vision of Worship*, p. 238.

and the prospect of the world to come. Victor Turner[55] pioneered anthropological studies on the importance of this transitional stage in changed behavior. Turner's work does not address the work of the Holy Spirit, but other studies from a Christian perspective have illuminated the significance of ritual and liminality for spiritual transformation.[56] The rituals were 'vitally important for the realization of the faith community's identity and vocation'[57] as a priestly kingdom and a holy nation (Exod. 19.6). They continue to serve the same function in the Christian community.

Nancy Ault contends that those of us who 'gather to publically worship God … are more than worshippers. We become participant learners.'[58] It is through worship that we are shaped and grow in our own faith. Worship is most effective when it connects with the heart (emotions), the mind (intellect), and the body of worshipers as a whole. Constance Cherry[59] is an advocate for carefully crafted worship experiences because she recognizes the powerful transforming influence that worship can have on Christians. She discusses at length the four major movements of a mainline Protestant liturgy: Gathering, Word, Table, and Sending. Each part must be done with intentionality in order to maximize the potential of worship to change lives. Verbal communication through singing, preaching, and praying are important aspects of a worship service. However, authentic worship experiences exhaust the limits of linguistic communication. Encountering the eternal and transcendent God demands images, signs, and symbols.[60] Yet, transformation requires more than well-planned liturgy; the real issue is, 'Do we allow the transforming power of the Spirit into our worship and into our lives?'[61] Liturgy and rituals are essential to worship but the Spirit is the true agent of transformation.

---

[55] Victor Turner, *The Ritual Process* (Ithaca, NY: Cornell University Press, 1969), p. 241.

[56] R. Jerome Boone, 'Community and Worship: Key Components of Pentecostal Christian Formation', *Journal of Pentecostal Theology* 8 (1996), pp. 135-42.

[57] Balentine, *The Torah's Vision of Worship*, p. 238.

[58] Nancy Ault, 'Worship as Information, Formation and Transformation', in Cohen and Parsons (eds.), *In Praise of Worship*, p. 177.

[59] Constance Cherry, *The Worship Architect: A Blueprint for Designing Culturally Relevant and Biblically Faithful Services* (Grand Rapids, MI: Baker Academic, 2010), pp. 35-122.

[60] Ault, Worship as Information, Formation and Transformation', p. 181.

[61] Ault, Worship as Information, Formation and Transformation', p. 189.

'The Torah envisions a truth about God and the world that successive generations of the community of faith have found to be especially pertinent for life at the border between past and future.'[62] The book of Deuteronomy in particular, depicts a people who must face the future in a radically different way than their community has dealt with life in the past. The Torah ends with openness to the future depicted by Deuteronomy. Failure and unfaithfulness characterize the past. The community of faith stands at the border to Canaan. Deuteronomy is the call to transformation. It is a call to covenant renewal. It is a call to obedience and blessing, a call to change for the future in order to re-create God's design for creation. The border is a place of liminality, 'betwixt and between' the past and future. In James Loder's[63] paradigm, it is a time of 'scanning'. It is a time to choose the 'holy' with new self-identity and responsibility. Balentine describes it as 'the "generative center" in the social drama of world-making'.[64] The Spirit works in the liminal space to create a community unregulated by social class and power structures. The transformed community of faith is released from the structures of the presumed world in order to create a new world, a world of God's own design. It is a passage from life dominated by the 'real' world to one directed by the values of the 'really real' world of God's design. The 'Torah's vision of worship summons all who would embrace its truth to love God absolutely and to live in the world in such a manner that this love is manifested in concrete deeds and acts'.[65]

The Torah prescribes a priesthood of persons who play a special role within the community of faith (Leviticus 8–10). These priests serve the community of faith in ways that support the overall *Missio Dei* in the world. However, it is the community of faith that is the primary agent of executing God's mission. The Protestant principle of the priesthood of all believers is grounded in this vision. To be Israel was a vocational call to be a priestly kingdom and a holy nation. Even though the vision and promise never quite actualized, it is indicative of the plan of God. The important issue is just what

---

[62] Balentine, *The Torah's Vision of Worship*, p. 240.
[63] James E. Loder, *The Transforming Moment* (Colorado Springs, CO: Helmers & Howard, 2nd edn, 1989), pp. 35-91.
[64] Balentine, *The Torah's Vision of Worship*, p. 241.
[65] Balentine, *The Torah's Vision of Worship*, p. 244.

was it that the Torah expected of the people of God? What was it that God envisioned for God's people?

Priests are people who are facilitators. They live and work at the boundary between the holy and the common, between the clean and the unclean. They 'extend the claims of the holy to the everyday so that the realm of God's presence on earth is enlarged and enhanced'.[66] They proclaim the revelation of God to others in word and deed. They image God in the very way that they live. At the crucial border between the holy and the common, they seek to sponsor the work of the Holy Spirit that transforms lives toward the image of God's creational design (Gen. 1.26-29). Priests set boundaries between the clean and the unclean. They live holy lives apart from immorality, deceit, covetousness, vulgarity, and corruption. They are people of personal piety and integrity. They take seriously God's command: 'You shall be holy for I the Lord your God am holy' (Lev. 19.2). When the people of God transformed to become those who come to faith in Jesus Christ, the expectation of their priesthood was unchanged (1 Pet. 1.16).

Holiness, as envisioned in the Torah, is not limited to personal purity. Holiness also includes righteousness and justice. Along with the demand to be 'holy' is the command 'you shall love your neighbor as yourself' (Lev. 19.18; Mt. 19.19; Mk 12.31-33). The Torah understands the propensity of human nature to be self-centered. It presupposes that humankind will seek its own wellbeing (*shalom*). The command requires that humankind be just as concerned about the wellbeing of others as it is about self. Therefore, do not murder, do not steal, do not commit adultery, do not lie to others, and do not strive for the possessions of others (Exodus 20; Deuteronomy 5). Moreover, the Torah has a special concern about the wellbeing of the poor and marginalized. Special laws about allowing a portion of each season's harvest for the needy provides for a necessary food supply (Deuteronomy 24).

The bottom line is that worship re-centers the world according to God's will. Worship is what shapes God's people into the priestly kingdom and holy nation that God desires. Worship is formative for priestly character and action. Worship generates the vision of the world of creational design. Worship is a call to enact the holi-

---

[66] Balentine, *The Torah's Vision of Worship*, p. 175.

ness of God. Worship motivates humankind to construct a reality of the world to come. In a real sense, it is this alternative reality to the presumed reality of culture that is what is 'really real' even if it is not seen with human eyes.

2

THE BOOK OF ISAIAH AND PENTECOSTAL WORSHIP

Jacqueline Grey[*]

The use of Scripture by early Pentecostals has been of increasing interest within contemporary scholarship. For some, such as Larry McQueen and Ken Archer, earlier Pentecostal readings have been utilized to highlight the hermeneutic of the embryonic movement.[1] In one sense, these scholarly works represent the search to uncover the 'heart' or theological values of the early Pentecostal community. These scholars have plumbed the depths of the recent past to provide a guide and prescription for current explorations of a viable Pentecostal hermeneutic. Within this approach, early readings have also been employed to highlight the development and evolution of Pentecostal hermeneutics from the grassroots.[2] Other scholars, such as Melissa Archer, have explored early Pentecostal readings of biblical texts to consider a history of effects; particularly the role of

[*] Jacqueline N. Grey (PhD, Charles Sturt University) is Associate Professor of Biblical Studies at Alpha Crusis College, Sydney, Australia.
[1] Larry R. McQueen, *Joel and the Spirit: The Cry of a Prophetic Hermeneutic* (JPTSup 8; Sheffield: Sheffield Academic Press, 1995), and Kenneth J. Archer, *A Pentecostal Hermeneutic for the Twenty-First Century: Spirit, Scripture and Community* (JPTSup 28; London: T&T Clark, 2004).

[2] See Jacqueline Grey, *Three's a Crowd: Pentecostalism, Hermeneutics, and the Old Testament* (Eugene, OR: Pickwick Publications, 2011).

Scripture in informing Pentecostal theology and practice.[3] Archer's work presents a survey of the literature of the early Pentecostal community in Northern America to see how their understanding of worship was influenced by the texts depicting worship in the Apocalypse of John. This present study combines both approaches. First, I will present a critical analysis of early Pentecostal readings of Isaiah; specifically readings that explore the topic of worship. This includes highlighting passages from Isaiah utilized to discuss the idea of worship as referenced in the literature of early Pentecostals in Australia. This analysis will provide a *description* of early Pentecostal perspectives of worship as understood through the lens of Isaiah. Secondly, I will discuss some of those same passages from Isaiah identified by the early Pentecostal readers to explore additional elements of worship (not highlighted by the earlier readers) that might speak to the current Pentecostal community. Utilizing texts from Isaiah, this analysis will explore the theme of worship to provide a *prescription* for the contemporary Pentecostal community to develop our understanding of worship. By looking backwards and forward through the lens of Isaiah, I hope to offer some contribution towards the development of a Pentecostal theology of worship.

Description of Early Pentecostal Approaches to 'Worship' through Readings of Isaiah

While it is difficult to identify with exactness the period of 'early' Pentecostalism in Australia, for the purposes of this project it will be defined generally as the period prior to the establishment of the now major national denomination,[4] the Assemblies of God in Australia (AG in Australia) in 1937. Pentecostalism prior to the formation of the AG in Australia was essentially a loose allegiance of

---

[3] Melissa L. Archer, 'The Worship Scenes in the Apocalypse, Effective History, and Early Pentecostal Periodical Literature', *Journal of Pentecostal Theology* 21 (2012), pp. 87-112. Archer surveys publications from the Wesleyan-Holiness and in the Finished Work traditions of the USA from the first ten years (1906–1916) of the Pentecostal Movement.

[4] Although there are various opinions as to whether Pentecostal groups such as the Assemblies of God in Australia such be referred to as a 'denomination' or 'movement', for the purposes of this paper I will hereafter refer to it as a 'denomination' unless quoting an author that specifically refers to it as a 'movement'.

individual churches and small groups. However, one major factor in the developing unity of these groups which eventually led to the formation of formal associations was the publishing of two key journals and sermon material from influential figures of that period in Australia. In the early years of Pentecostalism in Australia, there were two main journal publications that were distributed nationally. The first of the major journal publications was the *Good News* journal; a ministry of the Good News Hall, one of the first Pentecostal churches (based in Melbourne) led by 'Mother' Sarah Lancaster. The journal ran from 1913 to 1935. During the majority period of the publication there were no national denominational ties, rather fellowships were loosely affiliated through relational networks.[5] During this formative period, the Good News Hall was arguably the most influential church in Australia, primarily because of the publication and national distribution of this journal. The *Good News* journal featured articles, testimonies, and reports by Australian writers as well as articles from overseas centers of Pentecostalism of that time, including Keswick, Azusa, and South Africa. Unfortunately the *Good News* journal faded after the death of Lancaster in 1934 and eventually ceased circulation in 1935.[6]

The second major journal publication in this period classified as early Australian Pentecostalism was the *Glad Tidings Messenger*, later re-named as the *Australian Evangel*. This journal ran from 1927 to 1987 and was to become the official journal of the Assemblies of God in Australia. Again, while it contained articles, testimonies, and reports by Australian writers it also contained articles from other centers of global Pentecostalism, increasingly from the *Evangel* journal of the Assemblies of God (USA). These two journals represent the majority of literature produced by Australian Pentecostals in this formative period from the birth of Pentecostalism in Australia until the formalization of a national denomination in 1937. In addition to

---

[5] Shane Clifton, *Pentecostal Churches in Transition: Analysing the Developing Ecclesiology of the Assemblies of God in Australia* (Leiden: Brill, 2009), p. 57. As noted above, the Assemblies of God in Australia (the largest national Pentecostal group) was established in 1937. It is noted that prior to the establishment of the Assemblies of God in Australia in 1937 that there were various former formal links established among some Pentecostal churches, not least among them the Apostolic Faith Mission of Australasia in 1926.

[6] For a description of controversial ministry of Sarah Jane Lancaster, see Clifton, *Pentecostal Churches in Transition*.

the two journals, there were some limited sermon materials published in Australia. While there were various publications available of sermon material by Pentecostal preachers from around the world during this time, this study will focus only on those publications by Australians, or sermon material by non-Australians delivered in and published in Australia.

These journals and sermon material provide a rich repository of literature which assists contemporary scholars in describing the ethos and worldview of early Pentecostalism in Australia. This includes examination of the topics, issues, and concerns explored in the journals of interest to the early Pentecostals.[7] The specific texts from Isaiah highlighted by the early Pentecostal writers provide an indication of the values and emphases of the fledgling community. The texts from Isaiah were utilized by the early Pentecostal periodical writers primarily for the presentation of thematic or topical studies rather than for exegetical work. The articles highlighted in this study are mostly thematic studies that included or incorporated the topic worship, or where worship was referred to explicitly or implicitly. While other articles in these two journals may have referred to Isaiah, they have not been highlighted in this study as they were not referring (explicitly or implicitly) to worship. With this in mind, let us now turn to the study of the theme of worship in these journals and particularly the use of texts from Isaiah in these topical studies.

The interests of the early Pentecostal writers, as presented in their use of texts from Isaiah in their writing on the general topic of 'worship', can be summarized as concerns for true worship (referencing Isaiah 1 and 2), encountering God (referencing Isaiah 6 and 61), and defending the Pentecostal distinctive of speaking in tongues (referencing Isaiah 28). While some writers focused specifically on one of these concerns, others combine these interests. One such example is Rev. Dr. F.B. Meyer, described as a 'Minister, evangelist and Keswick promoter'.[8] In his sermon entitled 'With Thee is the Fountain of Life', published in 1923 from the collection of ser-

---

[7] It is insightful to examine both what these pioneers were interested in, as well as *not* interested in; however, an exploration of the absence of topics is, unfortunately, beyond the scope of this study.

[8] See http://webjournals.ac.edu.au/authors/f-b-meyer/. According to Professor of History, Mark Hutchinson, 'Meyer had quite an influence on early Pentecostals in Australia (especially Good News Hall), even though he himself was not a Pentecostal' (personal correspondence).

mons he preached during his tour of Australia, Meyer explored the topic of 'true worship'. He wrote:

> True worship, such as God seeks, must emanate from the spirit of worship. Is it irreverent to suppose that on each Lord's Day the Divine Spirit moves eagerly through cathedrals and churches, searching for loyal and true hearts that are offering the incense of the heart's love, the rhythm of their accordance with His Own? It may be that He turns away from many of our anthems and prayers, which please the taste but never reach beyond the vaulted roof. It might be well, at this point, to read Isaiah 1.[9]

From this reading of Isaiah 1, Meyer then goes on to say 'True Religion is the union of the Spirit of God with the spirit of man in and through Jesus Christ'. While it is unknown if there was a specific section of Isaiah 1 that Meyer read in his sermon, we can surmise several points. The reference to Isaiah 1 in this discussion of 'true worship' emphasizes the concern of Meyer to challenge the hearers not just to attend worship services or go through the ritual of worship but to have the right heart motivation. As Isaiah critiqued the Judean community for the empty form of their worship (particularly Isa. 1.10-17), so Meyer critiques the empty worship of his contemporary community. What Meyer draws from Isaiah 1 is that the people are worshiping, – for Meyer, they are attending the cathedrals and churches at this time just as Isaiah's community were attending the Temple to offer their sacrifices and incense – but their hearts are far from God. However, while Isaiah emphasizes that the reason for this rejection of their worship was due to the corruption and social injustice prevalent in the Judean community of that time, it seems for Meyer that this rejection of their worship is due to their lack of unity with the Holy Spirit. If the people want their worship to rise beyond the 'vaulted roof' they must engage in 'true worship'. This true worship is understood as the incense of 'the heart's love', being in rhythm with the Spirit and based on union with the Spirit. Utilizing this reading of Isaiah 1, Meyer is defining true worship as

---

[9] F.B. Meyer, 'With Thee is the Fountain of Life', http://webjournals.ac.edu. au/journals/HOM/meyer-f-b/6-with-thee-is-the-fountain-of-life/. This sermon collection was published in 1923 by Varleys Publishers, Melbourne and distributed in Australia.

an affective engagement with the Spirit through Jesus Christ and not determined by form or location.

The concern for true worship is also expressed in the 1924 *Good News* journal entitled 'The Coming Collapse of Civilisation'. The unknown author utilized Isaiah 2.12-17 to highlight the absence of proper acknowledgement of God in the broader society that they predict will result in the fall of present government structures:

> A collapse is predicted in the Word of God. There is one certain source to which men may turn, if they will, for an answer to their grave questionings. The Scriptures make very plain what is to be the end of the present form of society, and they declare in solemn tones the utter ruin and overthrow of the governmental structures of the whole world. One need only turn to Isaiah 2: 12-17 to see what is to be the end of things as they now are, in the coming Day of Jehovah.

The writer then goes on to quote the Isaiah passage directly from the Webster's Bible translation, inserting their own comments in verse 15: 'and upon every lofty tower (Eiffel, Woolworth) …'[10] The concern raised by the writer is understood as an issue of worship precisely because of the reference to and quotation of Isaiah 2. The text of Isaiah 2 emphasizes the pride and arrogance of those who exalt themselves above God and their consequential destruction. It is specifically due to the absence of correct worship of Yahweh and attitude of self-sufficiency that Isaiah announces the coming humiliation and devastation of the Judean community. The writer of this article identifies the words of Isaiah 2 as speaking directly to the global community of 1924,[11] reading Isaiah's prediction of the destruction of the Judean community as a prediction of the collapse of global post-WWI governments. The writer announces the severe consequences for this rejection of the worship of God. Instead, they look with eschatological hope and urgency for the Parousia, described in Isaian language as the 'coming Day of Jehovah'.

---

[10] Unknown, 'The Coming Collapse of Civilisation' *Good News* 15.8 (August 1924), http://webjournals.ac.edu.au/journals/GN/gn-vol-15-no8-aug-1924/06-the-coming-collapse-of-civilisation/

[11] No doubt influenced by the post-war context, this 'prediction' is interestingly published prior to the Great Depression of the 1930s.

In contrast to the concern for the absence of worship, early Pentecostal writers also emphasized positive examples and approaches to worship. In particular, the worship described in Isaiah 6 is highlighted as a constructive model of true worship. Rev. Dr. F.B. Meyer in his sermon 'The Dynamic of Pentecost' says,

> One of the best methods of quickening the life of the spirit is Worship. The repetition of Isaiah's Thrice-Holy, or of the Gloria in Excelsis, or of any of the outbursts of adoration recorded in the Book of Revelation, will at once bring us into contact with the world of reality.[12]

Ironically, having previously criticized empty form and ritual, Meyer provides a formula for entering into an attitude of worship. He recommends the replication and repetition of the chant by the attendants in the throne room of heaven[13] to assist the present worshiper to enter into worship. However this worship has the purpose of spiritual engagement or direct union with God (perhaps allowing Meyer's readers to fast-track to join the seraphs who are already in the throne room and presence of Yahweh). Meyer emphasizes that this spiritual realm, rather than the physical world, should shape our reality. It is also important to note at this point, that like the previous readings of Isaiah by early Pentecostals, the object of worship is Jesus Christ. Meyer equates the object of Isaiah's worship (Yahweh) with the object of worship in the Apocalypse of John, namely Jesus Christ. Yet, despite providing this formula for worship (by repetition of the liturgy of the Seraphs), Meyer attempts to capture the spontaneity and sincerity of the worship identified in the biblical texts. These are not empty repetitions but an 'outburst' of adoration, reflecting a key feature of enthusiasm often associated with Pentecostal worship. It seems the aim of Meyer is to guide his hearers toward a dynamic encounter with God, to enter the throne room, and commune with the Holy God.

Encountering God is a common topic and theme among early Pentecostal writers. For the embryonic community, this encounter with God inevitably resulted in doxology. Worship in this sense, is

---

[12] F.B. Meyer, 'The Dynamic of Pentecost', http://webjournals.ac.edu.au/journals/HOM/meyer-f-b/3-the-dynamic-of-pentecost/.

[13] Walter Brueggemann, *Isaiah 1–39* (WBC; Louisville, KY: Westminster John Knox Press, 1998), p. 58.

identified as a proper response to the revelation of God. This is reflected in a short story written by William Luff, entitled 'From Darkness to Light', as published in the 1935 *Glad Tidings Messenger.* In his story, the protagonist witnesses the funeral of Hope; but at the open grave, a beam of sunlight falls on the coffin. The story then continues:

> The blackness rolled back, the birds sang, the sun shone splendidly, and Jesus stood in our midst, saying, 'The Spirit of the Lord God is upon me; because the Lord hath anointed me to preach good tidings unto the meek; he hath sent me to bind up the broken-hearted … to give unto them beauty for ashes, the oil of joy for mourning, the garment of praise for the spirit of heaviness' (Isaiah 61:1-3).
>
> And at once a song burst forth –
>
> 'Jesus, my God, I know His name,
> His name is all my trust: Nor will He put my soul to shame
> Nor let my hope be lost'.
>
> So Hope was not dead after all! False hope may die, but God's Hope is immortal, and as I went away I caught myself singing a second hymn …[14]

In this story, the protagonist has a vision of Jesus Christ, who quotes Isaiah 61 (no doubt also an allusion to Luke 4). The result of this encounter or vision of Jesus Christ is worship. A song of praise and adoration bursts spontaneously from the protagonist as hope is restored. The text from Isaiah is utilized to encapsulate the work of Jesus in reversing the darkness (of sin, depression, etc.) to a new hope. Jesus is the recipient of the worship, as he is identified by the protagonist as the agent of transformation described by Isaiah. The spontaneous song is one of confidence, trust, and peace in the salvation of Jesus Christ. Similar to Meyer, the text of Isaiah is utilized to cause or stimulate worship. The story concludes with the protagonist continuing the enthusiastic worship with a second spontane-

---

[14] William Luff, 'From Darkness to Light' *Glad Tidings Messenger* (February 1935), http://webjournals.ac.edu.au/journals/AEGTM/gtm-1935-february/from-darkness-to-light-story/.

ous song. This emphasizes the concern of early Pentecostals for encountering God, which results in a newness of worship.

Among the early Pentecostals there was an expectation of a move of the Spirit in which God would be encountered. This expectation included the empowering of the Holy Spirit and endowment with spiritual gifts, none the least being the gift of speaking in tongues. The spiritual gifts, including speaking in tongues, tended to be experienced or practiced as part of the public worship service. This particular gift was generally considered the 'initial evidence' of the baptism in the Spirit. New members of the community would 'tarry' until this evidence of the Spirit was received. Upon receiving the gift of speaking in tongues, recipients would then rest from their tarrying – for that evening, at least! The emphasis on the gift of speaking in tongues was controversial within the broader Christian community at that time, as indicated by the proliferation of literature by early Pentecostals defending this experience in their worship services. Seeking biblical texts to validate their experience of speaking in tongues in their worship and community, the writers in this early period sometimes turned to Isaiah 28. Two such apologists were Stanley H. Frodsham and George Burns. In his 1929 article entitled "Interdenominational or Pentecostal?', published in the *Good News* journal, Frodsham wrote:

> And so we are not inter–Methodist–Congregationalist–Unitarian–Episcopalian–Seventh-Day–Adventist–Mormon–Etcetera–Etcetera–Etcetera. We are just plain Pentecostal people, belonging to that crowd of people who speak in other tongues, the crowd that are everywhere spoken against. David did not compromise with Michal when she rebuked him for dancing before the Lord. He told her, 'And I will yet be more vile than this.' And when the Lord comes forth with His 'strange work,' and His 'strange act' promised in Isaiah 28:21, it is possible that some us may do some things that are 'yet more vile' than speaking in tongues.[15]

Frodsham's argument subtly emphasizes key characteristics of early Pentecostal worship, including comparing the spontaneous and sin-

---

[15] S.H. Frodsham, 'Interdenominational or Pentecostal?', *Good News* 20.11 (November 1, 1929), http://webjournals.ac.edu.au/journals/GN/gn-vol20-no11 -nov-1929/15-interdenominational-or-pentecostal/.

cere worship of David's dancing with their own spontaneous speech of 'other tongues'. The argument also highlights the marginalization of early Pentecostals from the broader religious community; they were ridiculed as Michal ridiculed David. However, in aligning the early Pentecostal community with the scandalous behavior of David, they provide a heroic model of innocent suffering. Frodsham then connects the 'strange' behavior of the early Pentecostal community with the text of Isa. 28.21. While Isa. 28.21 speaks of a new and strange act of God, it is a message of threat to the recalcitrant Judean leadership for making a 'covenant with death', most likely an alliance against Assyria with Egypt.[16] It is not a positive passage! However, for Frodsham, it is an affirmative prediction of the outpouring of the Spirit among this embryonic Pentecostal community.

Another early Pentecostal writer who utilized Isaiah 28 for the defense of his Pentecostal experience, albeit from a different section of the chapter, was George Burns. As the first President of the Apostolic Faith Mission in Queensland, he wrote in the 1929 *Good News* journal:

> His outpoured Spirit here is God's proof that His blessed Son is there, seated and glorified at His Father's right hand. Jesus said: 'If I go not away the Comforter will not come, but if I depart I will send Him unto you,' and here, beloved friends, is the Comforter speaking to seventeen different nationalities of the wonderful works of God, revealing His presence in the very way that God hath said by the mouth of the prophet Isaiah that He would: 'With men of other lips and other tongues will I speak unto this people, yet for all that will they not hear Me, saith the Lord.' Isa. 28:11, 1 Cor. 14:21.
>
> Beloved, people criticise our speaking in tongues, and nickname it the 'Tongues Movement.' Listen! It was God Who said: 'I will speak unto this people with stammering lips and other tongues.' It was God, the Holy Ghost, Who spoke on Pentecost Day. God spoke, beloved, and God speaks still in the same way. 'This

---

[16] Brueggemann *Isaiah 1-39*, p. 227; John Goldingay, *Isaiah* (NIBC; Peabody, MA: Hendrickson, 2001), pp. 154-55.

is the rest and this is the refreshing' says God, 'Wherewith I will cause the weary to rest.' Isa. 28:12.[17]

Though not writing explicitly of worship, this article is included in the present study as it is a defense of the phenomenon and practice of speaking in tongues in the Pentecostal worship service. As noted above, throughout chapter 28, Isaiah is critiquing the Judean leaders for trusting in their 'covenant with death'. As the leaders would not listen to the guidance of Yahweh from the prophet's own message, Isaiah warns them that they will instead learn the hard way by hearing this message through the judgment of invasion from those that speak a different language ('stammering lips and other tongues'); most likely referring to a possible Assyrian invasion. He implores them to place their trust in Yahweh instead, who provides rest rather than place their trust in this unauthorized alliance. Again, it is a negative prediction in the original context that is read in a positive light by the early Pentecostal readers for their context. In this sense, Isaiah 28 acts as a proof text to validate their experience and theology. By use of this text, Burns attempts to transform a criticism of the community into a fulfillment of biblical prophecy. Burns identifies the 'stammering lips and other tongues' as being fulfilled on the Day of Pentecost (Acts 2) and continuing to be fulfilled by the current Pentecostal communities. As the Spirit was promised, so it has been received; the people can then enter the rest offered in Isaiah. It is through tarrying in the Spirit to receive the gift of tongues that rest and refreshing can be found. Yet, the use of Isaiah 28 by the early Pentecostal community does highlight important theological concepts valued by this community, particularly the democratization of the Spirit and the prophethood of all believers to hear God's voice.

In summary, it can be observed that early Pentecostal perspectives of worship as understood through the lens of Isaiah emphasize an affective engagement with the Spirit. Formal liturgies were critiqued and abandoned as empty worship in preference of spontaneous and therefore (supposedly) sincere expressions of worship. Of importance to most writers in this formative period of Pentecos-

---

[17] George Burns, 'We Preach: A Presidential Address' *Good News* 20.1 (March 1, 1929), http://webjournals.ac.edu.au/journals/GN/gn-vol20-no3-march-1929/10-we-preach-presidential-address/.

talism was the need for personal and dynamic encounter with God – to enter the throne room and meet with the Holy God. As we turn to consider the contribution of Isaiah to the future of worship within the Pentecostal community, it is interesting to note that many of these same values identified as important to the early Pentecostals are also identified as important to the current Pentecostal community globally. In a study of the charismatic, or spirit-filled, worship of young people in Scotland, Ward and Campbell made the following observation:

> There was a noticeable emphasis on the need or desire for youth to have the freedom to express themselves openly in their personal or corporate worship. The inference was that through worship – defined as shouts of praise to God along with spontaneous singing or dance/movement – would change the individuals present as well as youth across the nation.[18]

Theology-making occurs through the songs, testimonies, and the sharing of experiences with God.[19] While the opportunity for congregants to share spontaneously from the platform is decreasing in some Pentecostal churches, this informal 'theology-making' through songs and testimonies still occurs, albeit by the sharing of a chosen few. As Alvarado writes, 'The tenets of Pentecostal worship which are, in part, Spirit movement, passionate praise, emotional release, and spiritual gifts in operation, make its expression a transformative, vibrant, and moving encounter with the divine'.[20] It seems that the original values of early Pentecostal worship have been maintained by the subsequent generations. However, the question begs to be asked: what may the future hold?

---

[18] Peter Ward and Heidi Campbell, 'Ordinary Theology as Narratives: An Empirical Study of Young People's Charismatic Worship in Scotland', *International Journal of Practical Theology* 15 (Dec 2011), p. 231.

[19] W. Ma, 'Pentecostal Worship in Asia: Its Theological Implications and Contributions', *Asian Journal of Pentecostal Studies* 10.1 (2007), p. 151.

[20] Johnathan E. Alvarado, 'Worship in the Spirit: Pentecostal Perspectives on Liturgical Theology and Praxis', *Journal of Pentecostal Theology* 21 (2012), p. 139.

Prescription of Possible Pentecostal Approaches to 'Worship' through Readings of Isaiah

In this second section, I will explore through a brief discussion of these same texts from Isaiah some other concepts of worship, not highlighted in the earlier Pentecostal readings, which might contribute to the developing theology of worship within the Pentecostal community. Reflection on the description of worship adopted in the past provides a platform for prescribing an imagined and hoped-for future of worship. The concepts from Isaiah that will be explored in this section as a prescription for the Pentecostal community can be summarized as the link between worship and social justice (referencing Isaiah 1 and 2), the link between worship and poetic language (referencing Isaiah 6 and 61), and the development of worship in non-Western contexts (Isaiah 28) as indigenous approaches forge new ways of doing worship. These texts of Isaiah provide a potential contribution and possibility to shape the life and theology of the worshiping communities of global Pentecostalism.

While the origins of Pentecostalism were in many social contexts associated with the poor and marginalized (such as the Azusa Street mission) and birthed from socially-concerned Holiness movements, Pentecostals have generally tended to focus on evangelism to the detriment of social welfare. It may be surmised that the middle-class aspirations of these earlier generations have been realized as much of Pentecostalism in western contexts is now considered 'mainstream'.[21] Yet, within global Pentecostalism, the majority of adherents remain in contexts of poverty.[22] The current context of globalization means that the plight of the poor can no longer be ignored. In response, there has in recent years been a developing trend for Pentecostals (from diverse contexts including the Majority world or 'global south') to engage in public debate and advocating for social

---

[21] There is no doubt that the broader social acceptance of Pentecostals was aided by the charismatic movement and embracing of the Spirit by many in mainline denominations.

[22] For example, at least 80% of the world associate membership of the classical Pentecostal denomination 'Assemblies of God' are in the Majority World. See Allan Anderson, 'Towards a Pentecostal Missiology for the Majority World', *Asian Journal of Pentecostal Studies* 8.1 (2005), p. 30.

justice, including a practical concern for the poor.[23] This concern is not just for charitable acts but also to engage the systems that produce this situation of poverty. Yet while this concern has been explored in our public theology and practical mission, it has not been explored in connection to Pentecostal worship. As Cartledge observes, 'Questions regarding the political and structural issues in society are never addressed in worship; therefore worship does not spill out into the community with a view to changing the power structures'.[24] Yet, what might the connection between social justice and worship look like for the future Pentecostal community? The prophet Isaiah provides a model. In Isaiah 1, the prophet challenged the community of 'haves' to remember and associate with the 'have-nots' in their worship (particularly Isa. 1.10-17). By consideration of the plight of the poor during their Temple worship, the affluent worshiper was challenged to shift their frame of reference from being ego-centric to community-centric. In addition, Isaiah critiqued the worshiping Judean leadership for their personal responsibility and contribution to the suffering of the poor and marginalized, and called them not only to repent but reform. If we were to apply this model to the current Pentecostal community it might look like a shift from worship focused on individual needs and personal encounter with God to a more community-minded approach where the poor and persecuted are remembered in prayer and their needs incorporated into the worship. It invites those in contexts of comfort to join in the suffering of those that receive hostile treatment from political, religious environments. The worship service then becomes less about 'I' and 'me', but 'us' and 'we'; even those not physically present among the congregants. It also challenges those who benefit from the global and local power structures that keep the poor in their poverty to repent and reform. In this way, the 'haves' not only remember and associate with the

---

[23] An example of this is the recent publication of a position paper by the World Assembly of God Fellowship on a Pentecostal Theology of Compassion. See http://worldagfellowship.org/wp-content/uploads/2009/11/Pentecostal-Th eology-of-Compassion-WAGF-Position-Paper-Final-Revised-Version-from-1-Ma y-2012-with-new-cover.pdf

[24] Mark J. Cartledge, *Testimony in the Spirit: Rescripting Ordinary Pentecostal Theology* (Surrey: Ashgate Press, 2010), p. 45.

'have-nots' but also turn from their self-sufficiency to place their trust in God, rather than their own resources (Isa. 2.12-17).

Yet, it is difficult for worshipers in contexts that promote materialism and ego-centric behaviors to re-orientate their frame of reference to embrace others. Isaiah 6 provides a possible pathway to achieving this unselfing. In Isaiah 6, the prophet had a vision of the beauty and terror of Yahweh in the throne room that re-orientated him from a state of self-absorption to a state of 'opiated adjacency'. As Isaiah experienced this de-centering, he was motivated to repair the injustices he identifies in his community.[25] According to Alvarado, 'worship is a participatory event within which one loses him or herself'.[26] In this vision, Isaiah was absorbed into the holistic experience of sight, sound, touch, and smell in the throne room of Yahweh. However, I would like to consider briefly not just the role of the vision of Yahweh as an object of beauty, but the role of the oral contribution of the seraph in helping create this environment of worship. The 'repetition of Isaiah's Thrice-Holy' vocal performance aided the experience of the sublime in Isaiah 6. As described in Isa. 6.3-4, it is not just Isaiah that is impacted by this doxological cry of the seraph; the whole heavenly Temple itself responds with shaking and trembling to this oral expression. While the exploration of the power of the spoken word has been of historic interest to many Pentecostals, most controversially as a technique of some prosperity preachers to 'name it and claim it',[27] I would like to consider briefly the effect of the poetic expression such as the doxological cry of the seraph and the beauty of poetic speech.

Poetic language has the potential for creating beauty through words.[28] It is a creative and artistic expression using carefully crafted speech. The elevated language mirrors the elevation in subject and

---

[25] For a full exploration of this approach, see Jacqueline Grey, 'Beauty and Holiness in the Calling of Isaiah', in Lee Roy Martin (ed.), *A Future For Holiness: Pentecostal Explorations* (Cleveland, TN: CPT Press, 2013), pp. 47-56.

[26] Alvarado, 'Worship in the Spirit', p. 147.

[27] This is particularly associated with the Word of Faith expression of Pentecostalism.

[28] This could include either poetry or poetic prose. While the definition and even existence of poetry in the Hebrew Bible is debated, this study is not advocating for either position but acknowledging the use of poetic language or elevated speech in the Hebrew texts. For a more comprehensive discussion see the classic text: Robert Alter, *The Art of Biblical Poetry* (New York, NY: Basic Books, 1985).

feeling through the heightening of emotion. While meter and rhythm are not always obvious, the rhythmic flow of words delights the ear of the hearer. Like a vision of beauty, poetic language has the capacity to de-centre the hearer. While I am not aware of any formal studies regarding the connection between the use of poetic or elevated language in rhythmic flow and 'anointed' preaching or prophetic utterances, I hazard a guess that within Pentecostal circles there is a connection. Pentecostal preaching and reading of Scripture is more interested in creating a transformation (or encounter with God) than explanation.[29] Elevated language contributes to this experience of the sublime, perhaps as it mimics the transcendence of God. However, the concern to maintain the spontaneous and sincere worship of Pentecostalism may threaten the use of carefully crafted speech. Instead, there needs to be a balance – the requirement being sincerity. If there is a reliance on prepared speech, this does raise the issue of the role and use of formal liturgy within Pentecostal worship. According to Hollenweger, Pentecostalism can either move towards a formalization of worship with written liturgy and formal style, or it can discover a 'post-literary liturgy' with a focus on non-written texts such as testimonies and choruses.[30] While this disregards the wealth of poetic literature written in early Pentecostalism, such as the poems and stories found in the journals of the embryonic community, it also perhaps misrepresents the non-spontaneous crafting of the songs and speech that are used in wor-

---

[29] Melugin notes,

> Those who shaped the book of Isaiah (and other prophetic books as well) were not primarily interested in representing historical reality or depicting accurately the original meanings of earlier traditions that they used, but were fundamentally concerned with using language performatively or transformationally, namely, to shape or transform the life of the faith community. They used language more to do something that to explain or represent reality.

See Roy F. Melugin, 'Isaiah in the Worshipping Community', in M.P. Graham, R. Marrs, and S. McKenzie (eds.), *Worship and the Hebrew Bible: Essays in Honour of John T. Willis* (JSOT 284; Sheffield: Sheffield Academic Press, 1999), p. 250.

[30] Cartledge, *Testimony in the Spirit*, p. 44. Cartledge writes,

> By maintaining its oral roots, rather than attempting to become like traditional forms of Christianity (and perhaps resisting the 'textualisation' of Evangelicalism; cf. Smith, 1997), Pentecostalism will continue to connect with the majority of people who function, or prefer to function, within oral rather than literary media. In Hollenweger's view, it is this orality that will continue to facilitate the global spread of Pentecostalism.

ship services and disregards the increasingly reliance upon literacy in some Pentecostal (particularly western) contexts. There is a place for the deliberate and non-spontaneous crafting of beautiful, poetic speech to inspire and capture the imaginations of worshipers as well as a place for spontaneous worship. The newness that the utilization of poetic language, artistic forms, and creative expression bring is important for the vitality of future Pentecostal worship as we seek to trade 'beauty for ashes' (Isa. 61.3).

The opportunity for creative approaches and new artistic forms to revitalize Pentecostal worship can also be found by looking in non-Western contexts to provide new ways of doing worship. The possibility of sharing indigenous methods of creative expression is available to future Pentecostals more than any other group within Christianity. As Anderson notes, 'The "southward swing of the Christian center of gravity" is possibly more evident in Pentecostalism than in other forms of Christianity'.[31] Pentecostal worship is highly contextualized and its outworking, or practice, looks very different in diverse locations according to the social context. While this needs discernment to consider the appropriateness of adopting some indigenous forms of expression and ensuring that syncretism is not encouraged, this should not be approached out of a sense of superiority, as though Western forms of worship are not cultural. Non-western approaches to worship can and should also contribute to the developing theology of Pentecostal worship. For example, Wonsuk Ma emphasizes a typical Asian approach to worship. He writes,

> In Pentecostal worship, there is a high expectancy of experiencing God. Both 'expectancy' and 'experience' can immediately prompt enthusiastic responses. God is never abstract, but concrete; He is never static, but dynamic. And particularly to Asians, a deity is always acting, either bringing curses or blessings, thus constantly interacting with humans, deeply involved in human affairs.[32]

This and other perspectives are essential for scholars to consider in the development of a global Pentecostal theology. A corollary of

---

[31] Anderson, 'Towards a Pentecostal Missiology for the Majority World', p. 30.

[32] Ma, 'Pentecostal Worship in Asia', p. 141.

this is the importance of the development of Pentecostal theology, (not just the development of a Pentecostal theology of worship) which cannot be underestimated for the future of Pentecostal worship. Theology informs what we believe and consequently how and what we worship; worship informs theology through both the experiences of worshipers and the message of the content of the mechanism, such as songs. At the moment, there is a lack of clarity and consensus among Pentecostals on who (that is, which member of the Trinity) is worshiped, particularly as Old Testament texts such as Isaiah are utilized in worship. Should the Holy Spirit be worshiped? Should we consistently equate Jesus Christ with the visions of Yahweh from the Old Testament or do they include the Father? It is crucial that, as a global community, Pentecostals address these theological questions and discern the utilization of diverse indigenous methods of worship. As Isaiah warned the leaders of the Judean community who had forfeited their power of discernment[33] and proved unreliable visionaries in their context that they would be taught by those with 'stammering lips and other tongues' (Isa. 28.11), so the community of Pentecostal scholars needs to take heed to ensure that other non-biblical religious forms do not provide the direction for its worship. By avoiding syncretism, the Pentecostal community ensures that its local expression does not become a 'foreign tongue'. Instead, like Isaiah's community, the Pentecostal community needs to look for refreshing and vitality from God who provides rest, including through new expressions of worship from non-Western contexts, rather than place their trust in unauthorized alliances of syncretistic practice.

Conclusion

The book of Isaiah offers a wealth of theology and reflection for the formation of a Pentecostal theology of worship; this study only captures a small measure of the gold that it contains. For early Pentecostals in the context of Australia, the gold they unearthed in Isaiah emphasized the need for true worship. It presented a model of encountering God in the throne room of heaven and defending that experience as valid. These insights from the embryonic community

---

[33] Brueggemann *Isaiah 1-39*, p. 222.

are helpful for the contemporary community develop its theology and chart the direction of worship for future generations. However, as Pentecostalism grows, it is important that the locus of its theology-making not be contained by the cultural forms and expectations of its primarily Western scholarship. Instead, new forms and appropriate indigenous practices in worship need to be embraced and encouraged to celebrate the unpredictable moving of the Spirit globally and to speak immanently to these new contexts in their own language. This willingness to embrace other practices is enhanced when worshipers behold the beauty of God in their worship encounter – including the beauty of language in songs and speech that mimic the transcendence of God. While this poetic speech may be spontaneous, it is crucial that Pentecostals in their attempt to disassociate from traditional liturgical denominations do not undermine the power and beauty of non-spontaneous poetic speech in worship. Instead, embracing the power of language to transform and de-centre the worshiper opens the door to a more community minded approach to worship; one where egocentrism is abandoned while the poor and persecuted are embraced in prayer and their needs incorporated into the worship presented as an offering to God as part of the global church.

3

THE BOOK OF PSALMS AND PENTECOSTAL WORSHIP

Lee Roy Martin*

Introduction

Depictions of worship, encouragements to worship, and instructions for worship are scattered throughout the Bible – beginning with the offerings of Cain and Abel in Genesis 4 and concluding with the imperative 'Worship God' in Rev. 22.9.[1] It is the book of Psalms, however, that gives the most sustained attention to the topic of worship. Therefore, while any attempt to develop a theology of worship should include the study of a wide variety of biblical texts from both Old and New Testaments, the book of Psalms must be afforded serious consideration.

Unfortunately, the modern study of the Psalms, emerging primarily from the seminal work of Hermann Gunkel, has focused on historical backgrounds rather than theological construction. Gunkel's form-critical approach produced a classification of Psalm types and sought to understand the ancient function of the Psalter and

* Lee Roy Martin (DTh, University of South Africa) is Professor of Old Testament and Biblical Languages at the Pentecostal Theological Seminary in Cleveland, TN, USA.
[1] Cf. Tom Sterbens, 'Worship: The Journey to Worth', in R. Keith Whitt and French L. Arrington (eds.), *Issues in Contemporary Pentecostalism* (Cleveland, TN: Pathway Press, 2012), pp. 185-210 (p. 185).

the various *Sitze im Leben* of the individual psalms.[2] More recent studies in the Psalms have moved beyond the study of the ancient context and have demonstrated the Psalter's use throughout history and have offered helpful suggestions regarding the employment of the Psalms in the context of the contemporary liturgy. Therefore, for the most part, scholarship on the Psalms has emphasized their liturgical usage, either in ancient times or in contemporary times. What is missing from biblical scholarship, however, is an investigation into how the book of Psalms may contribute to a biblical theology of worship.

It should be pointed out that not everyone accepts the Old Testament as a valid source for Christian theology and practice. At least two questions arise whenever the Old Testament is appealed to in support of particular worship practices: 1. Can the Old Testament can be considered authoritative at all? 2. If we accept the authority of the Old Testament, how do we determine which practices are legitimate for Christian worship and which practices should not be included in Christian worship? I would argue that the role of the Old Testament in theological construction is a hermeneutical matter that impacts not just the question of worship but also the broader theological task. Pentecostalism, in agreement with most other Christian traditions, accepts the authority of the Old Testament in matters of theology, ethics, and practice (cf. 2 Tim. 3.16), with the proviso that certain practices (such as temple rituals, sacrifices, and cleanliness codes) have their theological fulfillment in the New Covenant of Jesus Christ. Therefore, Pentecostal scholar Gerald Sheppard can insist, 'The Psalms as scripture constitute a prime territory for our theological reflection, something far more than merely a prayer book among the artifacts of ancient Israelite religion'.[3] Another Pentecostal writer, P.A. Minnaar, in his article on 'Wor-

---

[2] See Hermann Gunkel, *The Psalms: A Form-Critical Introduction* (Facet Books Biblical Series, 19; Philadelphia: Fortress Press, 1967). Gunkel's approach was refined by later scholars including, for example, Sigmund Mowinckel, *The Psalms in Israel's Worship* (New York: Abingdon Press, 1967), and Claus Westermann, *Praise and Lament in the Psalms* (Atlanta, GA: John Knox Press, 1981).

[3] Gerald T. Sheppard, 'Theology and the Book of Psalms', *Interpretation* 46 (1992), p. 155. Cf. Leonard P. Maré, 'A Pentecostal Perspective on the Use of Psalms of Lament in Worship', *Verbum et Ecclesia* 29.1 (2008), pp. 91-109, who presents a convincing argument for the theological value of the Psalms.

ship', sees Psalm 95 as a 'guideline on the nature of worship and how to practice it'.[4]

Pentecostals are not the only ones who recognize the importance of the Psalms in discussions about Christian worship. Elizabeth Achtemeier argues that the Psalms tell us 'how properly to lament before the Sovereign Lord of the universe and how properly to praise him'. She explains further:

> And the hermeneutics behind that consists in the fact that the church is, according to Paul, the 'Israel of God' (Gal. 6:16), the wild branches grafted into the root of Israel (Rom. 11:7-24), or in Ephesians, those who, through the work of Jesus Christ, have been brought into the commonwealth.[5]

Ernest Gentile proposes that the Psalms were utilized by early Christians. He writes, 'The worship forms found in the book of Psalms provided an ideal way for the lively, Spirit-filled Christians of Bible days to express themselves in personal and corporate worship'.[6] John Lamb extends the paradigmatic function of the Psalms to contemporary worship: 'The Psalter which itself teaches the duty of praise, provides the necessary ideas and expressions'.[7] Renowned Psalms scholar Sigmund Mowinckel agrees that the Psalms have at least some paradigmatic use. He writes, 'The psalms are not only useful for performance in worship, they are useful as models for contemporary hymn writing'.[8] Michael Barrett suggests that the theology of worship is a prominent element in the book of Psalms and 'the Psalms are paradigms for worship'.[9] He argues, 'The Psalms give patterns for both individual and corporate worship'.[10]

When I first came into Pentecostalism, I heard the Psalms being used to validate the general loudness, exuberance, and bodily in-

---

[4] P.A. Minnaar, 'Aanbidding [Worship]', *Pinksterboodskapper [Pentecostal Messenger]* 8.9 (1983), pp. 2-5 (p. 3).

[5] Elizabeth Achtemeier, 'Preaching the Praises and Laments', *Calvin Theological Journal* 36.1 (2001), p. 104.

[6] Ernest B. Gentile, *Worship God!: Exploring the Dynamics of Psalmic Worship* (Portland, OR: City Bible Pub., 1994), pp. 3-4.

[7] John Alexander Lamb, *The Psalms in Christian Worship* (London: Faith Press, 1962), p. 163.

[8] Mowinckel, *The Psalms in Israel's Worship*, p. v.

[9] Michael P.V. Barrett, *The Beauty of Holiness: A Guide to Biblical Worship* (Belfast: Ambassador Publications, 2006), pp. 159-61.

[10] Barrett, *The Beauty of Holiness*, p. 160.

volvement in Pentecostal worship, as well as more specific Pentecostal practices like shouting, leaping, dancing, clapping, lifting the hands, and the use of musical instruments like the tambourine. For example, Pentecostals have justified their energetic worship by pointing to the following texts in Psalms:

'Shout for joy, all you upright in heart!' (32.11)[11]
'Clap your hands all people' (47.2).[12]
'Praise him with the … dance' (150.4).[13]
'Lift up your hands in the sanctuary and bless YHWH' (134.2).[14]
'Make a loud noise, and rejoice' (98.4).[15]
'Take up a song and bring the tambourine' (81.3).[16]
'Those who sow in tears will reap shouts of joy' (126.6).[17]

These examples demonstrate Pentecostalism's appreciation for and imitation of the worship practices found in the Psalter.[18] Furthermore, Pentecostals have adopted certain psalms as models of genuine biblical worship. Psalm 100, for example, is employed often as a paradigm for contemporary Pentecostal worship.[19]

---

[11] In regard to shouting, see also Pss. 47.2; 65.14; 66.1; 81.1; 95.1, 2; 98.4, 6; 100.1 (Heb. רוּעַ); 5.11; 20.6; 32.11; 17.1; 30.6; 33.1; 35.27; 42.5; 47.2; 51.16; 59.17; 61.2; 63.8; 65.9; 67.5; 71.23; 81.1; 84.3; 88.3; 89.13; 90.14; 92.5; 95.1; 96.12; 98.4; 98.8; 105.43; 106.44; 107.22; 118.15; 119.169; 126.2, 5; 132.9; 132.16; 142.7; 145.7; 149.5 (Heb. רָנַן). In this chapter, quotations from Scripture are the author's translation unless noted otherwise. Verse numbering follows the Hebrew text.

[12] Cf. Ps. 98.8. Concerning Pentecostal hand clapping, see David D. Daniels, III, '"Gotta Moan Sometime": A Sonic Exploration of Earwitnesses to Early Pentecostal Sound in North America', *Pneuma* 30.1 (2008), p. 18, who writes, 'The rhythmic pulse of Pentecostal musicality was sustained by clapping. For some early Pentecostals the sound of clapping communicated praise to God. Sometimes this was called praising God with Psalm 47 ("O clap your hands together"), a doxological form of clapping.'

[13] Cf. Pss. 30.11; 149.3.

[14] Cf. Pss. 28.2; 63.5; 119.48.

[15] Concerning loudness, see also Pss. 33.3; 150.5.

[16] Cf. Pss. 149.3; 150.4.

[17] Concerning weeping, see also Pss. 6.7; 30.6; 39.13; 56.9; 69.11.

[18] In the face of the Psalter's consistent call for expressive and passionate worship, I am quite astounded by Daniel I. Block, *For the Glory of God: Recovering a Biblical Theology of Worship* (Grand Rapids, MI: Baker Academic, 2014), who associates enthusiastic worship with idolatry (p. 226).

[19] I inserted my translation of Psalm 100 early on a Sunday morning while my family was getting ready for church. Imagine my astonishment when we arrived later at church and heard the worship leader reading this very Psalm and encouraging the congregation to worship according to its commands.

Psalm 100

A Psalm of thanksgiving
Shout to YHWH, all the earth.
Worship YHWH with gladness;
    Come before him with a loud cry.
Know that YHWH himself is God.
        It is he that made us, and we are his;
        We are his people, and the sheep of his pasture.
Enter his gates with thanksgiving, and his courts with praise.
        Give thanks to him, bless his name.
For YHWH is good;
        His steadfast love is forever,
        And his faithfulness endures to all generations.

The Psalm utilizes an impressive series of seven imperatives:

'shout joyfully' (הָרִיעוּ);
'worship with gladness' (עִבְדוּ בְּשִׂמְחָה);
'come with a loud cry' (בֹּאוּ בִּרְנָנָה);
'know that YHWH is God' (דְּעוּ כִּי־יהוה הוּא אֱלֹהִים);
'enter with thanksgiving ... praise' (בֹּאוּ בְּתוֹדָה בִּתְהִלָּה);
'give thanks to him' (הוֹדוּ־לוֹ);
'bless his name' (בָּרֲכוּ שְׁמוֹ).

These imperatives point to the importance of worship for God's people, to their intense involvement in the act of worship, to the affective dimension of worship, to praise as the indispensible intention of worship, and to God as the exclusive object of worship. It is clear that Pentecostals have used the Psalms as guides to worship, but it remains to be seen how a more comprehensive look at the Psalms might contribute to a Pentecostal theology of worship.

Given the Old Testament's authority in the Christian tradition generally and in the Pentecostal tradition specifically, I will proceed on the assumption that while the relative value of each specific worship practice in the Psalms may be assessed on its own merits, these practices and the broader and more basic theological concerns of the Psalter can be accepted as valuable for constructing a Pentecostal theology of worship. Interpreters will no doubt disagree as to what constitutes the essential concerns of the book of Psalms, but it is hoped that this study will at least generate a helpful discussion about Pentecostal worship and the Psalter.

This chapter will outline a theology of worship derived from the Psalms and suggest ways that the Psalter might contribute more specifically to a Pentecostal theology of worship. I will present my observations according to three categories: 1. observations regarding the book as a whole, 2. observations regarding the various psalm types, and 3. observations regarding the theology expressed in individual psalms.

The Theology of Worship Manifested in the Book of Psalms

The book of Psalms stresses the importance of worship.

We must be careful at the outset that we do not overlook the most obvious point that the Psalter expresses the value of worship both to the individual believer and to the community of faith. The importance of worship is registered in two ways. First, the very presence of the book of Psalms within the canon bears witness to the necessity of worship. It is not insignificant that one of the largest books in the Bible consists of words addressed to God rather than words that come from God. Nahum Sarna writes, 'In the Law and the Prophets, God reaches out to [humanity]. The initiative is His. The message is His ... In the Psalms, human beings reach out to God. The initiative is human. The language is human. We make the effort to communicate.'[20] Although not every psalm addresses God directly, even the indirect praises may be categorized legitimately as words of worship.[21] Therefore, the book of Psalms testifies to the

---

[20] Nahum M. Sarna, *On the Book of Psalms: Exploring the Prayers of Ancient Israel* (New York: Schocken Books, 1st paperback edn, 1993), p. 3. Sarna follows the lead of Gerhard von Rad, *Old Testament Theology* (2 vols.; New York: Harper, 1962), I, pp. 355-70, who speaks of the Psalms as 'Israel's answer' (*Antwort*) to Yahweh. Cf. H. Spieckermann, *Heilsgegenwart: eine Theologie der Psalmen* (Göttingen: Vandenhoeck and Ruprecht, 1989), pp. 7-20, and Hans-Joachim Kraus, *Theology of the Psalms* (trans. K.R. Crim; Continental Commentaries; Minneapolis, MN: Augsburg Pub. House, 1986), pp. 11-14.

[21] By my count, 109 of the 150 psalms include words addressed directly to God while the other 49 offer worship to God in a more indirect fashion (e.g. Psalm 150). Cf. Westermann, *Praise and Lament in the Psalms*, pp. 15-18, who argues that God is praised whenever his actions or attributes are commended either

importance of the human covenantal response to God's person and actions. Whenever God acts, the appropriate human response is worship, as may be witnessed not only in the Psalms but also in other texts such as Exodus 15, Deuteronomy 32, Judges 5, 1 Samuel 2, Jonah 2, and Habakkuk 3, where songs of praise and thanksgiving are recorded. However, these human words addressed to God become a word from God as the community participates through joining the dialogue and overhearing the interchange during times of worship.

Second, a multitude of texts in the book of Psalms attest to the importance of worship. Over and over, the psalms invite and command God's people to sing, to worship, to serve, to pray, to rejoice, to call out to God, to dance, to play instruments, to bring offerings, to enter the temple, and so on. For example, we read, 'Sing praises to YHWH, who dwells in Zion!' (Ps. 9.11); 'Worship YHWH in the beauty of holiness' (Ps. 29.2); 'Oh come, let us worship and bow down; let us kneel before YHWH our maker' (Ps. 95.6); 'Oh, give thanks to YHWH! Call upon his name' (Ps. 105.1); 'Exalt YHWH our God, and worship at his holy hill' (Ps. 99.9); 'Be glad in YHWH and rejoice, you righteous; and shout for joy, all you upright in heart!' (Ps. 32.11).[22]

In the Psalms, worship is both individual and communal. The first Psalm opens with a reference to the individual ('Blessed is the man', אִישׁ), but it concludes with statements about the community ('congregation', עֵדָה, and 'righteous ones', צַדִּיקִים). Throughout the Psalter, we find both individual prayers and communal prayers, individual testimonies and communal testimonies, individual praises and communal praises.[23] On the whole, there is a discernable progression from individualistic language at the beginning of the Psalter to communal language at the end of the Psalter. This progression corresponds to the movement from lament at the beginning of the Psalter to praise at the end of the Psalter.

---

directly or indirectly and that 'praise *occurs*' even in those psalms that lack explicit words of praise (emphasis original).

[22] Kraus, *Theology of the Psalms*, p. 12, states that the cult (i.e. worship) was 'the center of the life of the Old Testament people of God'.

[23] Lamb, *The Psalms in Christian Worship*, p. 3, declares, '[S]ome psalms are congregational, that is, that they were meant to be sung in the sanctuary, whether by a priest or a trained soloist … or by the whole company'.

Erhard Gerstenberger argues that the psalms are inherently communal. He writes,

Modern psalm-research has proved beyond reasonable doubt that Old Testament psalmody in no case was a private, poetic affair of closed-in individuals. There is nothing like our seemingly 'private' poetry in ancient times ... All Old Testament literature is community oriented, destined to be used in groups and congregations.[24]

Similarly, Teun van der Leer contends that the psalms 'teach us to believe and pray with and from within the community'. He adds,

However personal the Psalms can be (Ps. 27:7-14; 77:1-4), they are and remain songs of the faith community. There are quite a few Psalms with an illogical transition from 'I' to 'we', for example Ps. 122:1-2; 123:1-2; or they start with 'me' and conclude within the community, see for example Ps. 22. Many Psalms are even filled with longing for the community: Ps. 42:5.[25]

In anticipation of gathering together with God's people for worship, the psalmist writes, 'I will give you thanks in the great assembly; I will praise you among many people' (Ps. 35.18). Looking back on previous times of worship, the author of Psalm 40 declares, 'I have not concealed your steadfast love and your truth from the great assembly' (Ps. 40.11).

The book of Psalms grounds worship in covenantal commitment.

The corporate nature of Old Testament worship is generated by the covenant relationship between Yahweh and Israel,[26] and the book

---

[24] Erhard S. Gerstenberger, 'Singing a New Song: On Old Testament and Latin American Psalmody', *Word & World* 5.2 (1985), p. 157. Cf. Lamb, *The Psalms in Christian Worship*, p. 162, who writes,

The worshiper is not merely a human soul alone before his maker and father; he is a member of the family, of the body of Christ, of the communion of saints. He shares in the whole work of the church, whether in worship or in the proclamation of the gospel, or in the social advancement of the kingdom of God. The Psalter witnesses to this solidarity of the church.

[25] Teun van der Leer, 'The Psalms as a Source for Spirituality and Worship', *Journal of European Baptist Studies* 13.2 (2013), p. 26.

[26] Walter Brueggemann, *Worship in Ancient Israel: An Essential Guide* (Nashville, TN: Abingdon Press, 2005), pp. 7-9. I would like to express my appreciation to

of Psalms testifies to the importance of Israel's worship as a covenantal response to God's person and actions.[27] The worship of the Psalms, therefore, flows out of the covenant relationship between Yahweh and Israel. Worship is an expression of Israel's covenant commitment to Yahweh, and Israel's praises are in direct response to Yahweh's covenant faithfulness as embodied in Yahweh's חֶסֶד ('steadfast love').[28]

Mutual commitment is the heart of the covenant; and is, therefore, the foundation of genuine worship. Yahweh is fully committed to Israel, and Israel is fully committed to Yahweh. Yahweh promises to be present, 'enthroned on the praises of Israel' (Ps. 22.4), and every Israelite is required to be present in worship.[29] 'Thus worship in Israel consists in *a dialogic interaction* in which both parties are fully present, both parties are to some extent defined by the other, and both parties are put to some extent at risk by the transaction'.[30]

The covenant is exclusive, which means that Yahweh is the only legitimate object of worship.[31] All other gods are interlopers in the covenant relationship between Yahweh and Israel. The psalmist declares, 'For all the gods of the peoples are idols, but Yahweh made the heavens' (Ps. 96.5).[32] In their worship, the Israelites can affirm, '[W]e have not forgotten you, nor been disloyal to your covenant' (Ps. 44.18).

The importance of the covenant as the foundation of worship is expressed in the Psalter in at least three ways. First and most obvious are the numerous psalms in which the covenant is mentioned.[33] For example, the psalms of historical recital praise Yahweh's faith-

---

Pastor Guinn Green, whose questions about the commitment of the worshiper helped me to clarify my approach in this section.

[27] Cf. von Rad's above-mentioned characterization of the psalms as Israel's *Antwort* (*Old Testament Theology*, I, pp. 355-70).

[28] Brueggemann, *Worship in Ancient Israel*, pp. 7-9.

[29] Cf. Brueggemann, *Worship in Ancient Israel*, p. 13, who writes, 'Attendance to worship was not considered optional'.

[30] Brueggemann, *Worship in Ancient Israel*, p. 9 (emphasis original).

[31] Mutual commitment is implied in Exod. 6.7: 'I will take you as my people, and I will be your God'. Israel's commitment to worship Yahweh exclusively is required in the Decalogue: 'You shall have no other gods beside me … you shall not bow down to them nor serve them. For I, Yahweh your God, am a jealous God' (Exod. 20.3-5).

[32] Cf. Pss. 97.7; 106.36; 115.4; 135.15.

[33] The Hebrew word בְּרִית, which is translated 'covenant' occurs 21 times in the Psalter.

ful remembrance of the covenant. The psalmist exclaims that Yahweh 'remembers his covenant forever, the word which he commanded, for a thousand generations' (Ps. 105.8).[34]

Second, the praises that resound in the hymns are often motivated by Yahweh's covenant loyalty (Hebrew חֶסֶד). Translated as 'lovingkindness', 'mercy', 'faithfulness', or 'steadfast love', חֶסֶד is found 130 times in the Psalter.[35] The word חֶסֶד indicates the overarching covenantal, relational quality of Yahweh.[36] Therefore, the psalmist enters into worship with Yahweh's steadfast love in mind: 'But I, through the abundance of your steadfast love (חֶסֶד), will enter into your house' (Ps. 5.8).[37] Psalm 33 encourages the congregation to 'sing to [Yahweh] a new song' (v. 3) because 'the earth is full of the steadfast love (חֶסֶד) of Yahweh' (v. 5). Worshipers are encouraged to 'Give thanks to Yahweh, for he is good; his steadfast love (חֶסֶד) endures forever' (Ps. 107.1). From beginning to end, Psalm 136 repeatedly calls for the praise of Yahweh because 'His steadfast love (חֶסֶד) endures forever' (vv. 1-26).

Third, the pleas voiced in the laments grow out of the psalmist's covenant relationship to Yahweh. The psalmist cries out, 'My God, my God, why have you forsaken me?' (Ps. 22.1). The psalms of lament, therefore, are grounded upon the certainty of the divine–human relationship. John Eaton asserts that 'the emphatic "my God" expresses the covenantal bond with all its assurances'.[38] The phrase 'my God' (or 'Lord') occurs 60 times in the Psalter; and 'our God' (or 'Lord') is found 30 times.[39] The connection between covenant and lament is explored by Scott Ellington, who writes,

---

[34] See also Pss. 89.4, 29, 35, 40; 105.10; 106.45; 111.5, 9; 132.12. Moreover, all references to the Torah could be interpreted as references to the covenant.

[35] Francis Brown *et al.*, *The New Brown, Driver, Briggs, Gesenius Hebrew and English Lexicon: With an Appendix Containing the Biblical Aramaic* (trans. Edward Robinson; Peabody, MA: Hendrickson, 1979), p. 339; Ludwig Köhler and Walter Baumgartner, *The Hebrew and Aramaic Lexicon of the Old Testament* (2 vols.; Leiden: Brill, Study edn, 2001), I, pp. 336-37.

[36] Ernst Jenni and Claus Westermann (eds.), *Theological Lexicon of the Old Testament* (Peabody, MA: Hendrickson Publishers, 1997), p. 451.

[37] Cf. Ps. 100.4-5: 'Enter his gates with thanksgiving and his courts with praise … for Yahweh is good; his steadfast love (חֶסֶד) endures forever'.

[38] John Eaton, *The Psalms: A Historical and Spiritual Commentary with an Introduction and New Translation* (London: T & T Clark International, 2003), p. 235.

[39] Although the phrases 'my God' and 'our God' are connected mostly to Israel's prayers, they can also be associated with Israel's praises. For example, the

Biblical lament, while it does include tears, pleas, complaints and protests, is something more. It is the experience of loss suffered within the context of *relatedness*. A relationship of trust, intimacy, and love is a necessary precondition for genuine lament. When the biblical writers lament, they do so from within the context of a foundational relationship that binds together the individual with members of the community of faith and that community with their God.[40]

This covenantal foundation of worship includes a number of related elements such as devotion to Mt. Zion (e.g. Psalm 48), the centrality of the Jerusalem temple (e.g. Psalm 84), the role of sacrificial offerings as an expected part of worship (e.g. Ps. 50.5), and the enthronement of the royal Davidic heir (e.g. Psalm 2).[41]

The psalms anticipate and celebrate attendance to the temple. The psalmist writes,

One thing I have asked from Yahweh;
that will I seek:
that I may dwell in the house of Yahweh all the days of my life,
to gaze on the beauty of Yahweh
and to seek him in his temple' (Ps. 27.4)

My soul yearns, even faints, for the courts of Yahweh;
my heart and my flesh cry out for the living God' (Ps. 84.2).[42]

Although sacrificial offerings are both assumed and commanded in the Psalter, their efficacy is questioned in a number of texts. Several passages from the Psalter seem to suggest that sacrifice was not sufficient as an expression of worship. Psalm 40.6 reads, 'Sacrifice and offering you did not desire; my ears you have opened. Burnt

---

psalmist proclaims, 'Praise Yahweh. How good it is to sing praises to our God' (Ps. 147.1).

[40] Scott A. Ellington, *Risking Truth: Reshaping the World through Prayers of Lament* (Princeton Theological Monograph Series; Eugene, OR: Pickwick Publications, 2008), p. 7 (emphasis original).

[41] At least 32 different psalms pay tribute to Mt. Zion; 38 refer to the king or the throne; more than 40 psalms mention the temple; and at least 23 psalms include explicit references to sacrificial offerings. Psalm 50.5 views the sacrifices as integrally related to the covenant: 'Gather my holy ones together to me, those who have made a covenant with me by sacrifice' (cf. Ps. 4.6). These central elements of worship are discussed by Kraus, *Theology of the Psalms*, pp. 67-100.

[42] See also Pss. 5.8; 23.6; 26.8; 36.9; 42.5; 52.10; 55.15, 65.5; 66.13; 84.11; etc.

offerings and sin offerings you did not require'. A similar viewpoint is expressed in Ps. 51.16-17: 'For you do not desire sacrifice, or else I would give it; you do not delight in burnt offerings. The sacrifices of God *are* a broken spirit; a broken and a contrite heart – these, O God, you will not despise.' Psalm 27 anticipates the New Testament's perspective that some of the sacrifices have been fulfilled in Jesus Christ and others have been transformed into sacrificial praise. The psalmist writes, 'And now my head shall be lifted up above my enemies all around me; therefore I will offer sacrifices of joy in his tabernacle; I will sing, yes, I will sing praises to Yahweh' (Ps. 27.6). In this text, the 'sacrifices of joy' are parallel grammatically to the singing of 'praises' to the Lord, suggesting that singing can be conceived of as a sacrifice offered by the worshiper to the Lord.

Although Israel's theology of worship as found in the book of Psalms assumes the importance of Mt. Zion, the presence of God at the Jerusalem temple, the role of sacrificial offerings, and the continuation of the Davidic dynasty, these elements of worship must be filtered through the New Testament before they can be carried forward into Pentecostal worship. The New Testament shows that each of these Old Testament features has an underlying theology that should be part of our theology of worship. Both Mt. Zion and the Jerusalem temple bear witness to the ongoing presence of God in the midst of his people (Cf. Heb. 12.22-24; 1 Cor. 3.16). The sacrifices were fulfilled when Jesus offered himself (Heb. 7.27). However, the costliness of worship is registered through the expected offering of one's body (Rom. 12.1) and one's praises: 'Therefore, through [Jesus] let us continually offer the sacrifice of praise to God, that is, the fruit of our lips, giving thanks to his name' (Heb. 13.15). Finally, the Davidic king continues to reign in the person of Jesus of Nazareth, 'the root and offspring of David, the bright and morning star' (Rev. 22.16). To him we sing a new song, saying, 'You are worthy' (Rev. 5.9).

The book of Psalms views worship as theological expression.
The Old Testament is not a book of systematic theology. Instead, Old Testament theology is expressed in story and in song. The Psalms, therefore, are sung theology. Martin Luther declares that the book of Psalms 'might well be called a little Bible. In it is comprehended most beautifully and briefly everything that is in the en-

tire Bible.'[43] Erhard Gerstenberger expresses his amazement at the theological depth and breadth of the Psalms when he writes,

> [T]he Psalter does not contain a summa of theological thought or any kind of theological system ... Still, the Psalter is so vast in its theological dimensions that any systematizing effort must fall short. It will continue to stimulate our life of faith even in this different age, just as it has done for centuries.[44]

Lamb addresses the theological content of the Psalter by recounting a number of important themes that are found in it:

> One cannot read and meditate upon this book without reaching a particular and clear idea of God – a God with a creator's mastery over the universe, with a father's tender pity towards his children, with a judge's interest in righteousness, with a shepherd's care for the erring; a God whose glory is above the heavens, who counts the stars and names them, whose kingdom rules over all, yet whose mercy is from everlasting to everlasting.[45]

Worship, therefore, embodies our theology, celebrates our theology, and communicates our theology. When I first entered Bible college 40 years ago, my teachers complained that too much worship was grounded in bad theology, and I continue to hear similar complaints today. For example, Timothy Pierce observes, 'Music leaders, writers, and performers need to become better versed in theology ... Music must be immersed in proper theology precisely because it has a power to instruct and evoke in a manner that few mediums can.'[46] Consequently, the church's liturgy must be planned and executed with theologically faithfulness in mind. When evaluating our worship, we should ask what kind of theology our worship conveys.

---

[43] Martin Luther, 'Preface to the Psalter', in Jaroslav Pelikan (ed.), *Luther's Works* (55 vols.; Philadelphia: Fortress Press, 1960), p. 254.

[44] Erhard Gerstenberger, *Psalms: Part 1, with an Introduction to Cultic Poetry* (Grand Rapids, MI: Eerdmans, 1988), p. 36. Cf. Brevard S. Childs, *Introduction to the Old Testament as Scripture* (Philadelphia: Fortress Press, 1st American edn, 1979), who writes that the Psalms 'accurately reflect the theology of Israel' (p. 514).

[45] Lamb, *The Psalms in Christian Worship*, p. 160.

[46] Timothy M. Pierce, *Enthroned on Our Praise: An Old Testament Theology of Worship* (NAC Studies in Bible & Theology; Nashville, TN: B & H Academic, 2008), p. 239.

Moreover, while I agree wholeheartedly that worship must be grounded in good theology, I would also argue for the converse, which is that theology must be grounded in good worship. Samuel Terrien declares, 'Doxology is the key to theology'.[47] Unfortunately, many scholars have severed theology from worship by the creation of an academic version of *theology* that can be practiced apart from the worship of God, which has resulted in *logos* without *Theos*. The book of Psalms is a collection of songs, and these songs are deeply theological, a fact that calls for our intentional integration of worship and theology. Thus, when we consider the book of Psalms as a whole, we come to the conclusion that worship should be deeply theological and also that theology should be deeply worshipful.

The book of Psalms models the value of music in worship.
The Psalms may be read, recited, or chanted, but they were originally meant to be sung,[48] a fact that testifies to the value of music in worship. The Hebrew word מִזְמוֹר, translated 'psalm', is 'a song sung to an instrumental accompaniment',[49] and its root word, זָמַר, encompasses the broad idea of 'making music'.[50] The noun מִזְמוֹר ('psalm') occurs 57 times in the book of Psalms and the verb זָמַר ('make music') is found 41 times. The Psalter, therefore, places heavy emphasis upon music as a part of worship. Sigmund Mowinckel observes that in all ancient worship,

> song, music and dance play an important role. So they do in the Psalms … There can be no doubt that the Psalms were meant to be sung. They contain a number of allusions to singing, and they are often described in the titles as songs rendered to music, or as hymns.[51]

In worship we retell our story and share that testimony with our children and with other believers. It is important to note that many

---

[47] Samuel L. Terrien, *The Psalms: Strophic Structure and Theological Commentary* (Eerdmans Critical Commentary; Grand Rapids, MI: Eerdmans, 2003), p. 60.

[48] Kraus, *Theology of the Psalms*, p. 12.

[49] Köhler and Baumgartner, *HALOT*, I, p. 566.

[50] Brown *et al.*, *BDB*, p. 274.

[51] Mowinckel, *The Psalms in Israel's Worship*, p. 8. Cf. Lamb, *The Psalms in Christian Worship*, p. 6, who agrees with Mowinckel that 'the Psalms were intended to be accompanied by musical instruments', though we can say very little about the actual 'rendering of the Psalms in worship' (p. 7), that is, the musical notes etc.

of the Psalms are directed toward God, but most are directed toward the congregation. Our songs embody our communal memory and transmit our corporate ethos to new believers and to each new generation. The effectiveness of music is confirmed by the fact that I am unable to recall even one sermon that I heard before the age of 16, but I can sing any number of hymns that I had learned by the age of 10.[52]

I infer from the Psalms that worship through song is an end in itself and that singing does not necessarily lead to another, more important part of worship such as preaching or the Eucharist. Evangelical scholar Daniel Block, however, argues that since there is no reference to music in the instructions for the tabernacle (Exodus 25 through Leviticus 16) music is neither 'essential' to worship nor is it the main element in worship. I would point out, however, that music was later added to the sacrificial liturgy by divine command through the prophets Gad and Nathan (2 Chron. 25.29). Because the addition of music to the temple liturgy does not go along with Block's argument, he discounts Chronicles as less important than Exodus and Leviticus to a 'biblical' theology of worship. Block argues, therefore, that music is 'neither indispensible for nor the primary element in biblical worship' (p. 228). As we might expect, Block believes preaching to be the central act of worship.[53] If we were to follow Block's logic, we would note as well that there is no reference in the Exodus and Leviticus texts to either preaching or prayer. I also find it interesting that the writer of Hebrews re-envisions the Old Testament sacrifices by referring to Christian worship as 'a sacrifice of praise to God' (Heb. 13.15) not a sacrifice of preaching. Furthermore, as we will see later in Melissa Archer's contribution to this volume, the worship of heaven consists entirely of songs and praises to God. If music is as unimportant as Block suggests, then the worship of the Psalms and the heavenly worship of Revelation must be aberrations.

Daniel Block's work purports to be a 'biblical' theology of worship, but he complains about the movement away from the church organ (which is not found in Scripture) as the primary source of

---

[52] On the value of intergenerational worship, see Bob Bayles, 'Intergenerational Worship', in R. Keith Whitt and French L. Arrington (eds.), *Issues in Contemporary Pentecostalism* (Cleveland, TN: Pathway Press, 2012), pp. 223-40.

[53] Block, *For the Glory of God: Recovering a Biblical Theology of Worship*, p. 241.

worship music. I find it ironic that the instrument deemed by some early Baptists as 'the devil's instrument', should now be preferred over numerous instruments that preceded it in worship.[54] We might also lament the fact that worshipers before the Middle Ages apparently did not have appropriate musical instruments. While Block and others deem certain instruments to be more sacred than others and, therefore, more appropriate for worship, the book of Psalms seems to suggest that all musical instruments can be adapted as vehicles of worship.

The significant role of music in the Pentecostal tradition can hardly be overstated. In their book on global Pentecostalism, Donald E. Miller and Tetsunao Yamamori offer the following insight: 'Whether in a storefront building with bare florescent tubes hanging from the ceiling or in a theater with a sophisticated sound system, the heart of Pentecostalism is the music'.[55] Harvey Cox, in his celebrated study of Pentecostalism, devotes an entire chapter to the importance of music; and regarding Pentecostalism's openness to a broad variety of musical styles, Cox observes,

> Most pentecostals gladly welcome any instrument you can blow, pluck, bow, bang, scrape, or rattle in the praise of God. I have seen photos of saxophones being played at pentecostal revivals as early as 1910 … I have heard congregations sing to the beat of salsa, bossa nova, country western, and a dozen other tempos.[56]

Pentecostal historian David Daniels has explored music within the broader context of sound. He argues that a comprehensive approach to Pentecostal history must include more than spatial and

---

[54] Valdis Teraudkains, 'Leaving behind Imagined Uniformity: Changing Identities of Latvian Baptist Churches', in Ian M. Randall, Toivo Pilli, and Anthony R. Cross (eds.), *Baptist Identities: International Studies from the Seventeenth to the Twentieth Century* (Studies in Baptist History and Thought, 19; Eugene, OR: Wipf & Stock, 2006), pp. 109-22 (p. 116). For a thorough analysis of the controversy surrounding the pipe organ, see Randall D. Engle, 'A Devil's Siren or an Angel's Throat? The Pipe Organ Controversy among the Calvinists', in Amy Nelson Burnett (ed.), *John Calvin, Myth and Reality: Images and Impact of Geneva's Reformer, Papers of the 2009 Calvin Studies Society Colloquium* (Eugene, OR: Cascade Books, 2009), pp. 107-25.

[55] Donald E. Miller and Tetsunao Yamamori, *Global Pentecostalism: The New Face of Christian Social Engagement* (Berkeley, CA: University of California Press, 2007), pp. 23-24

[56] Harvey G. Cox, *Fire from Heaven: The Rise of Pentecostal Spirituality and the Reshaping of Religion in the 21st Century* (London: Cassell, 1996), pp. 142-43.

temporal data. Daniels proposes that 'historical writing on Pentecostalism should focus on the "sound and sense" that constitute early Pentecostalism between 1906 and 1932'. He writes,

> Silence and noise, chants and shouts, singing in the vernacular and in the spirit, instrumental and non-instrumental music, all were soundmarks of the Azusa Street Revival ... Music and music-making become a serious task in the production of early Pentecostal sound, which ranged from sounds described as heavenly to those described as lively.[57]

In his groundbreaking work, *Pentecostal Spirituality: A Passion for the Kingdom*, theologian Steven Land argues that the songs of Pentecostalism are forms of theological reflection, and they contribute to the distinctiveness of Pentecostal worship. Land argues,

> The dance of joy and the celebration of speech were evidence that victims were freed to become participants in salvation history. Music was and is very important in that celebration; it expresses, directs, and deepens that joy. The rhythmic and repetitive nature of much of the singing reflected this joyful celebration or feast of Pentecost in the light of the end, or, to come from the other direction, the marriage supper of the Lamb anticipated in every Lord's Supper. Hymns of revivalism, of the Holiness movement and of the Wesleyan renewal were sung along with new gospel songs which were usually a testimony, exhortation or chronicle of the journey toward 'home'. The oral-narrative liturgy and witness of Pentecostals was a rehearsal of and for the kingdom of God. They rehearsed for the coming of the Lord, the final event of the historical drama; and the songs, testimonies and so on were a means of grace used to sanctify, encourage, mobilize, and direct them on their journey.[58]

My own experience in the Pentecostal church confirms the research of the scholars cited above. My family was Baptist, and I had been raised in that context. We sang from the hymnal, and the only

---

[57] Daniels, "'Gotta Moan Sometime'", pp. 8, 17.

[58] Steven Jack Land, *Pentecostal Spirituality: A Passion for the Kingdom* (Cleveland, TN: CPT Press, 2010), p. 107. See also Josh P.S. Samuel, "'God Is Really among You!': The Spirit's Immediacy in Pentecostal Corporate Worship' (PhD, McMaster Divinity College, 2014), who examines the music of the Azusa Street revival and the contemporary worship music that is in vogue today (pp. 98-122).

accompaniment was simple understated piano music. I encountered quite a different approach to music at the Church of God, where we had a large choir that sang high energy gospel songs. Trios, quartets, and soloists were featured in almost every service, and we also had a teenage choir that sang contemporary Christian selections. The singing was accompanied by piano, organ, tambourine, and any other instrument that might be brought in. Our pianist, Carolyn McBrayer, played with such fierce self-abandon that the upright piano would shake and rock. Soon after I joined the Church of God, I invited my mother to attend church with me, and her initial response to the service was, 'I love the music'.

The Pentecostal emphasis upon music is affirmed by the presence of the book of Psalms within the biblical canon – 150 songs (not to mention the other songs scattered throughout Scripture). In light of the Psalms, I would argue that songs can function as the word of God just as surely as preaching can. God speaks to the Church through preaching, but God speaks through music also.

The book of Psalms witnesses to worship as spiritual formation.

Worship and discipleship are often separated as two different activities with two different goals, but Jerome Boone argues that worship contributes to discipleship. In fact, he insists that within the Pentecostal tradition, worship is the 'primary locus of Christian formation'.[59] According to Boone, all of the elements of Pentecostal worship move toward formation.[60] Marva Dawn agrees, arguing that worship's 'character-forming potential is so subtle and barely noticed, and yet worship creates a great impact on the hearts and minds and lives of a congregation's members'. It follows, therefore, that the worship of Pentecostals 'forms' who they are becoming.[61] We might infer, therefore, that the ultimate purpose and goal of

---

[59] R. Jerome Boone, 'Community and Worship: The Key Components of Pentecostal Christian Formation', *Journal of Pentecostal Theology* 8 (1996), p. 135.

[60] Boone, 'Community and Worship', pp. 135-42. Cf. Cheryl Bridges Johns, *Pentecostal Formation: A Pedagogy among the Oppressed* (JPTSup 2; Sheffield: Sheffield Academic Press, 1993), pp. 121-23; Johnathan E. Alvarado, 'Worship in the Spirit: Pentecostal Perspectives on Liturgical Theology and Praxis', *Journal of Pentecostal Theology* 21.1 (2012), pp. 135-51.

[61] Cf. Marva J. Dawn, *Reaching out without Dumbing Down: A Theology of Worship for This Urgent Time* (Grand Rapids, MI: Eerdmans, 1995), p. 4.

worship is to transform the worshiper into the image of God. The more we worship God, the more we become like God.

The observation that Pentecostal worship is a means to spiritual formation is echoed in the Psalms in at least three ways. First, the overall shape of the book of Psalms portrays the life of faith as dynamic rather than static, and it represents worship as a practice that generates progress toward spiritual growth and maturity.[62] Claus Westermann argues that life is a pendulum that swings back and forth between the extremes of lament and praise and that the Psalms take full advantage of that experiential movement to contribute to the believer's spiritual growth.[63]

Walter Brueggemann, refining and expanding on Westermann's thesis, argues that the psalms can be classified according to their functions as either psalms of orientation, psalms of disorientation, or psalms of reorientation.[64] The psalms of orientation set forth the foundational Hebrew world view. These psalms affirm that God is good and reigns over an orderly world that operates by dependable rules, in which good is rewarded and evil is punished (e.g. Psalm 1). Everything begins with this orientation, but the disruptions of life call into question the goodness of God and the assumption that the world is orderly and just. The psalms of disorientation, therefore, give voice to the complaints that surface when life is thrown into disarray (e.g. Psalm 13). The third category, the psalms of reorientation, are songs of new life that celebrate God's surprising acts of intervention and deliverance (e.g. Psalm 30). Brueggemann explains that the life of faith is a repeated movement through the cycle of orientation to disorientation to reorientation, a movement that should produce spiritual development.

Second, the concern for spiritual formation is reflected not only in the overall shape of the Psalms but also in the psalms of instruc-

---

[62] This function of the Psalms is explored by Walter Brueggemann, *The Psalms and the Life of Faith* (Minneapolis, MN: Fortress Press, 1995).

[63] Claus Westermann, *The Living Psalms* (Grand Rapids, MI: Eerdmans, 1989), p. 14.

[64] Walter Brueggemann, *The Message of the Psalms: A Theological Commentary* (Augsburg Old Testament Studies; Minneapolis, MN: Augsburg Pub. House, 1984). Of course, both Westermann and Brueggemann build upon Hermann Gunkel's groundbreaking form-critical work. See the above-mentioned Gunkel, *The Psalms: A Form-Critical Introduction*.

tion (sometimes called the wisdom psalms).[65] The entire Psalter might be considered instructional, but several psalms are aimed explicitly toward the shaping of world view and the transmitting of the Hebrew faith (e.g. Psalms 1, 32, 37, 49, 73, 78, 112, 119, 127, 128, 133, and 145). Prayer and praise are valuable aspects of worship, but the very first psalm emphasizes worship as a learning experience, and the curriculum for learning is the 'Torah of Yahweh' (Ps. 1.2). Thus, the book of Psalms begins with teaching and includes teaching throughout the book. The wisdom psalms point to the inclusion of instructional songs as a part of the liturgy. Timothy Pierce insists, 'There is little question that the book of Psalms views instruction as an integral part of worship'.[66] According to John Lamb, the Psalms 'might well be used in the worship of the synagogue where so much emphasis was laid on teaching'.[67] Leonard Maré agrees that the psalms were 'appropriated, conserved, and communicated as instruction to the faithful. The psalms should therefore also be read as teachings about God, the world, ourselves and the life of faith.'[68]

Third, the function of the psalms as aids to spiritual formation is implied by the hymns of praise for Torah (e.g. Psalms 1, 19, and 119). The word 'Torah' (תּוֹרָה) itself signifies instruction or teaching. The verbal form of 'Torah' is יָרָה (yarah) and means 'to point' or 'to show'. James Mays argues that the three major Torah psalms outline the way in which the entire book of Psalms should be read:

> Psalm 119 is a poetic inventory of the ways in which the instruction of the Lord in all its categories can become the agenda for virtually all the functions of psalmic hymn and prayer. Torah contains the mighty works of the Lord for which he is praised (vv 27, 18) and serves as a basis for and content of praise (vv 7, 62). It is the subject of thanksgiving for deliverance (v 46) and the fashion of sacrifice offered with thanksgiving (v 108). Involvement with torah creates the predicament in which prayer is uttered, excites the opposition of the wicked, and attracts their taunts (vv 22, 39). It is at once the motive for prayer and the an-

---

[65] Cf. Kraus, *Theology of the Psalms*, pp. 15-16.
[66] Pierce, *Enthroned on Our Praise*, p. 238.
[67] Lamb, *The Psalms in Christian Worship*, p. 4.
[68] Leonard P. Maré, 'Psalm 63: I Thirst for You, Oh God ...', *Ekklesiastikos Pharos* 95 (2013), p. 118.

swer (vv 28, 29). It is the subject of affirmation of trust (vv 33, 44) and furnishes the terms for the claim of innocence (v 69) and the content of vows (v 117) … The coherence of the psalter with its introduction becomes clearer. The psalms are the liturgy for those whose concern and delight is the torah of the Lord.[69]

The Psalter's overall shape, its inclusion of instructional psalms, and its praise of the Torah combine to show the power of worship to effect spiritual growth and transformation. One element of this spiritual formation is particularly impacted by the Psalms. As I have argued elsewhere, the book of Psalms is aimed in part at the formation of the affections:

Steven Land observes that while Pentecostals accept the necessity of orthodoxy (right doctrine) and orthopraxy (right practice), they see orthopathy (right affections) as the integrating center for both orthodoxy and orthopraxy.[70] Consequently, a Pentecostal approach would recognize the Psalms not only as a witness to right theology and practice, but also as an aide in the formation of the affections. The affections, not to be confused with transitory feelings or emotions, are the abiding dispositions and passions of the heart that characterize a person's deepest desires.[71] The psalms, therefore, teach us not only what to think (orthodoxy) and what to do (orthopraxy) but also what to desire (orthopathy).[72]

---

[69] James Luther Mays, 'The Place of the Torah-Psalms in the Psalter', *Journal of Biblical Literature* 106.1 (1987), pp. 3-12 (p. 9). Mays points also to Psalms 18, 25, 33, 78, 89, 93, 94, 99, 103, 105, 111, 112, 147, 148 as psalms that praise the Torah.
[70] Land, *Pentecostal Spirituality*, pp. 21, 34, 127-59. See also Mark J. Cartledge, 'Affective Theological Praxis: Understanding the Direct Object of Practical Theology', *International Journal of Practical Theology* 8.1 (2004), pp. 34-52 (p. 36).
[71] Land, *Pentecostal Spirituality*, p. 34. Cf. Thomas Ryan, 'Revisiting Affective Knowledge and Connaturality in Aquinas', *Theological Studies* 66.1 (2005), pp. 49-68 (55-58, 63). The affections, of course, play a key role in the creation of feelings and emotions.
[72] Lee Roy Martin, 'Longing for God: Psalm 63 and Pentecostal Spirituality', *Journal of Pentecostal Theology* 22.1 (2013), pp. 54-76. See also *idem*, 'Delight in the Torah: The Affective Dimension of Psalm 1', *Old Testament Essays* 23.3 (2010), pp. 708-27; *idem*, '"Oh Give Thanks to the Lord for He Is Good": Affective Hermeneutics, Psalm 107, and Pentecostal Spirituality', *Pneuma* 36.3 (2014), pp. 355-78.

Land argues that the Pentecostal experiences of regeneration, sanctification, and Spirit baptism generate the three affections of 'gratitude as praise-thanksgiving, compassion as love-longing, and courage as confidence-hope'.[73] Building on Land's approach, John Christopher Thomas names five affections that correspond broadly to the elements of the Fivefold Gospel: Salvation/Grat-itude, Sanctification/Compassion, Spirit Baptism/Courage, Healing/Joy, Return of Jesus/Hope. He writes,

> While it is possible to construe the relationship between the elements of the five-fold and the transformation of the affections differently, these should serve to illustrate the point that the Pentecostal interpreter's formation within the worshipping Pentecostal community, not only opens one up to interpretive possibilities based on his or her experience, but also has a deeply transforming impact upon the interpreter's affections.[74]

Leonard Maré pushes even farther and suggests that the spiritual formation of the individual will influence the entire community of faith. He writes that Psalm 63, for example, invites the worshiper to 'follow in the footsteps of the poet in the process of spiritual renewal … This will in turn lead to the transformation of the community of the faithful.'[75] It is time that we recognized the potential spiritual growth that can be realized through worship. Gordon McConville agrees: 'Within the context of worship, the psalmists are taking into their thinking the possibility that entire frames of reference may have to be reimagined'.[76]

---

[73] Land, *Pentecostal Spirituality*, pp. 47, 135-59.

[74] John Christopher Thomas, '"What the Spirit Is Saying to the Church": The Testimony of a Pentecostal in New Testament Studies', in Kevin L. Spawn and Archie T. Wright (eds.), *Spirit and Scripture: Exploring a Pneumatic Hermeneutic* (New York: T & T Clark, 2012), pp. 115-29 (p. 117). For more on a theological approach to the affections, see Gregory S. Clapper, *John Wesley on Religious Affections: His Views on Experience and Emotion and Their Role in the Christian Life and Theology* (Pietist and Wesleyan Studies; Metuchen, NJ: Scarecrow Press, 1989), and Daniel Castelo, 'Tarrying on the Lord: Affections, Virtues and Theological Ethics in Pentecostal Perspective', *Journal of Pentecostal Theology* 13.1 (2004), pp. 31-56.

[75] Maré, 'Psalm 63', p. 227.

[76] J. Gordon McConville, 'Spiritual Formation in the Psalms', in Andrew T. Lincoln, J. Gordon McConville, and Lloyd K. Pietersen (eds.), *The Bible and Spirituality: Exploratory Essays in Reading Scripture Spiritually* (Eugene, OR: Cascade Books, 2013), pp. 56-74 (p. 68).

The book of Psalms reveals worship to be a prophetic witness. The centerpiece of Walter Brueggemann's recent book on the Psalms, *From Whom No Secrets Are Hid*, is his chapter entitled 'The Counter-World of the Psalms', which he delivered at the 2013 Annual Meeting of the Society for Pentecostal Studies. In this essay, which Brueggemann considers to be his clearest formulation of the nature and function of the Psalms, he argues that the Psalms 'voice and mediate to us a counter-world that is at least in tension with our other, closely held world and in fact is often also in direct odds with that closely held world'.[77] Brueggemann identifies 'seven marks of the dominant ideology of our culture',[78] and then suggests contrasting marks that are found in the counter-world of the Psalms. The resulting contrasts are: 1. anxiety that is rooted in scarcity vs. trustful fidelity, 2. greed vs. a world of abundance, 3. self-sufficiency vs. ultimate dependence, 4. denial vs. abrasive truth telling, 5. despair vs. a world of hope, 6. amnesia vs. lively remembering, and 7. a normless world vs. normed fidelity.[79] Brueggemann then insists that it is the activity of Yahweh that makes this counter-world possible. The truth that we find in the Psalms, but which is absent from our present culture, is that Yahweh 'is a real agent, a lively character, and an agent of firm resolve who brings transformative energy and emancipatory capacity to all our social transactions'.[80]

At this point, Brueggemann inserts references to the Old Testament prophets, making clear a parallel that the reader may have noticed already. That is, Brueggemann's characterization of the theology of the Psalms is in fact quite similar to his description of the fundamental message of the prophets, as we find it described in his book, *The Prophetic Imagination*.[81] The theology of the Psalms, of course, is not structured in the form of judgment speeches and salvation speeches as we find in the prophets, but in the form of songs that imagine what the world is like when the preaching of the prophets is brought to real life.

---

[77] Walter Brueggemann, *From Whom No Secrets Are Hid: Introducing the Psalms* (Louisville, KY: Westminster John Knox Press, 2014), p. 9.

[78] Brueggemann, *From Whom No Secrets Are Hid*, p. 10.

[79] Brueggemann, *From Whom No Secrets Are Hid*, pp. 10-25.

[80] Brueggemann, *From Whom No Secrets Are Hid*, p. 27.

[81] Walter Brueggemann, *The Prophetic Imagination* (Philadelphia: Fortress Press, 1978).

What Brueggemann's insights bring to this study of worship is that in light of the fact that the Psalms are particular examples of worship, they can be a model for our contemporary worship. In many places, Pentecostal worship has begun to imitate the dominant culture of American society when, instead, worship should imagine an alternative community and alternative way of life for God's people. Brueggemann's vision is echoed by Elizabeth Achtemeier:

> I suppose only if a preacher has something of such a worldview – a view of human life and of a world from which God is never absent; a view of a world in which nothing is secular; of a life that is God-haunted and God-accompanied, do the psalms of praise and lament make much sense. For that is the context in which these songs occur.[82]

Furthermore, the prophetic nature of worship is realized in its public quality. The enactment of worship is a form of proclamation, as Patrick Miller has observed:

> Praise and thanksgiving, therefore, turn prayer into proclamation. The very heart of the act of giving thanks and praise is a declaration of what I, or we, believe and have come to know about the Lord of life. It is a declaration that thus calls others to a response to that reality, to see, fear, and trust in the Lord who has taken away my fears and helped me.[83]

We find in the Psalms 'the testimony by which those who sing, pray, and speak point beyond themselves, the "kerygmatic intention" of their praise and confession, their prayers and teachings'.[84] Pentecostals have always conceived of their preaching as prophetic speech, and they have practiced the prophetic charismata. I am suggesting, however, that we go even farther and recognize our entire

---

[82] Achtemeier, 'Preaching the Praises and Laments', p. 104.

[83] Patrick D. Miller, 'Prayer and Worship', *Calvin Theological Journal* 36.1 (2001), p. 62.

[84] Kraus, *Theology of the Psalms*, p. 13. The term 'kerygmatic intention' is borrowed from von Rad, *Old Testament Theology*, I, p. 106. Cf. Don Saliers, 'Liturgy and Ethics: Some New Beginnings', *Journal of Religious Ethics* 7.2 (1979), pp. 173-89 (p. 183), who asks, '… to what extent ought the church as liturgical community make moral and ethical transformation of persons and society the purpose of worship?'

liturgy as a prophetic witness to the transformative presence and power of God in this world.

The book of Psalms presents worship as an ethical act.

Theology, ethics, and worship are deeply and inextricably interrelated in the Psalter;[85] but in modern study, these three areas have too often been detached into discrete, exclusive categories.[86] Don Saliers laments this separation of ethical and liturgical studies:

> Questions concerning Christian ethics and the shape of the moral life cannot be adequately understood apart from thinking about how Christians worship. Communal praise, thanksgiving, remembrance, confession and intercession are part of the matrix which forms intention and action … But there has to date been a paucity of dialogue between liturgical studies and ethics, even though it seems obvious that there are significant links between liturgical life, the confession of faith, and the concrete works which flow from these. *How* we pray and worship is linked to *how* we live – to our desires, emotions, attitudes, beliefs and actions.[87]

Saliers' perspective on worship and ethics is easily comprehended by Pentecostals, who, according to Daniel Castelo, have instinctively integrated all aspects of human existence into one redeemed and transformed life, which is a 'living sacrifice' offered to God in worship (Rom. 12.1). Castelo writes,

---

[85] The following texts from the Psalter suggest a direct link between worship and ethics, addressing, for the most part, either the ethical condition of the worshiper, the ethical requirements of the covenant, or the ethical character of Yahweh: Pss. 1.2; 5.4-6; 7.4-6, 15-17; 9.19; 10.2-11, 14, 17-18; 12.2-9; 14.4-6; 15.1-5; 18.26-28; 24.3-4; 25.8-10; 26.2-3; 31.17-18; 32.6; 33.5; 34.14-15; 37.1-3, 8, 21, 28-29; 39.12; 40.9; 41.2; 49.1-20; 50.5, 16-20; 52.3-7; 53.5; 62.11; 68.6-7; 72.1-14; 73.1-19; 74.21; 82.2-4; 84.11; 92.9, 13; 94.2, 6, 12; 96.9, 13; 97.10; 99.4, 5; 101.5, 7; 107.40-41; 112.5-10; 118.18; 119.9, 19, 29; 125.3; 130.3-8; 141.3-4; 143.2, 10; 146.9; 147.6.

[86] For example, there is no entry for either 'liturgy' or 'worship' in John Macquarrie, *Dictionary of Christian Ethics* (Philadelphia: Westminster Press, 1967). Cf. Vigen Guroian, 'Seeing Worship as Ethics: An Orthodox Perspective', *Journal of Religious Ethics* 13.2 (1985), pp. 332-59, who observes the troubling 'separation, if not an outright divorce, of worship, belief, and ethics in much of American religious discourse' (p. 332).

[87] Saliers, 'Liturgy and Ethics' (p. 174) (emphasis original). Cf. Geoffrey Wainwright, 'Eucharist and/as Ethics', *Worship* 62.2 (1988), pp. 123-38.

For early Pentecostals, a conceptual divide did not exist between worship and ethics nor between private and public life; all of these subsequent distinctions and categories that compartmentalize life were incoherent to early Pentecostals, for they saw all of their life within an integrated scheme that originated in the context of God's altering and transforming presence.[88]

It should be clear from the earlier parts of this chapter that the Psalter represents worship as a thoroughly ethical practice.[89] Inasmuch as it flows out of the covenantal relationship between Yahweh and Israel, worship both celebrates and promulgates the covenantal ethical commitments of Israel to Yahweh and to the community. It is in the covenant that Israel finds its origin and purpose for existence. Guroian insists that 'ethics is possible because a new people has come into existence' by God's saving acts and is continually 'nourished' by their liturgical life together before God.[90] This vital connection between worship and covenant is recognized by LaVerdiere, who observes that 'the covenant penetrated and gave significance' to Israel's worship and that 'the covenant is cast in a liturgical context from its very inception'. Liturgy, therefore, 'would always be covenant liturgy, flowing from the express will of the Lord of the covenant and offered by the people of God'.[91] In its function as covenant renewal and remembering of Yahweh's acts, worship would 'strengthen their moral life'.[92]

Also, the above-mentioned function of worship in spiritual formation suggests that the moral life is shaped partially through the lifelong participation in the prescribed liturgy. Don Saliers describes the role of worship in forming the affections: *'the relations between liturgy and ethics are most adequately formulated by specifying how certain affections and virtues are formed and expressed in the modalities of communal prayer and ritual action. These modalities of prayer enter into the formation of the self in community'.*[93] Gordon Wenham adds that it is the act of *participation*

---

[88] Castelo, 'Tarrying on the Lord', p. 50.

[89] Cf. Theresa F. Koernke, 'Toward an Ethics of Liturgical Behavior', *Worship* 66.1 (1992), pp. 25-38 (p. 27).

[90] Guroian, 'Seeing Worship as Ethics', p. 335.

[91] Eugene A. LaVerdiere, 'Covenant Morality', *Worship* 38.5 (1964), pp. 240-46 (p. 240).

[92] LaVerdiere, 'Covenant Morality', p. 242.

[93] Saliers, 'Liturgy and Ethics', p. 175 (emphasis original). Cf. Castelo, 'Tarrying on the Lord', who writes, 'the inculcation and formation of the affec-

in prayer, praise, and confession that makes worship so effective in forming the moral life. He argues, for example, that 'if you pray ethically, you commit yourself to a path of action'.[94]

Furthermore, the Psalter's prophetic theology is weighted heavily toward ethical concerns. Therefore, worship in the book of Psalms aims for the 'moral and ethical transformation of persons and society'.[95] To put it another way, the psalms suggest that worship bears witness to an ethical world view. From the very beginning, the Psalter describes the ethical lives and destinies of the righteous and the wicked, because 'the Lord knows the way of the righteous, but the way of the wicked will perish' (Ps. 1.6). The righteous are like a 'tree planted by the rivers of water' (Ps. 1.3) and they 'flourish like the palm tree and grow like a cedar' (Ps. 92.12). Yahweh hears the 'cry' of the righteous, but Yahweh's face is 'against those who do evil' (Ps. 34. 15-16).

Righteousness is more than an abstract quality – it produces ethical actions. Positively, the righteous are generous, lending to their neighbors, and they give 'freely' to 'the poor' (Ps. 112.5-9). Negatively, the righteous 'turn away from evil' (Ps. 37.27). The wicked person, however, 'plots destruction' and loves 'evil more than good' (Ps. 52.1-5). Therefore, because 'Yahweh loves justice, he will not forsake his saints … but the children of the wicked shall be cut off' (Ps. 37.26-28). The Psalmist says to the wicked, 'God will break you down forever; he will snatch and tear you from your tent; he will uproot you from the land of the living' (Ps. 52.4-5).

Within this ethical world view, Yahweh takes up the cause of the oppressed. 'On every side, the wicked prowl', but Yahweh says, 'Because the poor are plundered, because the needy groan, I will now arise … I will place him in the safety for which he longs' (Ps. 12.1-8). Yahweh 'raises up the needy out of affliction and makes their families like flocks' (Ps. 107.41).

Although sometimes overlooked, the concern for justice is a significant theme in the book of Psalms. We find in the book of

---

tions arise from a context of worship' (p. 37). Cf. Philip J. Rossi, 'Narrative, Worship, and Ethics: Empowering Images for the Shape of Christian Moral Life', *Journal of Religious Ethics* 7.2 (1979), pp. 239-48 (p. 244).

[94] Gordon J. Wenham, 'Reflections on Singing the Ethos of God', *European Journal of Theology* 18.2 (2009), pp. 115-24 (p. 121).

[95] Saliers, 'Liturgy and Ethics', p. 183.

Psalms 97 references to 'justice' and 130 references to 'righteousness'.[96] Righteousness and justice are attributes of Yahweh, – 'He loves righteousness and justice' (Ps. 33.4-5) – and those attributes are also demanded in society. Israel is commanded, 'Give justice to the weak and the fatherless; maintain the right of the afflicted and the destitute. Rescue the weak and the needy; deliver them from the hand of the wicked' (Ps. 82.1-4). Along with the command comes a promise: 'Blessed is the one who considers the poor! In the day of trouble Yahweh delivers him' (Ps. 41.1). Worship, therefore, 'plays a very special part in telling the story of what we "should be" if we could only see ourselves "truthfully" in its light'.[97] In worship, the believer 'makes a commitment to service of others'.[98]

In this just society envisioned by the psalms, the weakest and most vulnerable members are afforded special consideration, and worship becomes a shaper of public policy. Therefore, 'We may investigate worship as motivator of moral behavior, or liturgy as political act. Liturgy can be viewed as the promulgator of an ideology, or at least of specific moral and ethical policies.'[99] Just as in other biblical texts, those weaker members are named as the alien, the fatherless, the widow, and the poor: 'Yahweh watches over the alien; he upholds the widow and the fatherless' (Ps. 146.9, cf. Pss. 39.12; 94.6; 119.19). Regarding Yahweh's concern for the poor, the Psalmist writes, 'Oh, Yahweh, who is like you, delivering the poor from him who is too strong for him, the poor and needy from him who robs him?' (Ps. 35.10).

As 'father to the fatherless and protector of widows' (Ps. 68.6), Yahweh not only cares about the weak, he requires that the community care as well. Israel is instructed, 'Give justice to the weak and the fatherless; maintain the right of the afflicted and the destitute' (Ps. 82.3). 'Blessed is the one who considers the poor!' (Ps. 41.1; cf. Pss. 10.2, 9; 37.14; 72.4).

---

[96] The words 'righteous' and 'righteousness' come from the צדק root, and the words 'justice', 'just', and 'judgment' come from the שפט root.

[97] Jeffrey Bullock, 'Forum: The Ethical Implications in Liturgy', *Worship* 59.3 (1985), pp. 266-70 (p. 269).

[98] Donald P. Gray, 'Liturgy and Morality', *Worship* 39.1 (1965), pp. 28-35 (p. 30).

[99] Saliers, 'Liturgy and Ethics', p. 187.

LaVerdiere observes that worship leads to the human 'imitation' of Yahweh's righteousness, justice, goodness, and faithfulness.[100] 'In theological terms, *tsedeq* ("justice") defines how God treats his people within the framework of the covenantal relationship and reveals how God expects humans to treat one another'.[101] In this imitation, the covenant faithfulness of Yahweh is brought together with the requirement for a just society. Yahweh's faithfulness is signified by the Hebrew term חֶסֶד (*hesed*), which can be translated 'steadfast love' (see discussion above). The חֶסֶד of Yahweh, therefore, inspires and shapes human חֶסֶד (cf. Pss. 18.25-27; 32.5-6; 50.4-5). Don Saliers argues,

> Of God, the Psalmist continually sings: 'for his love endures forever.' From this, intense affectivity may flow; and, upon occasion, from a proleptic experience the dispositions for more enduring love may be laid down in a life. That is, from an overwhelming experience of being mercifully loved and accepted, a person may find new capacities for steadfast love suddenly in place.[102]

The maintenance of a just society is the responsibility of every member of the community, but a greater burden is placed upon those who are in position of authority, namely, the king. The psalms include prayers that the king may judge righteously, that he may ensure justice for the poor, that he may 'defend the cause of the poor of the people, give deliverance to the children of the needy, and crush the oppressor' (Ps. 72.1-4; cf. Pss. 72.11-14; 99.3-4).

As a relational act, worship cannot be separated from the justice of Yahweh and the covenantal demand for justice within the com-

---

[100] LaVerdiere, 'Covenant Morality', p. 244.

[101] Elias Brasil de Souza, 'Worship and Ethics: A Reflection on Psalm 15', (accessed 25 Nov. 2015); available from https://www.academia.edu/3089608/Worship_and_Ethics_A_Reflection_on_Psalm_15_A_short_study_on_the_inextricable_relation_between_worship_and_conduct_in_Psalm_15, p. 4.

[102] Saliers, 'Liturgy and Ethics', p. 182. Paul Ramsey, 'Focus on Liturgy and Ethics', *Journal of Religious Ethics* 7.2 (1979), pp. 139-248, agrees. He writes, 'The notion of steadfast "covenant" love, or agape, in Christian ethics must obviously be constantly nourished by liturgy' (p. 150). It should be noted that Saliers and Ramsey are not without their critics; cf. William W. Everett, 'Liturgy and Ethics: A Response to Saliers and Ramsey', *Journal of Religious Ethics* 7.2 (1979), pp. 203-14; and Margaret A. Farley, 'Beyond the Formal Principle: A Reply to Ramsey and Saliers', *Journal of Religious Ethics* 7.2 (1979), pp. 191-202.

munity. Therefore, the genuineness or validity of worship is judged by ethical criteria that lies outside of the worship act itself. Yahweh accepts only worship that is offered in the context of a just and righteous community. Psalm 15 sets forth the ethical requirements for acceptable worship:

> O Yahweh, who shall sojourn in your tent?
> Who shall dwell on your holy hill?
> He who walks blamelessly and does what is right
>   And speaks truth in his heart;
> Who does not slander with his tongue
>   And does no evil to his neighbor,
>   Nor takes up a reproach against his friend;
> In whose eyes a vile person is despised,
>   But who honors those who fear the Yahweh;
> Who swears to his own hurt and does not change;
>   Who does not put out his money at interest
>   And does not take a bribe against the innocent.
> He who does these things shall never be moved (Ps. 15.1-5).[103]

Elias Brasil de Souza argues that 'Psalm 15 establishes the inextricable relation between worship and conduct and thus highlights important characteristics of the true worshiper'.[104] He adds, 'Such a theology, without denying the value of formal adoration, brings ethics to the foreground of worship and makes appropriate relationships with the neighbor a prerequisite to communion with Yahweh'.[105]

Further examination of the Psalter would bring to the surface a number of other ethical concerns,[106] but the texts that we have cited thus far are sufficient to illustrate the integration of worship and ethics. The book of Psalms, therefore, would seem to support the

---

[103] Cf. Pss. 5.3-7; 24.2-4; 50.15-20; 101.3-7.

[104] Souza, 'Worship and Ethics: A Reflection on Psalm 15', p. 1.

[105] Souza, 'Worship and Ethics: A Reflection on Psalm 15', p. 4. Cf. Ellen T. Charry, *Psalms 1-50* (Brazos Theological Commentary on the Bible; Grand Rapids, MI: Brazos Press, 2015), who writes that Psalm 50 rebukes those who have failed to practice the covenant's ethical demands for justice.

[106] For example, prayers for sanctification (Pss. 7.2-5; 26.1-3; 119.28-29; 141.2-4; 143.9-10), God's forgiveness of sin (Pss. 130.2-4; 143.1-2), God's ethical teaching (Pss. 25.7-10; 94.11-12; 119.8-9), and worship by those outside of Israel (Pss. 67.4; 72.17; 117.1).

assertion of Orthodox theologian Vigen Guroian that 'Christian ethics begins when the people of God gather to worship'.[107]

The Theology of Worship Embodied in the Psalm Types

In addition to the theology of worship that can be discerned from the book of Psalms as a whole, other helpful perspectives emerge from an examination of the various psalm types. Although the book of Psalms is often characterized as a book of praises to the Lord, the very first psalm does not contain a single word of praise to God. It is clear from the outset, therefore, that the book of Psalms contains songs of many different kinds. By employing a variety of psalm types, the Hebrew psalmists were able to respond in worship to the many different situations in their lives. Biblical scholars have identified five basic genres of psalms: the individual lament, the communal lament, the communal hymn, individual thanksgiving psalms, and royal psalms. Other scholars would also suggest categories such as wisdom psalms, psalms of Zion, historical psalms, and psalms of trust. These genres do not exhibit strict, ironclad structures, nor do they explain the nature of every song in the entire collection. Nevertheless, they are helpful guides to the basic forms of biblical psalmic expression.

The laments call for urgent prayer.
The most common type of psalm is the prayer psalm, which Bible scholars call 'the lament'. The lament is the worshiper's cry to God for deliverance from distress. The sufferer's trouble may take the form of sickness (Psalm 6), personal or corporate sin (Psalm 51), oppression (Psalm 10), or an accusation (Psalm 17). The lament usually begins with an address to God, followed by the specific complaint or need. The worshiper may then confess trust in God and offer up a petition to God. The lament may include a declaration of assurance that God has heard the prayer and conclude with a promise to praise God with a thanksgiving offering.

The laments suggest that worship is an opportunity for believers to express their deepest needs to God openly and honestly. We have learned in our religious circles to mask our true feelings, but the psalms teach us that we are permitted to reveal everything to

---

[107] Guroian, 'Seeing Worship as Ethics', p. 349.

God. According to Walter Brueggemann, 'The church at worship remains an uncommon and peculiar venue where deep secrets of exuberance and dismay can be voiced, a voicing that is indispensable for the social and economic health of the body of faith and the body politic.'[108] Similarly, Elizabeth Achtemeier argues cogently that both praise and lament ought to be part of the believer's worship:

> That genuine life before God includes lament can be surprising to some, of course. But those are the two poles of worship that we find in the Psalter – praise and lament – and indeed, lament makes up two-thirds of the Psalms. That fact … gives the lie to the characterization of worship as only celebration … We make little room in our worship services for sobbing, either inward or outward. But the psalmists sob, as did our Lord.[109]

Therefore, the psalms of lament teach us that we should make a place for prayer in our worship services. Many churches have turned worship into nothing but celebration, and they have relegated prayer to the back rooms. Leonard Maré observes:

> In the liturgy of Pentecostal churches there is virtually no room for lament. It is a fact that someone might attend a Pentecostal service and leave thinking that Pentecostals' lives are free from any kind of negativity or disharmony. Pentecostals tend to reject any expression of feelings of negativity, anger, revenge and complaint as a legitimate part of worship. This situation, to my mind, is an impoverishment of the full spectrum of human worship before God.[110]

In the psalms, however, worship provides a time and place for passionate prayer, for crying out to God.[111]

---

[108] Brueggemann, *Message of the Psalms*, p. xi. Cf. Samuel, '"God Is Really among You!": The Spirit's Immediacy in Pentecostal Corporate Worship', pp. 172-75, who argues for the value of lament songs in Pentecostal worship.

[109] Achtemeier, 'Preaching the Praises and Laments', p. 105.

[110] Maré, 'Psalms of Lament in Worship', p. 95. Cf. Ellington, *Risking Truth: Reshaping the World through Prayers of Lament*, pp. 4-14.

[111] The New Testament instructs us to include times of prayer for people in the congregation (Jas 5.13-18). We are to 'be anxious for nothing, but in everything by prayer and supplication, let [our] requests be made known unto God' (Phil. 4.6). Peter says, 'casting all your care upon him, because he cares for you' (1 Pet. 5.7). The early church prayed together in times of need (Acts 1.14; 2.42; 3.1; 4.31; 6.4, 6; 8.15; 12.5; 13.1-3; 14.23; 16.13, 25; 20.36).

Walter Brueggemann argues for the theological importance of the lament:

[T]he structure of plea and/or praise, when taken theologically and christologically, correlates with the Friday and Sunday of Christian faith. Therefore, it is precisely this psalm of lament genre that gives Christian faith its liturgical pattern of crucifixion and resurrection. One obvious implication is that the loss of the lament psalm in the worship life of the church is essentially the loss of a theology of the cross.[112]

We tend to ignore lament because we think it mitigates against praise. On the contrary, the pathos and passion of lament fuels and powers praise. Praise without lament is shallow, superficial, empty. Also, praise provides the foundation for lament. We are free to lament because we know the reality of a wonderful God. Having known praise, we feel free to lament. We know our pain will pass.

The practice of lament was commonplace in early Pentecostalism, taking the form of 'praying through' and 'tarrying'. However, this form of lament, which refers almost exclusively to seeking for salvation, has largely disappeared from present-day Pentecostalism.[113]

The lament psalms teach us that prayer is a vital component of genuine worship. Steven Land insists that 'it must be acknowledged that prayer – individual and corporate, human and "angelic", with sighs and groans, praise and petition – is at the heart of [Pentecostal] spirituality'.[114] On any given Sunday, a large portion of any congregation will consist of people who are hurting severely. The most meaningful and helpful thing we can do for them in the service is to reach out to them. They need more than a sermon. They need more than uplifting songs. They need the prayerful touch of caring brothers and sisters in Christ. They need a church that will spend time with them in prayer until the Holy Spirit breaks through to victory. Elizabeth Achtemeier writes:

---

[112] Walter Brueggemann, 'The Friday Voice of Faith', *Calvin Theological Journal* 36.1 (2001), p. 13.

[113] Scott A. Ellington, 'The Costly Loss of Testimony', *Journal of Pentecostal Theology* 16 (2000), pp. 48-59.

[114] Land, *Pentecostal Spirituality*, p. 24.

That opportunity to sob, to cry, to lament is moreover the most realistic of expressions to God. For human life is beset with miseries, fear, anxiety, and futility; with hatred and violence, cruelty and suffering; and with corruption and wasting and death. As one laywoman put it to a group of ministers, 'There's a lot of pain out there.' And it is precisely the pain of all our lives that lament lets us express – the awful, terrible upheavals and distortions caused by human sin. Until that is acknowledged, there is no reason for the gospel. Lament forms the prelude to the praise of the Lord.

The thanksgiving psalms call for times of testimony.
The song of testimony, often called the psalm of thanksgiving, is a public celebration of answered prayer (e.g. Psalm 30). It is a testimonial to all who are present that God has intervened in the life of the worshiper. The thanksgiving psalm is based upon the final element of the lament. At the end of the lament, the petitioner promises that when the prayer has been answered, he or she will offer a thanksgiving sacrifice. After God has answered the prayer and brought deliverance, the psalmist comes with his or her family and friends to the temple. At the temple, an offering or sacrifice is made in thanks to God, and a song of testimony is sung to commemorate the occasion in praise to God.[115]

The psalm of testimony teaches us the value of public thanksgiving and the expectation of bringing an offering to God. Patrick Miller writes,

> The prayers of thanksgiving are the primary Old Testament form of testimony. They are declarations to others of what God has done … To the extent that we have abandoned that personal testimony, we have forgotten the very character of thanksgiving as a liturgical act in Scripture. It is in the most profound sort of way a testimony to one person's experience of the power of God to deliver, to be present, to transform from death to life, to lift up from the depths to the heights.[116]

---

[115] Cf. R. Jerome Boone, *Let There Be Praise* (Bible Study Series; Cleveland, TN: Pathway Press, 1985), pp. 121-28.

[116] Miller, 'Prayer and Worship', p. 61

Public testimony, as it is called for in the thanksgiving psalms, was once a prominent practice in Pentecostal churches. Scott Ellington has suggested that perhaps the reason for the demise of testimony as a practice is that many Pentecostals have no liturgical opportunity for testimony.[117] However, could it also be true that the practice is less common because gratitude has diminished? Gratitude was once a ruling affection for Pentecostals (and it still is in many parts of the world), but here in the West, gratitude has been replaced by greed and autonomy.[118] We are affluent, educated, powerful, and self-righteous.[119]

The psalm of thankful testimony is meant to encourage the congregation who hear the song. John Goldingay insists that God's purposes in bringing deliverance are incomplete without our testimony. He states that 'if an Israelite sought and received God's deliverance and did not come to stand in the midst of the people of God to give God the glory, at least half of the point of that deliverance disappears'.[120] Our children need to hear that God has answered our prayers. Our friends and family need to hear what God has done in our lives. Some churches have become very impersonal, and the members of the congregation no longer share their lives with each other. These psalms demonstrate the value of sharing our testimonies with one another in the context of worship.

The hymns call for extravagant praise.

Another common type of psalm is the hymn. The hymn utters praise, glory, and honor to God. Walter Brueggemann writes, 'Israel's most characteristic utterance in worship is *praise*, the exuberant rhetorical act of gladly ceding one's life and the life of the world

---

[117] See Ellington, 'The Costly Loss of Testimony', pp. 48-59; Scott A. Ellington, '"Can I Get a Witness": The Myth of Pentecostal Orality and the Process of Traditioning in the Psalms', *Journal of Pentecostal Theology* 20.1 (2011), pp. 54-67. Cf. Boone, 'Community and Worship', pp. 140-41, and James K.A. Smith, *Desiring the Kingdom: Worship, Worldview, and Cultural Formation* (Cultural Liturgies, 1; Grand Rapids, MI: Baker Academic, 2009).

[118] J. Clinton McCann, 'Greed, Grace, and Gratitude: An Approach to Preaching the Psalms', in David Fleer and Dave Bland (eds.), *Performing the Psalms: With Essays and Sermons by Walter Brueggemann, J. Clinton McCann Jr., Paul Scott Wilson, and Others* (St. Louis, MO: Chalice Press, 2005), pp. 51-66.

[119] See Martin, '"Oh Give Thanks to the Lord for He Is Good": Affective Hermeneutics, Psalm 107, and Pentecostal Spirituality', pp. 370-78.

[120] John Goldingay, *Psalms* (Baker Commentary on the Old Testament Wisdom and Psalms; 3 vols.; Grand Rapids, MI: Baker Academic, 2006), I, p. 579.

over to Yahweh in joyous self-abandonment'.[121] In light of the Psalter's emphasis upon praise, Michael Barrett argues, 'Since true worship is all about God, praise and thanksgiving for His person and for His works are always integral elements in biblical worship'.[122]

While the psalm of thanksgiving offers praises to God because of a specific event in the life of the worshiper, the hymn offers praises to God because of his nature and attributes. It is a psalm that is uttered in praise of God's more comprehensive virtues (e.g. 'Praise him for his excellent greatness', Psalm 150.2). The hymns emphasize both God's majesty and his love. His majesty is expressed through affirmations of his sovereignty and his rule over creation. His love is expressed through statements about his works of salvation and provision. These hymns normally begin with an invitation to worship, followed by the reason for praise, and end with a concluding invitation to worship.

God is the God who is majestic and exalted, the King of kings, the Lord of lords, the God of gods; therefore, he is worthy of praise. God created the heaven, the earth, the angels, and all of humanity; therefore, he is worthy of praise. Not only is God majestic in holiness, but God is also loving, kind, and compassionate. God saved Israel from the bondage of Egypt; therefore, he is worthy of praise!

Regarding Psalm 150, Brueggemann writes,

[T]his Psalm is a determined, enthusiastic, uninterrupted, relentless, unrelieved summons which will not be content until all creatures, all of life, are 'ready and willing' to participate in an unending song of praise that is sung without reserve or qualification. The Psalm expresses a lyrical self-abandonment, an utter yielding of self, without vested interest, calculation, desire, or hidden agenda. This praise is nothing other than a glad offer of self in lyrical surrender made only to the God appropriately addressed in praise. The one who speaks in this Psalm is utterly ceded over to God in praise. Everything focuses on the God to be praised. The Psalter, in correspondence to Israel's life with God when lived faithfully, ends in glad, unconditional praise,

---

[121] Brueggemann, *Worship in Ancient Israel*, p. 43 (emphasis original).
[122] Barrett, *The Beauty of Holiness*, p. 166.

completely, and without embarrassment or distraction, focused on God.[123]

The hymns teach us that the goal of worship is praise; therefore, the Psalter concludes with a hymn of praise that declares 'Let everything that has breath praise the Lord!' (Ps. 150.6).

The psalms of trust call for hopeful worship.
One of the most beloved types of psalms is the psalm of trust. The psalm of trust is an expression of faith and trust that God is with his people and that God is their helper. Psalm 23 is a psalm of trust, and so is Psalm 27, which begins with these words:

The Lord is my light and my salvation.
  Whom shall I fear?
The Lord is the strength of my life.
  Of whom shall I be afraid?
When my enemies and foes came against me to eat up my flesh,
  they stumbled and fell.
Though an army would encamp against me,
  in this I will be confident (Ps. 27.1-3).

The psalms of trust suggest that through both its content and its atmosphere, worship should encourage believers to trust God. In a world where self-sufficiency is praised, the gospel demands that we admit our dependency upon almighty God. In a world characterized by despair, the worshiping Church proclaims a message of hope.[124] In a world of violence, ethnic conflict, and international power struggles, the worship of God's people should be a witness to the soon return of the Prince of Peace. In the midst of a chaotic world, worship provides a sacred space in which the heavenly voice can be heard saying, 'The Lord God omnipotent reigns!' (Rev. 19.6).

The historical psalms call for recitals of communal memory.
The historical psalms recount a portion of the history of Israel (see Psalms 78, 105, 106, and 136), and some of the historical psalms cover the story of Israel from the days of Abraham all the way up to the time when the psalm was written. Throughout these recitals of

---

[123] Walter Brueggemann, 'Bounded by Obedience and Praise: The Psalms as Canon', *Journal for the Study of the Old Testament* 50 (1991), pp. 63-92 (pp. 68-68).
[124] Brueggemann, *From Whom No Secrets Are Hid*, pp. 10-25.

Israel's story, the psalms will praise God because he helped the patriarchs and because he brought Israel out of Egypt. Like the psalms of testimony, these psalms teach God's faithfulness and provide encouragement to God's people. Furthermore, the identity and ethos of the people of God are embedded in the songs.

Therefore, the historical psalms teach us that reciting our common story builds community and transmits the ethos of the community to new members and to the next generation. Songs that remind us of God's involvement in our lives serve an important role in today's fast-paced world where we quickly forget our story. Claus Westermann argues that we now experience 'a great measure of *forgetting*, to a degree previously unknown in the history of the world'; therefore, 'the call not to forget' is as important now as it was when the psalms were written.[125]

Many of today's churches, particularly the mega-churches, are little more than a weekly convention of strangers, who sing, pray, and listen to a very generic sermon. Then they go their separate ways, often not even knowing one another's names. It is more vital than ever before that the Church's worship include frequent mention of the larger Christian story as well as the more particular story of the individual congregation and its families. This process of knowing one another will build community identity. It will also strengthen relationships so that everyone is less alone.[126]

The Theology of Worship Expressed in Individual Psalms

In addition to the theology of worship that can be discerned from the book of Psalms as a whole and from the various Psalm types, further insights into worship can be gained through the study of individual psalms. While space does not permit the full exploration of this category of observations, a few examples will be offered.

---

[125] Claus Westermann, *The Psalms: Structure, Content & Message* (Minneapolis, MN: Augsburg Pub. House, 1980), p. 7 (emphasis original).

[126] My pastor, Kevin Mendel, often remarks that even in the utopian environs of the Garden of Eden, it was 'not good that Adam should be alone' (Gen. 2.18); therefore, God created community.

Psalm 1 suggests the centrality of Scripture in worship.
Psalm 1 serves as an introduction to the entire book of Psalms, and it points to the central place of Scripture in worship. This first Psalm states,

> Blessed is the man
> who does not walk in the counsel of the wicked,
> nor stands in the path of sinners,
> nor sits in the seat of the scorner;
> but his delight is in the Torah of Yahweh,
> and in his Torah he meditates day and night' (Ps. 1.1-2).

The key phrase of Psalm 1 is found in v. 2: 'but his delight is in the Torah of Yahweh, and in his Torah he meditates day and night'. The first psalm, therefore, stands as an invitation to take 'delight' in God's Word and to 'meditate' on it. Before entering into the worship of the Psalter, the worshiper is encouraged to orient his or her affections toward the Torah. After the heart is attuned to the Torah, then the worshiper can sing and worship. Perhaps the singing of psalms (i.e. worship) is not the only way to 'meditate' on God's Torah, but it is one way to do so.[127]

Psalm 51 includes repentance as an act of worship.
For the most part, Pentecostals have emphasized repentance only in relation to conversion. The traditional Pentecostal affirmation that believers can 'live above sin' has resulted in a devaluation of post-conversion repentance. The psalms of repentance, and especially Psalm 51, however, point to the importance of repentance as a means whereby God's people can renew their covenant commitment to Yahweh. The psalmist writes boldly,

> Have mercy upon me, O God, according to your steadfast love; according to the multitude of your tender mercies, blot out my transgressions. Wash me thoroughly from my iniquity, and cleanse me from my sin. For I acknowledge my transgressions, and my sin is always before me … Create in me a clean heart, O God, and renew a steadfast spirit within me. Do not cast me away from your presence, and do not take your Holy Spirit from me. Restore to me the joy of your salvation (Ps. 51.1-12).

---

[127] See Martin, 'Delight in the Torah', p. 723. The centrality of Scripture is also attested in Psalms 19 and 119.

In light of the book of Psalms, Barrett argues that 'confession of sin' is an important ingredient in biblical worship.[128]

Psalm 63 conceives of worship as a longing for God's presence.

A passion for God is evident in from the beginning of Psalm 63:

> God, you are my God;
>   I will seek you earnestly;
>   my soul is thirsty for you;
>   my flesh longs for you in a dry and weary land without water.
> Thus in the sanctuary I have seen you,
>   beholding your power and your glory' (Ps. 63.2-3).

Here is an articulation of deep spiritual inclinations, an expression of the psalmist's intense desire to encounter God and to experience God's presence.

The longing for God is made more concrete through the metaphorical, yearning cry, 'My soul is thirsty for you; my flesh longs for you'. The language of hunger and thirst 'voices the intensity of emotional intimacy between the psalmist and God'.[129] The combination of 'soul' and 'flesh' signifies that the whole person is involved in the longing. The psalmist longs, body and soul, for his God. He longs deeply and passionately for God's presence, a presence that he has experienced in the past. In God's holy place, recounts the psalmist, 'I have seen you, beholding your power and your glory'.

The longing for God expressed in Psalm 63 brings to mind the affective component of Pentecostal spirituality, a spirituality that Steven Land has characterized as 'a passion for the kingdom', which is 'ultimately a passion for God'.[130] The Psalmist's 'hunger' and 'thirst' for God is consistent with Pentecostal spirituality and that the desire to encounter God in the sanctuary is consistent with the goals of Pentecostal worship. Chris Green insists that 'Pentecostal spirituality is nothing if not a *personal* engagement' with God,[131] a

---

[128] Barrett, *The Beauty of Holiness*, p. 168.

[129] James L. Crenshaw, *The Psalms: An Introduction* (Grand Rapids, MI: Eerdmans, 2001), p. 15.

[130] Land, *Pentecostal Spirituality*, pp. 2, 97, 120, 73-80, 212, 219.

[131] Chris E.W. Green, *Toward a Pentecostal Theology of the Lord's Supper: Foretasting the Kingdom* (Cleveland, TN: CPT Press, 2012), p. 289 (emphasis original).

'holy desire for God Himself'.[132] Like the Psalmist, the Pentecostal community is hungry and thirsty for God and seeks to behold God's power and glory, to lift up their hands in adoration, to testify of past blessings, to praise God with joyful lips, to shout for joy, to stick close to God, to rejoice in God, and to live in hope of the coming reign of God.

Psalm 103 demands that the entire self be engaged in worship.
Psalm 103 begins with these extraordinary words:

> Bless Yahweh, O my soul;
>   and all that is within me, bless his holy name!
> Bless Yahweh, O my soul,
>   and forget not all his dealings: (Ps. 103.1-2).

The hymns normally begin with a call to worship – 'Praise the Lord' – which is directed to the congregation. However, in Psalm 63, the exhortation is to the self. The psalmist calls upon himself to worship God. The words 'my soul' (נַפְשִׁי) mean 'my total self'.[133] The words 'all that is within me' confirm that the 'self' includes the inner totality of the person. Therefore, the psalmist is saying, 'Bless the Lord, Oh, my total self – my body, mind, emotions, and will'. In this psalm, therefore, worship is the directing of the entire self toward engagement with God in remembrance and praise. The worship of Psalm 103 is not half-hearted worship.

If we take seriously Psalm 103, then everything that is inside of us – our minds, hearts, feelings, thoughts, and will – should shout the praises of God. This is not shallow worship, outward ceremony, or empty ritual. This is not the kind of worship where we are only observers, while those who are on the stage perform worship. This is worship that is coming from deep inside, with all our hearts, all of our minds, and all of our strength. This is worship 'in spirit and in truth' (Jn 4.23-24).

Conclusion

We have seen that, when taken as a whole, the book of Psalms stresses the importance of worship, grounds worship in covenantal

---

[132] Castelo, 'Tarrying on the Lord', p. 53.
[133] Cf. Goldingay, *Psalms*, III, p. 166.

commitment, integrates worship and theology, conceives of music as an end in itself, sees worship as a location of spiritual formation, and presents worship as a form of proclamation. The major psalm types suggest that worship should include urgent prayer, frequent testimonies, extravagant praise, hopeful content, and recitals of the Church's story. We have observed four individual psalms that point to the centrality of Scripture in worship (Psalm 1), the inclusion of repentance as an element of worship (Psalm 51), the goal of worship as divine encounter (Psalm 63), and the call for total engagement of the self in worship (Psalm 103).

Furthermore, this study highlights a number of tensions that are found in the worship of Israel and that should be maintained in the Church's worship: Exuberant joy over against fearful awe, Transcendence over against immanence, Past remembrance over against future hope, The address to God over against the address to each other, and Liturgy over against liberty.

Obviously, the observations made in this chapter are not comprehensive; nevertheless, they are suggestive for a Pentecostal theology of worship. Many of the elements of worship that I have identified in the Psalms were present in early Pentecostalism, and they remain present in many churches, especially in the majority world. Pentecostal worship in the USA, however, has been influenced by contemporary evangelical currents, including the so-called seeker friendly, emergent, and missional models, which have pushed Pentecostalism closer in worship practices to mainline Protestantism. Unfortunately, if Pentecostalism loses the distinctive heart of its worship practices, it will also lose its distinctive spirituality, theology, and identity. Furthermore, history demonstrates that the growth of the Pentecostal church is linked to its depth of worship. Hopefully, constructive studies like this one will bring renewed attention to the heart of the Pentecostal tradition and will help to strengthen the movement. May Pentecostals continue to affirm with the Psalmist:

As the deer pants for brooks of water,
    so pants my soul for you, O God.
My soul thirsts for God,
    for the living God … (Ps. 42.2-3).

4

TOWARD A PENTECOSTAL THEOLOGY OF ANOINTED CLOTHS

John Christopher Thomas*

One aspect of Pentecostal worship practices that has drawn criticism by outsiders and generated a certain degree of consternation even amongst some insiders is the use of anointed cloths in its ministry of healing. The practice is based on Acts 19.12, where pieces of cloth that had come in contact with Paul's body were taken to sick and demon possessed individuals resulting in healing and exorcisms.

From the beginning of the movement, Pentecostals have made use of this means to facilitate healing. A survey of the testimonies of this practice found in early Pentecostal periodical literature provides evidence of its place in early Pentecostal life and thought.

Pentecostal Practice as Revealed in the Early Pentecostal Periodical Literature

Already at the Azusa Street Revival one finds evidence of the use of anointed cloths in the form of a testimony from 'The Apostolic

* John Christopher Thomas (PhD, University of Sheffield) is Clarence J. Abbott Professor of Biblical Studies at the Pentecostal Theological Seminary in Cleveland, TN, USA and Director of the Centre for Pentecostal and Charismatic Studies at Bangor University in Bangor, Wales, UK.

Faith Mission, 501 Alexander Ave.' in Winnipeg, Canada published in the *Apostolic Faith*.

> Winnipeg, Can. – There was a great Pentecostal Convention in Winnipeg beginning November 15th. Preachers and Workers from all parts of Canada were present. A band of workers who were in Portland at the time received a call from God to go to Winnipeg, and they were present at the convention: Sister Crawford and Mildred, Sister Neal, Brother Conlee and Brother Trotter. About twenty were baptized with the Holy Ghost and many were healed. The people brought handkerchiefs and aprons to be blessed as in Acts 19:12, and the Lord did wonderful signs through the simple faith of the dear ones that brought them. The Lord healed one young man of the tobacco habit, taking all the desire for the stuff away from him, through an anointed handkerchief, and he was saved in his own room. Demons were cast out of those bound by them.[1]

Several things are significant about this testimony. First, the activity of bringing cloths to be anointed occurs in the context of a great move of God. Second, the testimony indicates that it was the people in attendance that brought the items to be anointed and then taken to those in need. Third, Acts 19.12 is appealed to as biblical justification for this activity. Fourth, rather powerful signs are described as resulting from this means, such as deliverance, salvation, and exorcisms.

Sometime the next year a testimony of healing by means of an anointed handkerchief comes in the form of a letter from Clinton, South Carolina, written to Elizabeth Sexton, the editor of the *Bridegroom's Messenger*. Among the things testified to in the meetings held there was the following,

> Quite a number were prayed for and anointed in the name of Jesus, and shouted the victory.

> There was a lady at the Lydia Mill that took the smallpox; she sent for us to pray for her; we anointed a handkerchief and laid

---

[1] *The Apostolic Faith* 1.12 (1908), p. 1.

on hands and sent it to her. She was up the next day. Acts 19:12.[2]

An early issue of *The Latter Rain Evangel* also contains an account of this practice as it relates to the ministry of a Brother Bosworth.

Brother Bosworth has great faith in the use of the anointed handkerchief in praying for people at a distance. When in Dallas the Lord wonderfully blessed his ministry along this line as the following instances show.

One woman, the wife of a Presbyterian minister, writes that when she opened the letter containing the handkerchief the power of God came on her and she was instantly healed of a serious affliction. Another case is that of a man who was controlled by demon power. Unknown to him the wife placed a leaflet on which hands had been laid in prayer, under his pillow. It was done in faith and the result was deliverance from the evil spirit that had obsessed him. One woman was healed of cancer on the face and another instantly delivered from a cough.[3]

The three examples here offered underscore not only the healing of individuals but also the deliverance of one controlled by demonic power, reminiscent of the events of Acts 19.12, though no mention is made of the text.

Another testimony of healing in connection with an anointed cloth is found in *The Pentecostal Herald*, shortly after its founding in 1915 by George Brinkman in Chicago, Illinois. Under the heading, 'Healed of Tumor Through an Annointed [*sic*] Cloth (Read Acts 19:12)', a Mrs. Ayers writes,

I was attending Sister Etter's meeting at Long Hill, Conn., and when I saw the wonderful healings I remembered a dear sister in Fall City, Neb., who was afflicted with a large tumor. I desired that she should receive healing, and I had a cloth which I had sister Etter annoint [*sic*] and pray over, and sent to the sister in Nebraska. She bound it around the tumor, and now she is completely healed. It was an immense tumor, which was very un-

[2] 'Clinton, S.C.', *The Bridegroom's Messenger* 2.31 (Feb. 1, 1909), p. 3.
[3] *The Latter Rain Evangel* (May, 1913), pp. 13-14.

sightly, preventing the arms from coming into a natural position. Mrs. Ayers. Chicago, Ill., June, 1915.[4]

As with the previous example, several aspects of this account are significant. First, as before, the context in which the request for an anointed cloth is made appears to be extraordinary, a meeting in which wonderful healings were occurring. Second, once again, a member of the community bears a burden for someone who could not attend the meetings firsthand to receive ministry. On this occasion the person in need resided in another state hundreds of miles away from the location of the services. Third, the action is initiated by this person who brings a cloth to Sister Etter, requesting that she anoint it and pray over it. Fourth, more detail is given in this account of the way in which an anointed cloth was utilized by the one in need – it was wrapped around the woman's tumor. Finally, there is a direct connection drawn by the person testifying between the application of the anointed handkerchief and the healing that ensued.

In another example from *The Latter Rain Evangel*, a Sister Wanner reports of her husband's healing subsequent to the arrival of an anointed handkerchief from a friend from whom she had solicited prayer on her husband's behalf. Listed under the heading, 'A Very Present Help', Sister Wanner – formerly of Canada but living in Genesco, Illinois – offers an extended account of her husband's injury and subsequent healing.

> Early in the Spring Mr. Wanner, her husband, was employed by a young man to build a barn and house … As soon as the barn was completed Mr. Wanner began operations on the house and while shingling the roof the scaffolding suddenly gave way; he was thrown against the ladder and then fell to the ground with an awful shock, where he lay for a time unconscious. He finally walked into the house but was not able to speak to his wife in answer to her questions. A neighbor soon came in and told her of the accident and he was undressed and put to bed. As there was no doctor within thirty miles of the place they were forced to lean heavily on Him who has promised to 'be a very present help in time of trouble.'

---

[4] Mrs. Ayers, 'Healed of Tumor Through an Annointed [*sic*] Cloth (Read Acts 19:12)', *The Pentecostal Herald* 1.4 (July, 1915), p. 2.

These were days of deep trial as his wife, after careful examination, found that some of his ribs and also his shoulder blade were broken; his entire side and arm were so bruised that they were black and green; he had hemorrhages almost constantly for a week and the suffering was intense. Surely this was a time to prove God. Mrs. Wanner felt her need of co-operation in prayer and faith and wrote a number of letters to ministers and friends asking them to join her in this battle. About three weeks later they received a reply from a friend containing an anointed handkerchief which Mrs. Wanner applied to the afflicted parts of his body and claimed healing in the name of the Lord. Immediately the power of the Holy Spirit surged through his body and his heart was so filled with worship that he could not cease adoring Him who was able to save from death and destruction and the house was filled with the praise which ascended to the throne of God. The work was completed, he was entirely healed. On the following day he walked three miles to his own home and two days after he was again able to work. Truly this was nothing short of a miracle when one realizes that he was seventy-one years of age. Is God able to adjust broken bones in aged people? Many say He is not, but it was no harder for Him to knit his bones together than for Him to do it in a child.[5]

Several aspects of this article are significant for the current study. First, the severity of the injury suffered by Mr. Wanner is described in considerable detail – broken ribs, shoulder blade, terrible bruising on the left side, with continuous hemorrhaging. Second, as in other cases, the anointed handkerchief was secured by someone for the sufferer. Third, prayers from afar accompanied the anointed handkerchief and were joined by those of Sister Wanner. Fourth, the article was applied to the injured areas. Fifth, upon his initial encounter with the handkerchief Mr. Wanner was drawn into worship and within a day's time he was fully healed, making a three mile journey the following day and returning to work a couple of days later. The age of Mr. Wanner – seventy-one – was understood to underscore the extraordinary nature of the healing experienced.

---

[5] *The Latter Rain Evangel* (December, 1917), pp. 21-22.

Something of the prominence of this practice and the seriousness with which it was taken is revealed in an account of an event in
Cleveland, Tennessee described in the *Church of God Evangel.*

> There was a wonderful scene at church in this city last Sunday
> when it was announced that there were SEVENTEEN handker-
> chiefs to pray over. This meant that there were seventeen sick
> people that were calling for help. These handkerchiefs were laid
> out on the altar bench and the saints gathered around them and,
> what prayers! what prayers! All prayed, but some cried and
> screamed as if their hearts would break from compassion for the
> sick ones. Tender, loving hands were laid on these handkerchiefs
> under the power of the Spirit and the power of healing fell as it
> often does when people are healed in the sick room. For years
> we have been praying over handkerchiefs on Sunday about
> twelve o'clock, but we do not remember of having as many as
> seventeen at one time before. We have heard of many healings
> as a result of these prayers and handkerchiefs being sent forth in
> Jesus' name. We pray at the same time for many that do not sent
> handkerchiefs. Some times they send aprons to have them
> prayed over. Acts 19:12. These handkerchiefs are placed on the
> sick ones and often they wear them next to the skin for several
> days. Sometimes the sick are healed instantly when the handker-
> chief is applied in Jesus' name, sometimes the power of healing
> thrills through their bodies after several hours, sometimes the
> healing is gradual. John 4.52.[6]

There are several aspects of this testimony worthy of comment.
First, this account reveals something of the regularity with which
the saints in Cleveland anointed handkerchiefs and other items to
minister to those at a distance. Second, on this occasion the large
number of such instruments of mediation is thought to be significant by the community and the writer, with SEVENTEEN appear-
ing in all caps at one point. Third, this account makes clear that
such activity was not undertaken in a perfunctory fashion but underscores the intensity, empathy, sensitivity, and care exhibited by
the community when engaged in this practice. Fourth, the context
in which these items are anointed and prayed over is closely associ-

---

[6] *Church of God Evangel* 11.17 (April 24, 1920), p. 2.

ated with a mighty manifestation of the power of God. Fifth, in some contrast to the earlier accounts cited to this point, here it is implied that the sick are included among those sending in such articles for prayer, though in any case someone other than the sick person would have likely brought the items to the meeting. Sixth, as in the previous account, this recounting reveals a bit more about the way in which the items were applied by those in need, being worn in bandage-like fashion. Seventh, the testimony indicates that there was some flexibility of thought in how the resultant healings came about: some occurred instantaneously, while others occurred more progressively. Eighth, as in the other accounts, testimonies of healing are reported as a result of such activity, suggesting something of attitudes toward the efficaciousness of the practice.

This account is followed up two years later by another testimony that reveals both the increasing frequency of the practice in Cleveland as well as something of the existential experience of those who prayed over these articles.

> We pray for the sick every day, but on Sunday about 12:30 we have special prayer and every Sunday we have from twenty to forty handkerchiefs to pray over besides quite a number of requests. When the time comes we spread the handkerchiefs out on the altar and the saints gather around and the prayers are offered up in the earnestness of our souls. We are often reminded of the experience of the apostles when the sick folks were brought in on couches and beds and placed in the street with a hope that even a shadow of Peter might fall upon them. We think of every handkerchief representing a sick person, and when we have forty or fifty handkerchiefs we think of being in the midst of that many sick folks. And oh, how the saints pray.[7]

Several aspects of this recounting are worthy of note. First, this account makes plain the regularity with which the community prayed for the sick and the regularity with which praying over anointed articles was part of this time of prayer. Second, it is clear that the number of such anointed items had grown from the account two years earlier. In point of fact, the number of requests had nearly tripled. Third, prayer for these items occurred in sacred space, as

---

[7] *Church of God Evangel* 13.23 (June 10, 1922), p. 1.

they have been spread out upon the altar for the activity of anointing and prayer. Fourth, the earnestness of the saints' intercession on behalf of the sick is again cited. Fifth, the account also speaks of the believers' existential identification with actors in the Acts narrative as participants in the biblical story through their shared experience with Peter.[8]

A series of references to anointed cloths occurs in three separate issues of *The Bridal Call*, a publication arm of the ministry of Aimee Semple McPherson. The first is found in the February issue of that year.

ANOINTED HANDKERCHIEFS – We gladly anoint and pray over handkerchiefs sent through the mail for the sick, according to Acts 19:12. Enclose same in self-addressed envelope stamped. In the past few weeks many scores have been prayed over in the meetings from place to place, and wonderful reports come in of healing.

One lady states that her acute indigestion stomach trouble was gone. Others healed of open sores, lung trouble, and many other ailments.

One man had a dying mother who suffered excruciating pains from cancer which had been operated upon and had grown again. She was an elderly lady and the time had come for the Lord to take her home. But children of the Lord do not need to *suffer* so. In olden days they who died 'fell asleep and were gatherer to the Fathers.'

Unable to go to this poor dear soul ourselves, an anointed handkerchief was sent, placed upon the sufferer's side, and from that hour the pain left. She lived over a week after that, then sweetly, consciously, and without pain, fell asleep in the arms of Jesus, whose ear is open to our cry and always answers prayer.[9]

As with other accounts, this one is relevant for this broader study in several ways. First, in some ways the announcement that the ministry welcomes handkerchiefs to anoint and pray over seems a bit less

---

[8] Cf. K.E. Alexander, *Pentecostal Healing: Models in Theology and Practice* (JPTSup 29; Blandford Forum: Deo, 2006), p. 207.
[9] 'Anointed Handkerchiefs', *The Bridal Call* 3.9 (February, 1920), p. 16.

like an advertisement for such but more of an acknowledgement of the reality the ministry is experiencing. It appears that so many of the items are being submitted to them that the phenomenon has necessitated instructions about how to submit the items. Second, as with other accounts, this one makes clear the biblical basis for the practice by citing Acts 19.12. Third, the account reveals that the context for such items to be anointed and prayed over is the believing community in worship, specifically in prayer. It might not be going too far to suggest that these words imply the reception of the anointed handkerchief is a means by which the sick person is physically connected to the community. Fourth, it appears that those who submit items for prayer include both the sick as well as those who bear a burden for the healing of others. Fifth, as usual a number of healings are cited as examples of the efficaciousness of this means of healing.

The regularity of such activity is evidenced in the next issue of *The Bridal Call* in a description of what occurred at a series of meetings in Baltimore.

> It is estimated that as many as two hundred and fifty to three hundred sick people (besides numerous anointed handkerchiefs which were sent according to Acts 19:12) were prayed for upon each of such days.[10]

Both the regularity of the practice and its biblical basis is underscored.

The extraordinary numbers of handkerchiefs to be anointed and something of the evolving theology of this practice is exhibited in an account published in *The Bridal Call* a mere two months later in a report of the events that transpired at a series of meetings in Washington.

> The services were not concluded until nearly 2 o'clock this morning. Mrs. McPherson, after praying for the last cripple and sick person, went into the parsonage, and early this morning, before she arose there were many men and women gathered in front of the parsonage waiting for her to come.

---

[10] Aimee Semple McPherson, 'Wonderful Down-pour in the Baltimore Churches', *The Bridal Call* 3.10 (March, 1920), p. 8.

Several hundred handkerchiefs were brought to the church to be prayed over. The handkerchiefs were anointed with oil yesterday, prayed over, and will be returned to the senders today.

With each handkerchief that was returned Mrs. McPherson sent this letter:

'Dear Child of God:

'These are wonderful days in which we live. Days in which faith is springing up in the hearts of the children of God. Days in which our God is proving that "His arm is not shortened that he cannot save, neither His ear heavy that He cannot hear." Days in which he is answering, as of old, the simple prayer of a humble, sincere, believing heart.

'Today, as in days of His earthly ministry, we are seeing continually His wonderful love for humanity. His sympathy, ability and willingness to heal all human ailments. Many are being healed in answer to the "Prayer of Faith." Bless His dear Name! (James 5:15.)

'As it is impossible for you to be present in these services, we are enclosing you a handkerchief (in accordance with Acts 19.12) which has been prayed over by Sister McPherson with the prayer that, as it is applied to the diseased part of your body, in Jesus' precious name, living faith in Christ may spring up in your heart, and that, as you consecrate your life to His will and service, perfect healing shall be the result. Remember always that Jesus wants, first of all, to save your soul, and then to heal your body that you may have a strong body in which to live for His glory. Praise be to His own dear Name! "By His strips we are healed." Isaiah 53:5.

'Believe that when you pray you shall receive that for which you are asking. Mark 11:24. "Jesus Christ is the same yesterday, to-day, and forever." Heb. 13:8. Remember that he has the same compassion today that he had when, in His earthly ministry, He had compassion on the multitudes, "and healed all that were sick with divers diseases."[11]

This entry reveals a number of relevant details. First, it makes clear that the context for the practice of anointing handkerchiefs and praying over them continues to be that of worship. Second, the account reveals that the numbers of handkerchiefs brought for anointing appears to coincide with the phenomenal response to Sister McPherson's ministry in general. Third, again it is evident that individuals in need or who bore burdens for the healing of others are the ones responsible for bringing items for such purposes. Fourth, the story suggests that a somewhat organized approach has emerged in terms of the reception of the handkerchiefs, their anointing and being prayed over, and their return/distribution to those who brought/sent them. Fifth, related to this previous point is the fact that now a letter accompanies the return of the handkerchiefs with an explanation of the biblical basis of the practice, instructions about how to use the handkerchief in order to achieve healing, an acknowledgement that spiritual healing should precede physical healing, and encouragement to the believer in question to allow faith to be made manifest in his or her life.

In a section entitled 'Jesus Heals the Sick – Testimonies in Our Recent Mail', that appeared four months later in *The Bridal Call*, a sister gives evidence of how this process worked in a short testimony that follows the heading 'OBSTINATE SORE HEALED'.

> It has been ten days now since the healing of the sore which I feared was an incipient cancer. I have taken the Lord for my body, and, as I could not attend Sister McPherson's meetings, I stamped and addressed an envelope to myself and enclosed in it a handkerchief for Sister McPherson to pray over, according to Acts 19:12. In as little time as possible from the many demands upon her she did so. I received the handkerchief the morning of June 18th, 1920. I put the handkerchief on the sore and it was healed, and the scab has vanished. I am praising Jesus for his wonderful works to the children of men. – Mrs. C.A.M.[12]

---

[11] 'Jesus the Physician Heals the Sick Today', *The Bridal Call* 3.12 (May, 1920), p. 18.

[12] 'Obstinate Sore Healed', *The Bridal Call* 4.4 (September, 1920), p. 20.

In addition to beginning and concluding with reference to the healing of a sore feared to be cancerous, this testimony acknowledges the biblical basis for the practice by citing Acts 19.12, praises Sister McPherson for her prompt attention to the request, reveals that she acted in a way consistent with the instructions given earlier in *The Bridal Call*, and offers praise to the Lord for such healing activity. This case provides additional support for the use of anointed cloths in early Pentecostal worship.

To these voices might be added a testimony in the *Pentecostal Evangel* by a Mrs. H.F. Ecker that appears under the heading, 'HEALED THROUGH A HANDKERCHIEF (Acts 19:12)'.

> I want to praise the Lord for defeating all my enemies. My soul is rejoicing in Him. I received the anointed handkerchief for which I thank you. God wonderfully healed my body and all in the house were blessed. My 2 children had boils and my husband feeling very poorly but we are all well and praise God for it. Please keep on praying for me. – Mrs. H.F. Ecker, Ruxton. Md.[13]

Similarly, in the *Church of God Evangel*, in a section entitled 'FINE WORK – 40 MEMBERS' under the heading, 'The Lord Miraculously Healing and Blessing Exhilarants', the following testimony occurs.

> Pelzer, S.C. – ... About two months ago I had a sore foot which the doctor said was pellagra, and I sent a handkerchief to Cleveland, Tennessee, according to Acts 19:12, which reads: 'So that from his body were brought unto the sick handkerchiefs or aprons, and the disease departed from them, and the evil spirits went out of them.'

> Since that time I have not taken any medicine or called for a doctor, but have been trusting the Lord for both soul and body, and I am a well woman today by the Lord's help and in answer to prayer. ... Edna Haney, Pelzer, S.C.[14]

As with many of the other citations this account appeals to Acts 19.12 and testifies to the fact of a healing by means of an anointed

---

[13] *The Pentecostal Evangel* 518 (October 20, 1923), p. 11.
[14] 'FINE WORK – 40 MEMBERS: The Lord Miraculously Healing and Blessing Exhilarants', *Church of God Evangel* 15.35 (September 13, 1924), p. 1.

handkerchief. It also functions as evidence that the practice continues amongst Church of God constituents in Cleveland, Tennessee.

Anointed Cloths and Acts 19.11-12

These examples from the early Pentecostal reception history of Acts 19.12 indicate that the practice this text generates is both widespread and potent. But can the text of Acts 19.11-12 bear the weight of such an interpretation? To gauge its strength, a reading of Acts 19.11-12 is here offered. However, before turning to the text it should be noted that many biblical scholars would answer this question in the negative. Part of the interpretive challenges of this text are hinted at in the observations of Ernst Haenchen offered nearly half a century ago,

> Scholars have advanced different explanations of how this second type of miracle [through scarves and handkerchiefs] came about. But whether they were 'liberal' like Wellhausen or 'conservative' like Zahn, one perceives in most of them a certain uneasiness and the attempt to excuse the Apostle.[15]

What would a narrative reading of the text reveal? It is to that attempt that the next section of this study is directed.[16]

The broader context of Acts 19.11-12 reveals a number of extraordinary things with regard to Paul's missionary activity, two of which would no doubt be impressive to the reader. The only healing account described in the run up to this text is that of the lame man in Acts 14, which causes such a stir that the people of Lystra take Barnabas and Paul to be the gods Zeus and his messenger Hermes. There is also one account of an exorcism. In Philippi, Paul and Barnabas are followed around by a young woman with a Phythian Spirit (πνεῦμα πύθωνα), who kept shouting, 'These men are servants of the most high God, they are proclaiming to you the way

---

[15] E. Haenchen, *The Acts of the Apostles: A Commentary* (trans. B. Noble, G. Shinn, H. Anderson and R. McL. Wilson; Philadelphia: Westminster Press, 1971), p. 562.

[16] The following section is informed by and in places draws heavily from J.C. Thomas, *The Devil, Disease, and Deliverance: Origins of Illness in New Testament Thought* (Cleveland, TN: CPT Press, 2010), pp. 274-77.

of salvation'. One day Paul turned upon her and, speaking to the spirit, cast it out in the name of Jesus (Acts 16.16-18).

Upon arriving in Ephesus Paul discovers certain disciples who, like Apollos, know only the baptism of John. After hearing Paul they are baptized in the name of the Lord Jesus. When Paul lays hands upon them the Holy Spirit comes on them and they speak in tongues and prophesy (19.1-6). Paul's preaching activity, which begins in the synagogue, eventually moves to the lecture hall of Tyrannus and results in the word of God being heard by the Jews and Greeks who live in Asia. At this point the text reads:

> God did unusual deeds of power through the hands of Paul, so that even upon those who were sick were brought handkerchiefs and aprons which had touched him and the diseases departed from them, and the evil spirits came out.

Verse 11

The reader learns that accompanying the preaching of the word of God are extraordinary miracles. Nearly every aspect of v. 11 serves to underscore the remarkable nature of the events. First, the Greek sentence begins with the word δυνάμεις ('mighty works'), a term that to this point in the Lukan narrative is used to describe the mighty works which Jesus (Lk. 10.13; 19.37; Acts 2.22), Stephen (Acts 6.8), and Philip (8.13) have performed. The appearance of this term indicates to the reader something of the powerful nature of Paul's ministry. Second, these mighty works are described as unusual (οὐ τὰς τυχούσας).[17] In other words, although mighty works are unusual enough, the reader is told that Paul's (unusual) mighty deeds are unusually unusual. Third, it is clearly stated that God did these things, a causation that in some cases in Acts is merely assumed. Finally, these deeds are said to come through the hands of Paul, a phrase the reader is likely to understand as meaning that Paul is the channel through whom God does such mighty acts. It may include the idea that Paul laid hands on those who were in need,[18] but should not be understood as indicating this means of

---

[17] G. Haufe ('τυγχάνω', *EDNT*, III, p. 372) observes that this meaning results from the adjectival use of the intransitive participle with negation. For a similar usage cf. Acts 28.2.

[18] For this interpretation cf. F.J. Foakes-Jackson and K. Lake, *The Beginnings of Christianity Part I: The Acts of the Apostles* (Grand Rapids: Baker Book House, 1965) IV, p. 239; W. Barclay, *The Acts of the Apostles* (Philadelphia: Westminster, 1976),

healing alone, as v. 12 reveals. Nevertheless, the statement does convey the idea that Paul is especially used by God in this fashion.

Verse 12

However, this extraordinarily emphatic description of Paul's mighty works looks understated when it is compared to what is revealed in v. 12. Paul's mighty works were so extraordinary that (ὥστε καὶ) even pieces of cloth that touched his body were taken to the sick and demon possessed, and the diseases and evil spirits left. The reader learns that these clothes are likely the handkerchiefs (σουδά-ρια) and aprons (σιμικίνθια) a tent maker would normally use in the course of his or her work,[19] perhaps suggesting 'that even the most despised objects associated with Paul were [thought to be] potent'.[20] The powerful presence of God in Paul's ministry is so pervasive that direct contact is not any more required with him than with Jesus (Lk. 6.19; 8.44) or Peter (Acts 5.15-16).[21] Observations about the superstitious nature of such a practice[22] and questions about whether or not Paul gave his approval to this action[23] miss

---

p. 143; Haenchen, *Acts*, p. 561 n. 2; and W. Neil, *The Acts of the Apostles* (NCB; Grand Rapids: Eerdmans, 1981), p. 204. G.H. Twelftree (*In the Name of Jesus: Exorcism among Early Christians* [Grand Rapids: Baker Academic, 2007], p. 148 n. 119) takes the phrase as indicating agency exclusively, apparently ruling out the idea that Paul laid hands on any individuals who were healed.

[19] Cf. F.F. Bruce, *Commentary on the Book of Acts* (NICNT; Grand Rapids: Eerdmans, 1954), p. 389. However, cf. T.J. Leary, 'The Aprons of St. Paul – Acts 19.12', *JTS* 41 (1990), pp. 527-29, for evidence that σιμικίνθια is a belt rather than a leather-worker's apron.

[20] On this whole issue cf. the helpful discussion in C.S. Keener, *Acts: An Exegetical Commentary 3* (Grand Rapids: Baker Academic, 2014), pp. 2840-41.

[21] Foakes-Jackson and Lake, *The Beginnings of Christianity Part I: The Acts of the Apostles*, IV, p. 240; J. Munck, *The Acts of the Apostles* (AB; New York: Doubleday, 1967), p. 192; J.W. Packer, *Acts of the Apostles* (Cambridge: Cambridge University Press, 1966), p. 161; Neil, *Acts*, pp. 204-205; J. Crowe, *The Acts* (Wilmington, DE: Michael Glazier, 1979), p. 146; R.C. Tannehill, *The Narrative Unity of Luke-Acts A Literary Interpretation volume two: The Acts of the Apostles* (Minneapolis: Fortress Press, 1990), p. 237; and L.T. Johnson, *The Acts of the Apostles* (Sacra Pagina 5; Collegeville, MN: Michael Glazier, 1992), p. 340.

[22] R.B. Rackham, *The Acts of the Apostles* (London: Methuen, 1901), p. 353; F.J,F Foakes-Jackson, *The Acts of the Apostles* (London: Hodder & Stoughton, 1931), p. 179; E.M. Blaiklock, *The Acts of the Apostles* (Grand Rapids: Eerdmans, 1959), p. 156; J.D.G. Dunn, *Jesus and the Spirit* (Philadelphia: Westminster, 1975), p. 168; and I.H. Marshall, *The Acts of the Apostles* (Grand Rapids: Eerdmans, 1980), p. 310.

[23] E.M. Knox, *The Acts of the Apostles* (London: Macmillan, 1908), p. 306 and D.J. Williams, *Acts* (Peabody, MA: Hendrickson, 1990), p. 333.

the point that for the reader these events indicate the powerful presence of God in Paul's ministry. When he comes up against illness or the work of demons the totality of God's victory is demonstrated.[24]

The expulsion of evil spirits accompanies the healing of the sick in this verse. It is not altogether clear whether the reader is to understand the healing of the sick and the expulsion of the evil spirits as two separate events. Although Luke can blur the lines between the two conditions, on this occasion, given the fact that two different infinitives are used to describe the results of diseases leaving and evil spirits going out, it would appear that here two distinct categories are recounted.[25] Such is the extent of God's presence with Paul that exorcisms are accomplished, not through direct contact with him, but by cloths that had contact with his skin.

Theological Implications from a Reading of Acts 19.11-12

Given this reading, what might be deduced from this text about the theological significance of the use of anointed cloths in this text?

First, it should be observed that the extraordinary miracles here attributed to Paul are not a one-off series of events in Luke-Acts but are integrally connected to the broader narrative in which continuity of the powerful presence of God's Spirit is being underscored. This theme goes back at least as far as Luke 8.42b-48 to the story of the woman with an issue of blood who, desperate for a healing from her twelve year malady, is healed when she touches, not Jesus' body, but the hem of his garment. On that occasion, Jesus' question about who touched him was owing to the fact that he was aware power left his body when the hem of his garment was touched. The fact that healing came via contact with the outer part of his clothing suggests that he was so specially anointed by the Spirit – Luke's language would be 'full of the Spirit' – that healing power was somehow conveyed by means of his clothing, emphasizing the extent of the presence of God's powerful presence in his life.

This theme continues in Acts 5.12-16, where in the aftermath of the events involving Ananias and Sapphira, extraordinary miracles

---

[24] S.R. Garrett, *The Demise of the Devil: Magic and the Demonic in Luke's Writings* (Minneapolis, MN: Fortress, 1989), p. 91.

[25] E. Jacquier, *Les Actes des Apôtres* (Paris: J. Gabalda, 1926), p. 573.

were wrought at the hands of the apostles.[26] The most spectacular aspect of these verses occurs in the latter part of v. 15, where it is disclosed that the hope of those who brought the sick for healing is not that Peter should lay hands upon them, which might be expected from v. 12, but that perhaps even his shadow might fall upon them. Clearly, such action indicates the extent to which the people regarded (ἐμεγάλυνεν) the believers, especially Peter. It is possible, of course, to take this detail as highlighting the superstition of the people[27] and/or attempt to shield Luke from the embarrassment of affirming this view himself.[28] However, to do so ignores the ideas surrounding the power of the shadow in the Graeco-Roman world[29] and the fact that Luke does indicate in the very next verse that numbers of healings and exorcisms take place (some presumably through precisely this means).[30] Such misgivings also ignore the significance of the Greek verb used here (ἐπισκιάσῃ), which in the Lukan writings, means 'to overshadow'. In Lk. 1.35, this term is used when Mary is told by the angel, 'The power of the Most High will overshadow (ἐπισκιάσει) you'. In Lk. 9.34, the verb reappears to describe the cloud which overshadows (ἐπεσκίαζεν) the three disciples during the Transfiguration.[31] As its previous occurrences in Luke have conveyed a sense of the divine presence and power, so the reader is here likely to understand the appearance of the term (ἐπισκιάσῃ) in the very same way. While technically it is Peter's shadow with which the sick want contact, the reader understands this overshadowing as very closely connected to, if not representa-

---

[26] On this text cf. Thomas, *The Devil, Disease, and Deliverance*, pp. 237-43.

[27] Blaiklock, *The Acts of the Apostles*, p. 71; A.C. Winn, *The Acts of the Apostles* (Richmond, VA: John Knox, 1960), p. 52; Dunn, *Jesus and the Spirit*, pp. 165-66; and D. Williams, *Acts*, p. 103.

[28] Some scholars observe either that it is not clear whether Luke approved of this belief or that Luke does not record the outcome of such a belief. Cf. W.C. Carter and R. Earle, *The Acts of the Apostles* (Grand Rapids: Eerdmans, 1973), p. 75; Neil, *Acts*, p. 96; Marshall, *Acts*, p. 116; and J.B. Polhill, *Acts* (Nashville: Broadman, 1992), p. 164.

[29] P.W. van der Horst, 'Peter's Shadow: The Religio-Historical Background of Acts V. 15', *NTS* 23 (1976-77), pp. 204-12.

[30] F.L. Arrington, *The Acts of the Apostles* (Peabody, MA: Hendrickson, 1988), p. 60.

[31] C.S.C. Williams, *The Acts of the Apostles* (London: A. & C. Black, 1964), p. 89; Arrington, *Acts*, p. 60; and J.R.W. Stott, *The Message of Acts* (Leicester: IVP, 1986), p. 113.

tive of, the power of God.[32] Clearly, one of the implications of this text is that the same Spirit with which Jesus is full is present and operative in Peter and other charismatically anointed believers in the early church.

Part of the significance of such extraordinary events in Acts 5 is the identification and legitimation of Jesus' followers as the true people of God, despite Jewish rejection of his messianic claims. A similar rationale is at work in Acts 19.11-12, where the description of the extraordinary miracles attributed to Paul are part of the boarder Lukan emphasis on the legitimacy of the place of the Gentile believers as part of the people of God.[33] While a variety of other characters are identified as being charismatically anointed in the Acts account,[34] special emphasis is placed upon Paul as he is the primary agent though whom the witness of the Gospel is taken to the heart of the Roman Empire, where he preaches the Kingdom of God and teaches the things concerning Jesus Christ unimpeded (Acts 28.30).

Second, the reader would likely conclude that Paul was not aware – in the first instance – of the distribution of such strips of cloth to the sick and possessed, or at least that he plays 'no active role in the apparent involuntary release and transfer of spiritual power or in healings and exorcisms'.[35] Such an understanding would be consistent with the involuntary mediation of Jesus and Peter described before him.

Third, at the same time it is clear that as with the response of those desirous of facilitating healings who brought the sick and afflicted for possible contact with Peter's shadow, the community of believers around Paul were intentional about retrieving and transporting these strips of cloth for others in need. It might be worth observing that ironically these pieces of cloth resulted in exorcisms

---

[32] Neil, *Acts*, p. 96; G.W.H. Lampe, 'Miracles in the Acts of the Apostles', in *Miracles: Cambridge Studies in their Philosophy and History* (ed. by C.F.D. Moule; London: Mowbray, 1965), p. 175; and G.A. Krodel, *Acts* (Minneapolis, MN: Augsburg, 1986), p. 125.

[33] Johnson, *The Acts of the Apostles*, p. 344.

[34] Cf. esp. R. Stronstad, *The Prophethood of All Believers* (Cleveland, TN: CPT Press, 2010) and J.C. Thomas, 'The Charismatic Structure of Acts', in *The Spirit of the New Testament* (Blandford Forum: Deo, 2005), pp. 223-32.

[35] Twelftree, *In the Name of Jesus: Exorcism among Early Christians*, p. 149.

while in the following text would-be exorcists – the seven sons of Sceva – lose their clothing to a demon![36]

Fourth, despite arguments to the contrary, the text reveals that such pieces of cloth functioned as mediating substances through which the Holy Spirit worked from the Spirit anointed Paul to those in need of healing and exorcism. As far as the text is concerned, these phenomena are not to be explained simply as an example of God honoring the faith of individuals despite their superstitious worldview, but rather are seen as an extension of the Spirit's power through a mediating substance.[37]

Implications for Pentecostal Theology and Practice

Despite their widespread utilization, little attention has been given to the theology and use of anointed cloths by Pentecostal scholars. On those occasions when comment is offered, it is normally an observation about the occurrence of the phenomenon without much elaboration. French Arrington's words are representative, 'Showing that Paul was a true servant of the Lord, God healed the sick though everyday articles that had touched the apostle's body'.[38] Going a bit further, in a section entitled 'Special Miracles Through Handkerchiefs and Aprons', Guy P. Duffield and Nathaniel M. Van Cleave offer a slightly more extensive reflection on the practice after citing the text of Acts 19.11-12,

> These were 'special miracles' in that there were no scriptural instructions concerning them. Paul must have simply been guided by the Holy Spirit in this matter. Many churches have followed a similar pattern and have given out small pieces of cloth, over which prayer has been made, and sometimes they have been anointed with oil. Some most remarkable miracles have been reported from the use of this method. It is understood that the 'prayer cloth' has no virtue in itself, but provides an act of faith

---

[36] I am indebted to my graduate student Jacob Edgeman for this observation.

[37] Cf. the esp. helpful discussion of this issue in J.F. Tipei, *The Laying on of Hands in the New Testament: Its Significance, Techniques, and Effects* (Lanham, MD: University Press of America, 2009), pp. 145-47.

[38] F.L. Arrington, *Christian Doctrine: A Pentecostal Perspective Volume Two* (Cleveland, TN: Pathway Press, 1993), p. 258.

by which one's attention is directed to the Lord Who is the Great Physician.[39]

But even these somewhat more extensive comments leave a number of questions and perhaps contain some conclusions that are at odds with the narrative itself. Ray H. Hughes offers perhaps the most extensive theological reflection on the practice in his book *Church of God Distinctives*. In a section entitled 'Other Media of Healing', he writes of Acts 19.11-12 in particular:

> This is a medium of contact with the sick. When the apron or handkerchief is laid on the body through faith in the name of the Lord, the sick recover. Since all healing comes from God, who is omnipresent, it should not be thought a thing incredible that God would honor such a method to show His power. This medium simply assists the sick in making contact with the Healer.[40]

The weakness of Hughes' assessment is owing more to its brevity than its insight.

The remainder of this study will be devoted to raising a few issues that might merit inclusion in a future, more comprehensive, construction of a theology and use of anointed cloths. First, despite the misgivings of and embarrassment felt by any number of scholars – and even some practitioners – there should be no question about the biblical underpinning of and support for the use of anointed cloths in worship. Not only is there sufficient biblical precedence for the practice, but the phenomenon is also part of a more comprehensive set of divinely sanctioned activities that reflect the powerful presence of the Holy Spirit amongst the people of God. As such, the practice of the church in this regard should reflect that this practice is associated with unusual workings of the Spirit and thus the church should resist any temptation to routinize this activity. One of the ways early Pentecostals seemed to have maintained this dynamic understanding was by means of the intensity of their prayers over such anointed articles and their existential connection with both the Spirit anointed individuals described in Scripture and those who would receive such cloths. It appears that

---

[39] G.P. Duffield and N.M. Van Cleave, *Foundations of Pentecostal Theology* (Los Angeles: L.I.F.E. Bible College at Los Angeles, 1983), p. 398.

[40] R.H. Hughes, *Church of God Distinctives* (Cleveland, TN: Pathway Press, 1968), p. 46.

such anointing often occurred in what could be described as 'sacred space'.

Second, in this practice it would appear to be significant for the church to keep an intentional focus on those in need rather than upon the one(s) from whom the cloths originate. Initially, such an observation would appear to be counter-intuitive for, on the one hand, in Acts 19.12 Paul's anointing by the Spirit is underscored. But, on the other hand, a closer examination of the text reveals that the narrative focus is not so much on Paul for Paul's sake but upon the Spirit who anoints him. Paul is the instrument through whom such Spirit empowered events are mediated. However, it should be remembered that throughout the Acts narrative a variety of individuals are described as being charismatically anointed by the Spirit – some in unique ways – such as Philip who is transported physically by the Spirit. On this occasion, what is being underscored is the presence of the Spirit in Paul's life to effect such extraordinary works, not simply the fact that it is Paul through whom they are mediated. The parallels between the lives and ministries of Jesus, Peter, and Paul are indeed significant for they the agents through whom the story of salvation for all nations – including Gentiles – is told. As such, this trajectory ensures the legitimacy of the Gentile mission. In this sense Paul *is* important for he is the one through whom the kingdom of God and the teachings of Jesus will be made known in Rome, but in another sense – consistent with the broader Acts narrative – Paul is one of many charismatically anointed figures. Thus, the focus on those in need and the Spirit anointed origins of the cloths helps keep the focus upon the Spirit who is active rather than an unhealthy focus upon a Spirit anointed individual. At the same time, it is a reminder to contemporary believers that the same powerful presence of the Spirit is available and present even now amongst God's people.

Third, another important component for the use of anointed cloths is the role of the community in this practice. As seen in Acts 19.12, Paul is not described as playing an active role in the sending out of such strips of cloth to those in need, but rather the community is the entity that is underscored as being primarily responsible for such ministry on behalf of others. As such the practice functions as a physical sign of the conveyance of the presence of God in the community to those on its margins owing to physical infirmity or demonic affliction. The anointed article serves to extend the community's pastoral care and concern for those in need.[41] As in Acts 19.12 it would appear that in this practice the onus is upon members of the community to discern the needs around them and to become active in requesting, obtaining, and delivering these articles to those in need. This communal emphasis seems borne out in early Pentecostal approaches to the practice, where communal requests seem to have driven the practice.[42] Significantly, this communal practice does not appear to have been commercialized or commoditized in any way, but was viewed as a ministry of the church or the broader believing community. The various entities simply requested that the sent items be accompanied by a self addressed stamped envelop.

Fourth, rather than understanding this practice as some kind of suspect magical rite, it appears time for the Pentecostal church to re-embrace and re-appropriate the use of anointed cloths in its ministry of healing. Perhaps the place to begin is by re-visioning the practice from the ground up. Pentecostal New Testament scholar John Tipei offers a starting point by reflecting theologically on the phenomenon:

> Luke's reports about the use of 'mediating substances' in healing are not necessarily an indication that he condoned magical practices or that he entertained superstitious beliefs. As long as the sick person recognized the true source of the healing power mediated through these pieces of material, there would be nothing superstitious about such practice. In fact, one may even consider that for Luke a healer's hand functioned like a 'mediating substance,' interposed between the real source (God) and the receiver; they are both carriers of numinous power. The only difference between a healer's hands and a mediating substance is that the symbolism attached to the former is much stronger than that attached to the latter. The positive side of the use of mediating substances is that the attention of the sick person is diverted

---

[41] On this idea cf. Alexander, *Pentecostal Healing*, p. 207.

[42] Cf. K.E. Alexander, 'The Pentecostal Healing Community' in J.C. Thomas (ed.), *Pentecostal Ecclesiology: The Church and the Fivefold Gospel* (Cleveland, TN: CPT Press, 2010), pp. 183-206 (pp. 193-94).

from the healer (Acts 5.13) to God who actually performs the miracle (Acts 19.11).[43]

This judicious judgment reveals something of what may be gained by serious theological reflection on this topic. Rather than being embarrassed by the practice Pentecostals should be encouraged to devote additional intentional theological reflection on a variety of aspects of the practice.

In this light, as a way of pushing the conversation forward a bit, I would like to suggest that anointed cloths be understood sacramentally. Nearly two decades ago I proposed that when Pentecostal ecclesiology is re-visioned from the ground up it would likely take shape around the fivefold Gospel that proclaims Jesus is Savior, Sanctifier, Holy Spirit Baptizer, Healer, and Soon Coming King. I further proposed that in such a constructive paradigm, each ecclesiological component would be accompanied by a sacramental sign: the Church as Redeemed Community (water baptism), the Church as Holy Community (footwashing), the Church as Empowered Community (glossolalia), the Church as Healing Community (anointing with oil), and the Church as Eschatological Community (the Lord's Supper), respectively.[44] If anointing with oil indeed functions as the sacramental sign of healing for Pentecostals, then anointed cloths may well be a physical extension of this primary sign.[45] If so, far from being viewed as a quasi-magical embarrassment, the anointed cloth could function robustly as a sign of healing that connects the one in need with the healing community from which they have been separated by distance and or infirmity. If this 'mediating substance' comes from the believing community and is sent with the prayers and anointing of that community from a sacred space, its physical presence would not only convey the healing power of the Spirit, but also point beyond the materiality of the sign to the Spirit who heals.

---

[43] Tipei, *The Laying on of Hands in the New Testament*, p. 147.

[44] J.C. Thomas, 'Pentecostal Theology in the Twenty-first Century', *Pneuma* 20 (1998), pp. 3-19.

[45] On the sacramental significance of anointed handkerchiefs, cf. Alexander, 'The Pentecostal Healing Community', pp. 197-202, esp. pp. 197-98.

A Final Word

In this study I have sought to offer a short reception history of Acts 19.11-12 in early Pentecostal periodical literature, offer a narrative reading of this text, reflect upon Acts 19.11-12 theologically, and offer some suggestions about a few of the significant aspects of possible contemporary practice. If this modest study contributes to a better understanding of the use of anointed cloths, or to a resurgence of their usage in Pentecostal worship, or serves as a catalyst for additional studies that result in a more comprehensive theology of anointed cloths, I will consider my effort to have contributed in some small way.

5

WORSHIP IN THE BOOK OF REVELATION

Melissa L. Archer[*]

Introduction

When asked to name places in Scripture containing worship passages, many come easily to mind: the Psalms, Isaiah 6, the Lukan canticles, or perhaps the Christ hymn of Phil. 2.6-11. One rarely thinks of the book of Revelation, at least not beyond the worship scene in Revelation 4–5. Revelation is the go-to-book for end time scenarios – it is *The Apocalypse*, after all. Pentecostals in particular have poured over dispensational charts and have been terrorized by films depicting the Rapture and the horrors of being 'left behind'. Tragically, it is the rich theology of the Apocalypse that has been *left behind* in many Pentecostal circles. This is true when thinking about a theology of worship based on the Apocalypse; however, as the simple title of this essay suggests, I believe that Revelation has a great deal to offer its readers about worship; indeed, the whole of the Apocalypse can be explored as a *liturgical* text. As such, it has much to contribute to a biblical theology of worship for Pentecostals.

Although it is beyond the scope of this essay to engage fully in a narrative analysis of Revelation, much of the essay is based on my

* Melissa L. Archer (PhD, Bangor University, Wales) is Associate Professor of Biblical Studies at Southeastern University in Lakeland, FL, USA.

understanding of the book's structure.[1] In recent years, many scholars have given serious attention to the four ἐν πνεύματι ('in the Spirit') phrases found throughout the Apocalypse. As literary markers, these phrases guide the hearers[2] through the phases of John's vision while at the same time providing continuity to the whole of the narrative. These phrases also ground the Apocalypse pneumatologically by highlighting the role of the Spirit. Liturgically, the phrases point to the role of the Spirit as the facilitator of worship for both John and his hearers. Along with the prologue and epilogue, these phrases suggest the following large units as a way of structuring the narrative:[3]

---

[1] It seems prudent to lay out some of my presuppositions concerning the Apocalypse. I maintain that the implied author of the Apocalypse is someone named John, who is a part of the Johannine community and likely a prophetic figure familiar to the implied audience, the seven churches of Asia identified in Rev. 1.11. The author himself is a Jewish follower of Jesus Christ who receives visions while apparently exiled on the island of Patmos 'for the word of God and the testimony about Jesus' (Rev. 1.9). The Apocalypse was written sometime in the late first century, possibly during the reign of the emperor Domitian. Whether or not the author or the audience was experiencing persecution is a continual matter of scholarly debate; nevertheless, the narrative at the very least anticipates and depicts persecution and even death for one's witness to Jesus. The Apocalypse shares affinities with other apocalyptic literature and contains numerous echoes of and illusions to Old Testament scripture. The genre of the Apocalypse is a contested issue. The Apocalypse consistently identifies itself as a prophecy (Rev. 1.3; 22.7, 10, 18-19), but it also features apocalyptic elements and is set in an epistolary format; thus, it seems sufficient to suggest that the Apocalypse is an apocalyptic prophecy.

[2] I am using *hearers* rather than *readers* to emphasize the important biblical concept of hearing (*shema*) as well as to highlight the emphasis on hearing found in the Apocalypse. The Apocalypse itself identifies both a reader and hearers (Rev. 1.3), yet there is a clear emphasis placed on hearing, especially hearing what the Spirit has to say to the churches (Revelation 2–3). The idea of hearing is clearly tied to obeying, which is another key concept in the Apocalypse. My commitment to hearing thus reinforces the oral/aural nature of Scripture. On this I am deeply indebted to L.R. Martin, *The Unheard Voice of God: A Pentecostal Hearing of the Book of Judges* (JPTSup 32; Blandford Forum: Deo Publishing, 2008), p. 53). Additionally, as a fourth generation North American Pentecostal, I have been shaped in Pentecostalism's oral nature. On the oral theology and liturgy of Pentecostalism, see C. Bridges Johns, *Pentecostal Formation: A Pedagogy among the Oppressed* (JPTSup 2; Sheffield: Sheffield Academic Press, 1993), pp. 87-91; W.J. Hollenweger, 'The Black Roots of Pentecostalism' in A. Anderson and W.J. Hollenweger (eds.), *Pentecostals After a Century: Global Perspectives on a Movement in Transition* (JPTSup 15; Sheffield: Sheffield Academic Press, 1999), p. 36.

[3] Many scholars recognize the ἐν πνεύματι phrases as having a significant role in the Apocalypse. R.J. Bauckham, *The Climax of Prophecy: Studies in the Book of Revelation* (Edinburgh: T&T Clark, 1993), p. 3, identifies them as denoting 'three ma-

I.   Prologue (1.1-8)
II.   ἐν πνεύματι – 'On the Lord's Day' (1.9–3.22)
III. ἐν πνεύματι – 'In Heaven' (4.1–16.21)
IV.   ἐν πνεύματι – 'In the Wilderness: Babylon' (17.1–21.8)
V.   ἐν πνεύματι – 'On a Mountain: New Jerusalem' (21.9–22.5)
VI.   Epilogue (22.6-21)

A Pentecostal Reading of Worship in the Apocalypse

Worship is a central feature of Pentecostalism.[4] In worship, Pentecostals expect to have an encounter with God. Worship for Pentecostals is a *felt* experience of being in the presence of God – an experience made possible by the Spirit. The Spirit orchestrates the worship encounter between the Divine and the human; indeed, true worship takes place in *Spirit* and *Truth* (Jn 4.24).[5] At the heart of Pentecostal worship and spirituality is the knowledge that the worshiper is engaging in a personal encounter with the Holy Spirit.[6] The

---

jor transitions within the whole vision'. J.A. Filho, 'The Apocalypse of John as a Visionary Experience: Notes on the Book's Structure', *JSNT* 25.2 (2002), p. 229, suggests that the phrases indicate 'the most important moments in the visionary experience that the book presents, involving changes of place and subject'. For scholars who use the phrases to outline Revelation, see J.L. Trafton, *Reading Revelation: A Literary and Theological Commentary* (Macon: Smyth & Helwys, Inc., 2005), p. 10; R. Waddell, *The Spirit of the Book of Revelation* (JPTSup 30; Blandford Forum: Deo Publishing, 2006), pp. 148-49; J.C. Thomas, *The Apocalypse: A Literary and Theological Commentary* (Cleveland: CPT Press, 2012), pp. 5-6.

[4] For studies on Pentecostal/Charismatic worship see D.E. Albrecht, *Rites in the Spirit: A Ritual Approach to Pentecostal/Charismatic Spirituality* (JPTSup 17; Sheffield: Sheffield Academic Press, 1999), J.H.S. Steven, *Worship in the Spirit: Charismatic Worship in the Church of England* (Carlisle, Cumbria: Paternoster Press, 2002); D.E. Miller and T. Yamamori, *Global Pentecostalism: The New Face of Christian Social Engagement* (Los Angeles: University of California Press, 2007); K. Warrington, *Pentecostal Theology: A Theology of Encounter* (London: T&T Clark, 2008), pp. 219-26; M. Cartledge, *Testimony in the Spirit: Rescripting Ordinary Pentecostal Theology* (Farnham, UK: Ashgate Publishing Limited, 2010), pp. 29-54.

[5] Pentecostals understand 'Spirit' to be a reference to the Holy Spirit. J.C. Thomas, 'The Spirit in the Fourth Gospel', *The Spirit of the New Testament* (Blandford Forum: Deo Publishing, 2005), p. 161, suggests that in the Fourth Gospel 'Truth' is a 'subtle reference to Jesus' based on the associations between truth and Jesus in Jn 1.14, 16, 17; 3.21 and the explicit claim of Jesus in Jn. 14.6.

[6] D.E. Albrecht, 'An Anatomy of Worship: A Pentecostal Analysis', in W. Ma and R. Menzies (eds.), *The Spirit and Spirituality: Essays in Honour of Russell P. Spittler* (JPTSup 24; London, T&T Clark, 2004), p. 74.

liturgy of Pentecostalism[7] is vibrant, dynamic, and grounded in holy expectancy. The book of Revelation can be experienced as a narrative about worship – about true worship *in the Spirit*. This essay will discuss some of what the Apocalypse reveals about worship and suggest ways in which it can contribute to a Pentecostal theology of worship.[8]

On a structural level, worship is woven into the very fabric of the narrative. Every section of the Apocalypse contains liturgical material. In the prologue, a liturgical blessing is pronounced upon the reader (lector) and the hearers of the prophecy (1.3).[9] This suggests a liturgical context – a worship service – in which the Apocalypse would be read to the church as part of their worship. All within the community are invited to participate, suggesting that reading and hearing (and keeping) the prophecy are to be considered liturgical activities within the churches.[10] The epistolary greeting to the churches (1.4-5) is infused with liturgical language as grace and peace are extended to the churches from God ('the one who is, was, and is to come'), from the Spirit[11] before God's throne, and from

---

[7] While Pentecostals see themselves as anti-liturgical, they, like all traditions, have a distinct liturgy and are thereby liturgical. On this see, J.K.A. Smith, *Desiring the Kingdom: Worship: Worldview, and Cultural Formation* (Grand Rapids: Baker Academic, 2009), p. 152. See also Albrecht, *Rites in the Spirit*, p. 22: 'The Pentecostal service lies at the heart of the Pentecostal/Charismatic spirituality and with its attending rites and practices constitutes the most central ritual of Pentecostalism'. See his Appendix B (pp. 254-59) for a listing of what he identifies as 'liturgical rites, foundational rites, and microrites'.

[8] What is presented here is adapted from the final chapter of my monograph, *'I Was in the Spirit on the Lord's Day': A Pentecostal Engagement with Worship in the Apocalypse* (Cleveland: CPT Press, 2015). The monograph is a slightly revised version of my PhD thesis (Bangor University, Wales).

[9] L. Thompson, *The Book of Revelation: Apocalypse and Empire* (New York & Oxford: Oxford University Press, 1990), p. 54; W.H. Gloer, 'Worship God! Liturgical Elements in the Apocalypse', *Review and Expositor* 98 (2001), p. 38. See also O.K. Peters, *The Mandate of the Church in the Apocalypse of John* (New York: Peter Lang, 2004), p. 47.

[10] M. Gorman, *Reading Revelation Responsibly* (Eugene: Cascade Books, 2011), p. 82. See also Thompson, *The Book of Revelation*, p. 72, 'Reading and listening to the Book of Revelation are themselves liturgical acts in the worship life of Christians in western Asia Minor'.

[11] Although a point of scholarly debate, it would seem that John's reference to the 'seven spirits' would most likely have been understood by his hearers as a reference to the Holy Spirit, particularly given the close connections between God, Jesus, and the Spirit throughout the Fourth Gospel and in Revelation. See J.L. Resseguie, *The Revelation of John: A Narrative Commentary* (Grand Rapids: Baker Academic, 2009), p. 66 who states that such 'dynamic imagery emphasizes the

Jesus (the faithful witness, firstborn from the dead, and ruler of the kings of the earth). The prologue continues with a liturgical doxology to Jesus (1.5b-6), a prophetic word of Jesus' return cast in liturgical form (1.7), and a direct word from God (1.8). The powerful self-revelatory word from God closes out the prologue by taking the hearers back to the 'originating being of God'.[12]

Following the prologue, the use of the ἐν πνεύματι phrases that divide the phases of the vision as discussed above suggest that the Spirit be seen as facilitating John's visions. John's claim that he received the vision 'in the Spirit on the Lord's Day' (Rev. 1.10) is key. Richard Bauckham, who writes at length on John's experience, states: 'John was ἐν πνεύματι in the sense that his normal sensory experience was replaced by visions and auditions given him by the Spirit'.[13] For Bauckham, the phrase highlights the Spirit's role as 'agent of visionary experience' and links John's experience with Old Testament figures such as Isaiah, Ezekiel, Zechariah, and Enoch.[14] It is possible, however, that more is being communicated in John's statement of being *in the Spirit*, particularly given the Apocalypse's liturgical setting and the profusion of liturgical material in the prologue. John's statement of being in the Spirit on the Lord's Day seems to suggest two things. First, John was observing, in solidarity with the churches, the day for worship; thus, just as the churches would be gathered for worship on the Lord's Day, so too was John worshiping – even while exiled on Patmos. Second, being *in the Spir-*

---

active presence and power of the Spirit of God in the world'. For a thorough treatment of the Spirit in the Apocalypse, see Waddell, *The Spirit of the Book of Revelation.*

[12] S.S. Smalley, *The Revelation to John* (Downers Grove: InterVarsity Press, 2005), p. 38.

[13] Bauckham, *Climax of Prophecy*, p. 152.

[14] Bauckham, *Climax of Prophecy*, p. 154. For many early interpreters, the phrase was indicative of a trance-like or ecstatic state. So R.H. Charles, *A Critical and Exegetical Commentary on the Revelation of St. John* (Edinburgh: T&T Clark, 1920), I, p. 24, 'In this passage, then, ἐγενόμην ἐν πνεύματι denotes nothing more than that the Seer fell into a trance. It was not until he was in this trance that Christ addressed him.' Also G.B. Caird, *The Revelation of St. John the Divine* (New York: Harper & Row, 1966), who translates all the ἐν πνεύματι phrases as 'in a trance'. See also P. Prigent, *Commentary on the Apocalypse of St. John* (trans. W. Pradels; Tübingen: Mohr Siebeck, 2001), p. 128, who says that the phrase 'undoubtedly refers to a phenomenon more or less resembling that of ecstasy'.

it on the Lord's Day was a normal experience of worship for John.[15] The simple and unassuming nature of his statement indicates that John fully expects his audience to understand what it means to be *in the Spirit.* Johannine hearers might recall Jesus' statement about worship being in Spirit and in truth (Jn 4.24). In describing himself as being *in the Spirit,* John is making a statement about the significance of worship as the point of contact between heaven and earth. Thus, John is *in* worship *when* he receives the apocalypse. He did not worship *in the Spirit* in hopes of receiving an apocalypse; he worshiped *in the Spirit* because that is how worship takes place. This is not to take away from the significance of John receiving the revelation or the agency of the Spirit in giving the revelation; rather, it is to emphasize the *context* in which John received the revelation. It is in worship that Spirit-inspired revelation is given both to John and to the seven churches, as seen in the prophetic messages (Revelation 2–3).

The narrative is filled with liturgical vocabulary, such as λατρεύω ('worship, service'; 7.15; 22.3) and forms of προσκυνέω ('worship'; 4.10; 5.14; 7.11; 9.20; 11.1, 16; 13.4 (2x), 8, 12, 15; 14.11; 16.2; 19.4, 10, 20; 20.4; 22.8), as well as the liturgical acclamations of Ἀμήν ('amen'; 1.6, 7; 3.14; 5.14; 7.12 (2x); 22.20) and Ἀλληλούϊα ('hallelujah'; 19.1, 3, 4, 6). Traditional liturgical forms – doxology (1.5b-6), blessings (1.3; 14.13; 16.15; 19.9; 20.6; 22.7, 14), and benediction (22.21) – combine with liturgical images of incense, altar, and temple, suggestive of formal elements within a service of worship with which the hearers would be familiar. Over and over, the hearers are confronted with images of worship designed to affirm and bolster their own worship practices. Further, the Apocalypse is replete with hymns of worship (4.8, 11; 5.9-10, 12, 13; 7.10, 12, 15-17; 11.15-18; 12.10-12; 15.3-4; 16.5-6; 19.1-2, 3, 5; 6-8) and the liturgical posture of prostration (1.17; 4.10; 5.14; 7.11; 19.4, 10; 22.8). Worship scenes are embedded in the narrative (4–5; 7.9-17; 11.15-19; 12.10-12; 14.1-5; 15.1-8; 19.1-8). These scenes are directly tied to the narratives around them and aid the hearers in interpreting and discerning them – always from heaven's perspective. The juxtaposition of

---

[15] J.N. Kraybill, *Apocalypse and Allegiance: Worship, Politics and Devotion in the Book of Revelation* (Grand Rapids: Brazos Press, 2010), p. 28, describes John as being in 'an attitude of waiting on God' as he normally would during regular worship ('on the Lord's day').

scenes of heavenly worship with scenes of judgment upon the inhabitants of the earth is intended to demonstrate to the hearers that whatever they might face while on earth, true reality is what is taking place in heaven. It is only from heaven's perspective, where God and the Lamb rule and are just in all their judgments, that the scenes of judgment can be properly assessed. The alternate reality created by the worship scenes is differentiated from the earthly reality of false worship that is given to and demanded by the Dragon, the beasts, and, even, Babylon in Revelation 13–18. Throughout the Apocalypse, it is worship that reveals one's allegiance. Revelation presents worship as 'the definitive act of Christian resistance' to any and all that are opposed to God.[16]

The epilogue (22.6-21) bears similarities to the prologue,[17] yet even the epilogue's rehearsal of key elements in the Apocalypse is expressed through liturgical language that reinforces the liturgical framework of John's writing as well as the liturgical setting of John's churches in which it is heard and experienced. In the epilogue, liturgical blessings are pronounced by Jesus (22.7, 14), thus assuring the churches that he is still standing in their midst (1.12-16). Their response to Jesus' thrice-repeated announcement of his soon return (22.7, 12, 20) couples the liturgical Ἀμήν with a liturgical prayer of longing for the return of their Lord, Jesus.[18] The closing benediction (22.21) both reflects the Revelation's epistolary nature[19] and serves as a conclusion to the entire worship setting of the narrative, likely based on the benediction spoken as the conclusion to the churches' own worship services. The benediction upon *all* is communal,[20] an open-ended offer of grace to all who would hear

---

[16] S. Saunders, 'Revelation and Resistance: Narrative and Worship in John's Apocalypse', in J.B. Green and M. Pasquarello III (eds.), *Narrative Reading, Narrative Preaching* (Grand Rapids: Baker Academic, 2003), p. 118.

[17] Parallels between the prologue and epilogue are as follows: the revelation 'to show to his servants what is necessary to take place quickly' (1.1 = 22.6); the beatitude (1.3 = 22.7, 9); the identification of the work as prophecy (1.3 = 22.7, 10, 18, 19); John's name (1.1, 4 = 22.8); John hearing and seeing these things (1.2 = 22.8); 'the time is near' (1.3 = 22,10); the use of 'testimony' (1.1-2 = 22.16); 'I am the Alpha and Omega' (1.8 = 22.13); the Spirit (1.4 = 22.16, 20); the Parousia (1.3, 7 = 22. 7, 12, 20); the keeping of the words of the prophecy (1.3 = 22.7).

[18] Along with 22.21, this is the only occurrence of 'Lord Jesus'.

[19] Thompson, *The Book of Revelation*, p. 55.

[20] Thompson, *The Book of Revelation*, p. 56.

and respond, and thus become followers of the Lamb.[21] The benediction, then, is not a perfunctory ending to John's letter but a profound theological statement of hope for all who would worship God and the Lamb.

This initial observation about the liturgical structure of the Apocalypse is instructive for Pentecostals if for no other reason than it opens up the possibility of a fresh reading of the Apocalypse that is freed from the chains of a dispensationalist reading. Early Pentecostals were profoundly affected by the worship found in the Apocalypse. In their own encounters with the Spirit, they *experienced* the Apocalypse in ways not unlike John.[22] In recognizing the liturgical fabric of the Apocalypse, contemporary Pentecostals can both re-discover and retrieve it as a resource for their own worship.

While this point has been mentioned above, it is so essential that it bears repeating. John's statement of being *in the Spirit* is a profound statement both about worship and the central role of the Holy Spirit. Worship is an engagement with and participation in the Spirit of God. Worship *in the Spirit* turns ordinary places like Patmos and the seven churches of Asia into sacred spaces and ordinary time into eschatological time.[23] Worship is not confined to a designated time or place; rather, true worship takes place whenever and wherever one is communing with God *in the Spirit*; thus, John stands in solidarity and *in the Spirit* with the seven churches in worshiping God even though exiled on Patmos. John is *in the Spirit* because worship takes place *in the Spirit*. It is *in the Spirit* that John is granted a vision of the living Jesus (1.9-18). In the prophetic messages to the churches (Revelation 2–3), it is *in the Spirit* that the churches hear the voice of Jesus who is in their midst. Although each message indicates that it is Jesus, the one who appeared to John, who is speaking to them[24] and revealing intimate knowledge of their wor-

---

[21] B.K. Blount, *Revelation: A Commentary* (Louisville: Westminster John Knox Press, 2009), p. 417.

[22] For the use of the Apocalypse by early Pentecostals as attested in the early Pentecostal periodicals (1906–1916), see M.L. Archer, 'The Worship Scenes in the Apocalypse, Effective History, and Early Pentecostal Periodical Literature', *Journal of Pentecostal Theology* 21.1 (2012), pp. 87-112. All references to the practices of early Pentecostals in the remainder of this essay can be found in this article.

[23] C. Bridges Johns, 'The Light That Streams from the End: Worship Within the Coming Christendom', *The Living Pulpit* 12.3 (2003), p. 14.

[24] Each message provides an ascription that is connected in some way to Revelation 1 and John's inaugural vision of the exalted Christ. Each ascription is a

ship practices, each message concludes with an imperatival call to hear what the *Spirit* is saying to the churches (2.7, 11, 17, 29; 3.6, 13, 22). In this way, the words of Jesus and the words of the Spirit are co-terminus. To hear what the Spirit is saying is to hear the very words of Jesus! It is *in the Spirit* that the transcendent God is made immanent[25] and the churches find themselves, along with John, in the realm of heaven where they see, hear, and experience its liturgy (e.g. Revelation 4–5). It is *in the Spirit* that the churches ascertain their true identity as New Jerusalem, the wife of the Lamb (21.2, 9), despite the fact that they currently find themselves living in Babylon, the consort of the Dragon (Revelation 17–18). Worship *in the Spirit* creates a context for pneumatic discernment – a crucial liturgical task for the people of God.

The Apocalypse's claim that worship takes place in and through the Spirit is quite conducive for Pentecostals who, above all, define themselves as people of the Spirit[26] and understand their worship to be Spirit directed.[27] Pentecostals view worship as an experiential encounter; thus, they value *experiences* in worship. Pentecostals can find in the Apocalypse confirmation that true worship *is* experiential, involving the whole person – body, mind, and spirit – in encounter with God *in the Spirit*. In the Apocalypse, the experience of worship is that which will *mark* the hearers as followers of the Lamb, as theologically formed worshipers who understand that their own worship is to be a proleptic participation in the sights, sounds, and activities of the heavenly realm. In this way, *Spiri*ted worship engages the imagination. Pentecostal worship should be a

---

description of or declaration about Jesus that takes on meaning particular to each message. Coupled with the specificity of what Jesus knows about each church, the ascriptions demonstrate that Christ indeed *is* in the midst of each community – just as John saw Jesus standing in the midst of the lampstands. Collectively, the ascriptions create a liturgy – a doxological confession about Jesus. As each message unfolds, the churches discover another reason to worship Jesus.

[25] R.J. Bauckham, *The Theology of the Book of Revelation* (Cambridge: Cambridge University Press, 1993), p. 46, notes that God as transcendent does not mean that God is distant from God's people; rather, 'The transcendent God, precisely because he is not one finite being among others, is able to be incomparably present to all, closer to them than they are to themselves'.

[26] S.J. Land, *Pentecostal Spirituality: A Passion for the Kingdom* (JPTSup 1; Sheffield: Sheffield Academic Press, 1993), p. 169.

[27] Warrington, *Pentecostal Theology*, p. 220; Steven, *Worship in the Spirit*, p. 183; R.J. Boone, 'Community and Worship: The Key Components of Pentecostal Christian Formation', *Journal of Pentecostal Theology* 8 (1996), p. 138.

holy imaginative experience. *Spirit*ed worship is also sensory; John sees the Lamb, hears the trumpets, smells the incense, tastes the scroll, and touches the measuring rod. In the same way, Pentecostals can find an invitation to a *Spirit*ed sensory experience of worship – an experience of worship as 'ritual play' whereby the Spirit takes them into the throne room to worship before God and the Lamb.[28] Early Pentecostals testified to receiving songs and poems *in the Spirit*, and the inclusion of these in their published periodicals attests to their understanding that these were Spirit-given and intended for worship.[29] In the same way, present-day Pentecostal communities should encourage and intentionally incorporate artwork, poetry, banners, incense, or other items designed to engage both the imagination and the senses as expressions of *Spirit*ed worship.

Worship creates a context for the prophetic activity of the Spirit. The Apocalypse itself is a prophecy, given to John, a prophetic figure (10.11; 22.9), for churches in which prophets appear to function (10.7; 19.10; 22.9). Jesus' solemn warning for adding or taking away from the words of the prophecy (22.18-19) confirms the necessity of prophecy, or at the very least this particular prophecy, for the churches.[30] That the Apocalypse is also a liturgical narrative sug-

---

[28] For the idea of worship as ritual play, see S. Chan, *Pentecostal Theology and Christian Spiritual Tradition* (JPTSup 21; Sheffield: Sheffield Academic Press, 2000), pp. 116-19; also P. Althouse and M. Wilkinson, 'Playing in the Father's Love; The Eschatological Implications of Charismatic Ritual and the Kingdom of God in Catch the Fire World', *Arc* 39 (2011), pp. 93-116.

[29] Antionette Moomean, *Apostolic Faith* 1.11 (October-January, 1908), recounts her experience of Spirit baptism in which the Lord showed her the cross. She then relates the following:

One morning the Spirit dealt with me, singing through me –
Must Jesus bear the cross alone,
And all the world go free:
No, there's a cross for every one,
And there is one for me.

The last line He just seemed to burn into my soul by repeating it over and over again. *Sometimes the Spirit would sing a line and then sob out a line.* Although I wept and was in anguish of soul, it was all in the Spirit (emphasis mine).

Her testimony speaks to the sense amongst Pentecostals that worship afforded a deep connection to the Spirit and that they were giving voice to the words and longings of the Spirit.

[30] Thomas, *The Apocalypse*, p. 686:

The seriousness with which the resurrected Jesus treats the words of this prophecy is indicated in part by the fact that four times reference is made to

gests an integral connection between worship and prophecy. Because the Apocalypse is meant to be read and heard when the churches gather for worship, worship becomes the context for the giving and receiving of prophetic revelation. Because worship is intimately linked to the Spirit, prophetic words and visions are a means by which the Spirit communicates to the churches.[31] Moreover, calls for pneumatic discernment in the prophetic messages (2.7, 11, 29; 3.6, 13, 22) and throughout the rest of the narrative (11.8; 13.18; 14.12) suggest that discernment is an essential activity in relation to prophecy. The Apocalypse calls on the churches to discern both their *own condition*, as evidenced in Jesus' words of correction in the prophetic messages, and the *culture* of Babylon around them. It is by means of the words of the prophecy that the Spirit aids the churches in properly discerning the insidious workings of the Dragon and the beasts (Revelation 12–13), even while the inhabitants of the world are enticed by them. Thus, the churches can worship and sing the song of Rev. 12.10-12 knowing that the Dragon is overcome by the blood of the Lamb and the word of their testimony. By means of the words of the prophecy, the Spirit aids the churches in properly discerning their true identity as the Bride of the Lamb, so that in their worship they can sing the songs of Rev. 19.6-8, celebrating God's destruction of Babylon and their own wedding feast with the Lamb. The words of the prophecy are to be received *in the Spirit* because John received them *in the Spirit*. The climatic statement – 'the testimony of Jesus is the S/spirit of prophecy' (19.10)[32] – fuses together prophetic proclamation and worship.

Pentecostals value prophecy and believe that the Spirit speaks prophetically to the church. While Acts 2.17-18 and 1 Corinthians 12 and 14 are favorite texts, Pentecostals should also look to the

---

what is written in this book within the span of two verses. There could be no mistaking that one's response to the words of the prophecy of this book are of eternal consequence …

[31] R.L. Jeske, 'Spirit and community in the Johannine Apocalypse', *New Testament Studies* 31 (1985), p. 463.

[32] It is likely that the hearers would associate τὸ πνεῦμα (spirit) with the Holy Spirit, given all the ways that the Spirit has functioned in the Apocalypse up to this point in the narrative in relationship to God and the Lamb. Further, the close alignment of the words of Jesus and the Spirit in the prophetic messages strengthens the idea that 19.10 is a reference to the Holy Spirit.

Apocalypse for its dynamic concept of prophecy and prophetic discernment. The refrain of the prophetic messages to *hear* what the Spirit is saying is as crucial now as it was for John's hearers. Early Pentecostals frequently wrote down the words of the Spirit – often in song or poetry – so that the community could *hear* the voice of the Spirit. Some of the early issues of the *Latter Rain Evangel* even published transcriptions of messages given by the Spirit during the services at Stone Church to enable the body of Christ to hear the Spirit. Present-day Pentecostals, who believe that the Spirit desires to speak a present word to the community, should consider ways to ensure that in those moments – particularly experienced in worship – when the Spirit speaks, the words of the Spirit are given their full due. Writing the message of the Spirit down or allowing for several moments of silence to meditate on the Spirit's words would allow obedient response to the voice of the Spirit. Further, Pentecostals might re-imagine the giving and receiving of prophetic words and visions (as well as discerning them) as essential to their corporate worship experience.

The Apocalypse demonstrates that worship is the central purpose for all of creation, whether in heaven or on earth. It is not insignificant that the first thing John sees and hears when taken to heaven via the Spirit is worship rendered unto God and the Lamb (Revelation 4–5). The songs of worship begun by the 24 elders and four living creatures (4.8, 11; 5.9-10) crescendo as the angels add their song (5.12) only to be followed by all of creation adding their voices to produce a symphony of praise to God and the Lamb (5.13). This worship scene anticipates the eschatological goal for all creation to worship God and the Lamb.[33] As the vision progresses, John is shown scene after scene of heavenly worship where God and the Lamb continue to be lauded for their character and their works. In many of the worship scenes, John also sees the martyrs – those who, while on earth, gave their lives for the Lamb – worshiping in heaven (7.9-17; 14.1-5; 15.1-8).[34] That those who refuse to worship the beast on earth are put to death but then found to be alive in heaven reinforces for the hearers the primacy of worship

---

[33] Bauckham, *The Theology of the Book of Revelation*, p. 33.

[34] S. Pattemore, *The People of God in the Apocalypse: Discourse, Structure and Exegesis* (Cambridge: Cambridge University Press, 2004), pp. 114-16 has an excellent discussion on Revelation's portrait of the church as a martyr church.

both while on earth *and* continuing in heaven. This portrait of the overcomers alive in the presence of God and fully engaged in worship bolsters the hearers in their own practice of worship in the midst of potential suffering. The worship scenes are thereby paradigmatic and pedagogical. Paradigmatically, they provide the pattern for the churches' own worship practices and thereby become an evaluative instrument. Pedagogically, they instruct the churches as to their primary task of the worship of God and the Lamb. Indeed, worship forms a crucial component of the churches' witness in the world – calling all to the worship of God.[35] Additionally, the Apocalypse portrays for the hearers the goal of worship: to *be* New Jerusalem – the *wife* of the Lamb (21.2).[36] The city is just not *for* the people of God, it *is* the people of God;[37] thus, John is afforded a glimpse of the people of God fully united with the Lamb. New Jerusalem is the glorious fulfillment of the churches' expectation when gathered for worship. In their worship, they encounter the living Jesus *in the Spirit*; through their worship, the Spirit prepares them for the coming day when they will fully live in God and God will dwell in them (21.3). John's hearers are invited to enter into an alternate reality – an escape from their present situation, for in worship the boundary between the present and the future is breached as the Spirit transports the worshipers back and forth between heaven and earth revealing what is and what will be. This is what makes the connection between the promises to the overcomers in the prophetic messages (2.7, 11, 17, 26-28; 3.5, 12, 21) and the vision of New Jerusalem so vital for the churches. Worship *in the Spirit* collapses the *time* between the present and the future. The rewards promised to the overcomers are not 'put off' until the end of the book where John sees the new heaven and earth and the New Jerusalem; rather, the eschatological promises are a *present* reality for those keeping the words of this prophecy. It is in worship and *in the Spirit* that the churches receive a foretaste of what awaits them *in full* as New Jerusalem. It is this foretaste that enables them to continue in their wor-

---

[35] M.M. Thompson, 'Worship in the Book of Revelation', *Ex Auditu* 8 (1992), p. 47.

[36] Bauckham, *The Theology of the Book of Revelation*, pp. 136-43, argues that New Jerusalem functions as a multivalent symbol for people, place, and presence. See also R.H. Gundry, 'The New Jerusalem: People as Place, Not Place for People', *NovT* 29 (July 1987), pp. 254-64; Richard, *Apocalypse*, p. 161.

[37] Pattemore, *The People of God in the Apocalypse*, pp. 199-200.

ship and witness to Jesus. Worship thus serves as an apprenticeship for that day when worshipers from *every* tribe, language, people, and nation (7.9) will join the heavenly residents in worshiping before the throne of God and the Lamb.

Pentecostals understand the idea of worship as the nexus between heaven and earth; and in worship, Pentecostals 'imagine a different world'.[38] The testimony of early Pentecostals of experiences in worship in which they suddenly found themselves transported to the throne of God or saw the table spread for the Marriage Supper affirms what the Apocalypse has portrayed; namely, that in worship, the boundary between the present and the future is breached. The Apocalypse invites Pentecostals not to envision a future *world* of material prosperity – mansions and streets of gold – but a future *union* with God and the Lamb, where *all* will worship. Accordingly, Pentecostal worship must not be reductionistic or shallow but formational and catechetical. Cheryl Bridges Johns calls the Pentecostal church to see itself as 'the primary agent of conscientization' – helping believers to understand reality in a new way. She further suggests that the liturgical elements of Pentecostalism – water baptism, communion, footwashing, testimony, healing rituals, Spirit baptism, and songs and dances – work to both construct and maintain this new reality.[39] It is through their rituals that Pentecostals experience communally a foretaste of the future and invite others to participate in that for which they were designed – worship.

The Apocalypse establishes that God alone is to be worshiped. This is so because of who God is. In the Apocalypse, God is holy (4.8) and the creator of *all* things that are (4.11; 10.6) and all things that will *be* (21.1, 5). God as holy and creator identifies the 'most elemental forms of perception of God' and requires a response of worship.[40] To offer worship to anyone or anything else constitutes idolatry – a practice that is anathema in the Apocalypse (9.20; 13.4, 8; 21.8; 22.15; also 19.10; 22.9). God is the one who is, who was, and who is to come (1.4, 8; 4.8; also 11.17; 16.5 [who was and is]), the Almighty (1.8; 4.8; 11.17; 15.3; 16.7; 19.6, 15; 21.22), the Alpha

---

[38] Althouse and Wilkinson, 'Playing in the Father's Love', p. 96; also R. Jaichandran and B.D. Madhav, 'Pentecostal Spirituality in a Postmodern World', *Asian Journal of Pentecostal Studies* 6.1 (2003), p. 59.

[39] Bridges Johns, *Pentecostal Formation*, pp. 125-29.

[40] Bauckham, *The Theology of the Book of Revelation*, p. 33.

and Omega (1.8; 21.6) who sits on the throne (4.2; 5.1; 6.16; 7.10; 19.4; 20.11; 21.5) and who lives forever (4.9; 10.6; 15.7). God is Father (1.6; 2.27), Sovereign Lord (6.10), and Judge (15.3; 16.5, 7; 18.20; 19.2; 20.11-15) who from the throne reigns over all (11.17; 19.6). It is this God who reigns supreme and whose will and plan is unveiled; it is this God who will inaugurate a new heaven and earth where God will dwell with God's people (21.3). They will see God's face and bear God's name upon their foreheads (22.4). For who God is and for all that God has done, is doing, and will do, God is worthy of worship; thus, worship must be oriented *theo*logically.

The Apocalypse also reveals that Jesus is worthy of worship. Like God, Jesus is given various titles in the Apocalypse. The dominant designation is Lamb (Revelation 5; 6.1, 3, 5, 7, 16; 7.9, 14, 17; 12.11; 14.1, 4, 10; 15.3; 17.14; 19.7; 21.22; 22.3), which symbolizes Jesus' supreme role as redeemer. Jesus is also the Faithful Witness, Firstborn from the dead, and Ruler of the kings of the earth (1.5). To John and the seven churches, Jesus identifies himself as the First and the Last, the Living One, and the One who holds the keys to Death and Hades (1.17-18; also 2.8; 3.14; 22.13). Further, Jesus is 'one like a son of man' (1.13-16; 14.14), the Son of God (2.18), the Amen (3.14), Shepherd (7.17), Christ (1.1-2; 11.15; 12.10; 20.4, 6), King of kings and Lord of lords (17.14; 19.16), Faithful and True (19.11), and Word of God (19.13). Jesus is the Root and Offspring of David (22.16), the Morning Star (22.16; also 2.28), and Lord (22.20-21). It is this Jesus who is coming soon (1.7; 16.15; 22.7, 12, 20). In Revelation 5, Jesus is afforded worship in the same way that God is worshiped in chapter 4. The profound implications of the hymn in 5.13 can scarcely be overstated; that is, worship to the One on the throne includes the worship of the Lamb, Jesus – not as two separate objects of worship but as one; thus the worship of God *and* Jesus re-defines monotheistic worship.[41] It is this perspective that is adopted throughout the remainder of the Apocalypse. Evidentiary of this is that throughout the Apocalypse, Jesus acts and speaks as God acts and speaks; in fact, the hearers can scarcely distinguish John's divine referents, which is surely the point! For example, in the hymn of Rev. 11.15, the singular verb βασιλεύσει (he

---

[41] Thompson, 'Worship in the Book of Revelation', pp. 50-51: 'Worship of Christ was not a development in early Christianity that occurred at the expense of monotheism, but precisely within an unrelenting monotheistic framework'.

will reign) is employed even though God and Christ are mentioned together. Similarly, in 22.3-4, singular forms of αὐτος (he) are used when God and the Lamb are the antecedent for the pronouns. God and the Lamb *is* the Alpha and Omega (1.8; 22.13). God and the Lamb *is* the temple within New Jerusalem (21.22). Worship and worshipers must be oriented *theo*logically and *christo*logically and not to the exclusion of one or the other. The worship of God and the Lamb would not be complete without giving consideration to the worship of the Spirit. While this is not made explicit in the Apocalypse, the very fact that the Spirit is depicted in intimate relation to God (1.4; 4.5) and to the Lamb (5.6) clearly links the Spirit with God and Jesus, both of whom receive worship. The Spirit is the one who enables worship since true worship takes place *in the Spirit*. It does not seem to be a stretch to suggest that the worship of God and the Lamb *includes* the worship of the Spirit.[42]

The implications of this point for Pentecostal worship is very important. Pentecostal worship is about an encounter with the Divine. As noted by Land, for Pentecostals, 'God is the *last thing* … Therefore Pentecostals should focus their attention and theological efforts on an understanding of God as the eschatological Trinitarian presence and not on speculative end-time sequences'.[43] The Apocalypse provides Pentecostals with a plethora of descriptors for the Triune God in combination with a rich liturgy that extols the character and works of God that can inform all aspects of Pentecostal worship. Pentecostal worship in song, in prayer, and in preaching must be grounded theologically, christologically, and pneumatologically. Pentecostal worship must be centered on the Triune God as the object of worship rather than centered on the worshiper. As Smith states, 'Worship is not *for me* … worship is about and for God'.[44] Pentecostals should ensure that their worship proclaims the narrative of God and God's works in the past, the present, and the future.

The Apocalypse differentiates between legitimate and illegitimate worship. This is a theme which permeates the Apocalypse. Fundamental to the Apocalypse is that God alone is to be worshiped, which includes the worship of Jesus (and the Spirit). The twice-

---

[42] See Thomas, *The Apocalypse*, pp. 226-30.
[43] Land, *Pentecostal Spirituality*, p. 197.
[44] Smith, *Desiring the Kingdom*, p. 150.

repeated injunction – 'Worship God' (19.10; 22.9) – reverberates as the heart of the narrative. John's attempt to worship a being other than God (19.10; 22.9; also 17.6b) gives indication to the hearers of the subtle nature of false worship. The theme of false worship first appears in the prophetic messages when the hearers are confronted with the realization that false worship has infiltrated their sacred spaces through the false teachers/prophets 'Balaam' (2.14) and 'Jezebel' (2.20) who intentionally seek to lure the churches into idolatrous practices.[45] Then, after the events connected to the sixth trumpet, John records that the inhabitants of earth did not stop *worshiping* demons and idols (9.20). In Revelation 12–13, illegitimate worship is fully exposed as the hearers encounter the Dragon and his beasts. This evil trinity – a perverse parody of the Triune God[46] – launches a full-scale campaign aimed at turning all of humanity from the worship of God by demanding worship of the beast. It is at this point that humanity is divided into two camps: those who give their worship to the beast and sing, 'Who is like the beast?' (13.4) and those who refuse to worship the beast and are killed (13.15). As if this were not enough, in Revelation 17, the hearers are confronted with another entity demanding their worship and allegiance – Babylon the harlot. The sight of her is so wondrous that John's amazement teeters on worship (17.6b-7)[47] – even while fully cognizant that she is drunk on the blood of the saints (17.6-7). Worship becomes a decisive test of allegiance; that is, the followers of God and the Lamb and the followers of the Dragon, beasts, and Babylon are *marked* by their worship.[48]

---

[45] These prophetic or teaching figures are given the names 'Balaam' and 'Jezebel' by Jesus intentionally to cause the hearers to think of the biblical stories of these notorious characters who led Israel astray.

[46] G.R. Beasley-Murray, *Revelation* (Grand Rapids: Eerdmans, 1981), p. 207; Thomas, *The Apocalypse*, pp. 382-403.

[47] The verb θαυμάζω was used in 13.3 to express the wonderment of the whole world when the wounded head of the beast is healed. This sense of awe and wonder leads the world to worship the Dragon and the beast (13.4). Thomas, *The Apocalypse*, p. 502.

[48] In the Apocalypse the 144,000 bear the seal of God upon their forehead (7.3). In 13.16, the followers of the beast worship him and are thereby identified by his mark upon their hand or forehead (13.16), while those who refuse to worship are killed but then portrayed in 14.3 having the name of God and the Lamb on their foreheads (see also 22.4), just as promised to the overcomers in 3.12.

True and false worship leads people to specific eternal destinies in the Apocalypse. The followers of the beast are cast into the lake of fire (20.11-15); the followers of the Lamb enter into and are New Jerusalem (Revelation 21–22). The fate of the followers of the beast is not pre-determined, as evidenced in the proclamations of the three angels in Revelation 14 who proclaim the same message to everyone: 'Worship God' (14.7). Further, they announce the fate of Babylon (14.8) and the fate of those who choose to worship the beast (14.9-11). *Whom* to worship thereby becomes a conscious and informed choice on the part of the worshiper. The thread of what constitutes true and false worship woven throughout the Apocalypse is not just to show the fate of those who follow the beast, for the Apocalypse is written for the churches. It is the people of God who must diligently guard against the subtle *and* blatant pressure to render worship to anyone or anything other than God and the Lamb. This is why the churches are first taken up into heaven, along with John, to fall before the God of all creation and the Lamb, their redeemer. They hear and participate in the thunderous worship given to God and the Lamb. To them is shown the outcome of their perseverance and their refusal to worship the beast. It is in the context of dying for refusing to worship the beast that the hearers realize the true *blessedness* of 'those who die in the Lord' (Rev. 14.13), for it is the martyrs – those who refuse to worship the beast – who are alive in heaven, singing the song known only to them (14.3) and the song of Moses and the Lamb (15.1-4). It is by engaging in the liturgy of heaven that John's hearers are to counter the false liturgies around them.

For Pentecostals, the temptation toward false worship might seem irrelevant; after all, Pentecostals seek above all else an authentic and experiential encounter with God. Pentecostals, however, should constantly discern whether or not they are unwittingly engaging in or being led into false worship. It can come in the guise of elevating Pentecostal pastors or leaders onto platforms from which the glory reserved for God is wrongly ascribed to them. It can happen in worship where style is worshiped more than the Triune God. It can happen when buildings are built 'to the glory of God' but then the community has no resources or desire to engage the world outside its doors. The rising popularity and growing acceptance of Pentecostalism into the mainstream of American culture likely offers the most subtle temptation. While the Apocalypse calls John's hearers to resist the trappings of Babylon, it calls present-day Pentecostals to resist the trappings of current culture.[49] The liturgies of the culture around John's hearers had the potential to lure them away from the true worship of God; thus, the urgent call to 'Come out of Babylon' (18.4) sounds forth. Similarly, the liturgies of modern culture wear away at Pentecostal self-identity by demanding that Pentecostals accommodate themselves to the trends of contemporary culture. The Apocalypse advocates for the followers of the Lamb to refuse to engage in false worship and to self-identify as overcomers – those willing to lose their lives for the sake of the Lamb. Early Pentecostals shared this understanding,[50] yet present-day Pentecostals are uncomfortable with this perspective. Pentecostals must engage in critical self-reflection to ensure that they are not participating in or fostering any type of false worship. They might also reflect on ways in which their liturgy can engage the imagination of the worshipers so that the culture of New Jerusalem so fills their hearts and minds that the contemporary culture of Babylon loses all allure. The call of the Spirit to come out of Babylon is for every generation of hearers to heed. Ever in the hearts and minds of Pentecostal worshipers must be the mantra of the Apocalypse: 'Worship God!'

The Apocalypse describes numerous activities which are expressions of worship. Due to the constraints of space, only a few of the many liturgical activities found in the Apocalypse will be discussed. The most recognizable are the hymns found throughout the narrative. The hymns heard in heaven are exclusively focused on the person and work of God and the Lamb. The hymns are profoundly theological and thereby become melodic vehicles for catechesis. Thereby, it is in the hymn of Rev. 5.9-10 that the worthiness of the

---

[49] Smith, *Desiring the Kingdom*, pp. 90-91, identifies modern cultural practices as secular liturgies: 'We need to recognize that these practices are not neutral or benign, but rather intentionally loaded to form us into certain kinds of people – to unwittingly make us disciples of rival kings and patriotic citizens of rival kingdom'.

[50] William Seymour, *Apostolic Faith* 1.10 (September, 1907), p. 2, wrote: 'O beloved, our reigning time has not come yet. We are to be with the Babe from the manger to the throne. Our reigning time will come when Jesus comes in great power from the throne. Until then we are to be beaten, to be spit upon, and mocked. We are to be like His son.'

Lamb and the significance of his work of redemption is made explicit; it is in the hymn of 12.10-12 that the radical definition of what it means to follow the Lamb is rehearsed; it is in the hymn of 15.3-4 that God's desire for the conversion of the nations is declared. Because John claims to hear these hymns sung in heaven, the hymns have divine sanction and approval; thus, the hearers are encouraged to agree with and, indeed, adopt the 'premises' established in the hymns.[51] To sing them or to pattern songs on them is of utmost importance. The hymns assist the hearers in reinterpreting present reality. Many of the hymns are embedded in the midst of narratives depicting trouble and danger for the people of God; nevertheless, the songs never devolve into dirges acutely focused on pain and suffering. Instead, the hymns locate the present in the Apocalypse's theme of the coming of God's kingdom (7.10-12; 11.15-18; 12.10-12; 19.1-8). The suffering inherent in the reality of martyrdom is not denied or ignored (7.15-17; 16.6) but assuaged with the assurance that God will wipe away every tear, and the Lamb will be their shepherd. The hymns reorient reality and remind the hearers that worship in song interprets all earthly existence from heaven's perspective. It is the martyrs – those who have imitated their Lord in death and thereby become overcomers, like their Lord – who can sing 'Great and marvelous are your deeds, Lord God Almighty' (15.3). The hymns become the churches' language of resistance in the face of evil and even death (12.10-12). The hymns are prophetic – declaring what is and what will be. By this, the hearers are encouraged to be steadfast and to endure for despite the seeming unending reach of the Dragon and the beasts, salvation belongs to God and the Lamb (7.10; 19.2); the kingdom of our Lord and of his Christ has come (11.15); rewards will be given to the people of God (11.18); the accuser has been cast down (12.10); the smoke of Babylon goes up forever (19.3); and the wedding of the Lamb is to come (19.7). The hymns inform and sustain the worshipers on their journey through difficulties knowing that New Jerusalem – the final goal of worship – is just ahead. At the heart of the prophetic nature of the hymns is the Spirit, for it is *in the Spirit* that John and the churches hear the hymns.

---

[51] M. Harris, *The Literary Function of the Hymns in the Apocalypse* (Ann Arbor: UMI Dissertation Service, 1989), p. 284.

Musical instruments are also present in the Apocalypse as John sees and hears trumpets and harps. Harps, particularly, are used exclusively in the worship scenes (5.8; 15.2; also 14.3). The acknowledgement of musical instruments suggests their suitability in worship and points to the presence of musicians. The living creatures, elders, and overcomers all seem to be singers *and* musicians. While the verbal worship found in the hymns is that which is most noted in the Apocalypse, the creation of instrumental worship is often overlooked. Worship is a performance, in its most positive sense, for God and the Lamb. The presence of musical instruments suggests creativity in worship.

Pentecostals *love* music and song; indeed, Pentecostal worship is often defined in terms of music.[52] From the Apocalypse, Pentecostals can find affirmation for both as avenues of worship. The hymns of the Apocalypse are theological expressions of praise directed to God. This feature of the hymns should encourage Pentecostals to evaluate both the content and function of their own hymnody. Warrington points out that lyrics in Pentecostal music 'have increasingly taken the form of more directional expressions to God than doctrinal reflections on his character'.[53] The hymns of the Apocalypse are focused on the clear exultation of God; they neither make use of first person pronouns nor offer the worshipers' perspectives or desires. As such, they can serve as a helpful corrective to the tendency within contemporary Pentecostal worship to become preoccupied with individual concerns.[54] The hymns of the Apocalypse form the hearers into theological singers. If Pentecostals sing their theology, then a robust theology should ring out loud and clear from their music. Pentecostal worship that is saturated in the Spirit will produce music that is unapologetically robust in its theology so that the person and work of the Triune God is the focus. The prophetic nature of the hymns of the Apocalypse should encourage Pentecostals to engage the prophetic through music. To this end, as early Pentecostals discovered, singing in the Spirit can be a means for the Spirit to sing a prophetic word in the midst of the worship-

Robust theology in lyrical expressions of worship

---

[52] Albrecht, *Rites in the Spirit*, pp. 155-56.
[53] Warrington, *Pentecostal Theology*, p. 224.
[54] Smith, *Desiring the Kingdom*, p. 150; Chan, *Pentecostal Theology*, p. 118.

ing community.[55] As for musical instruments in Pentecostal churches, the more the better! The harps of the Apocalypse have been replaced in most Pentecostal churches by the guitar (acoustic, electric,
and/or bass), and to it are often added keyboards and drums, as
well as any number of brass and woodwind instruments.[56] Undoubtedly the instruments found in the Apocalypse contribute to
the *loudness* of the book in much the same way that Pentecostal worship services are usually loud; however, the performance of worship
is for God alone. Just as instruments serve to express creative worship to God in the Apocalypse, Pentecostal musicians should maintain this singular focus and see the valuable contribution they add to
the creation and expression of worship. Early Pentecostals testified
to receiving the gift of suddenly being able to play an instrument for
which they had no prior training, and they insisted that this gift
came from the Spirit who played through them. Contemporary
Pentecostal musicians in tune with the Spirit should see themselves
as musicians who play *in the Spirit*. The creative and spontaneous
flow of music that connects the musician to God in a worship experience that is deep and unexplainable is the Spirit playing through
them. Pentecostals should seek intentional ways both to foster this
sense of playing *in the Spirit* and to encourage the community to *hear*
what the Spirit is saying through instrumental worship.

The Apocalypse depicts kinesthetic movement as an appropriate
liturgical response to God. Throughout the narrative, various characters fall down or prostrate themselves before the throne of God
and the Lamb (4.10; 5.14; 7.11; 19.4). The repetition of this liturgical posture by the elders and living creatures confirms that prostration is, at least for the Apocalypse, the most appropriate response
to the presence of God. In all of their liturgical activities – singing

---

[55] S. Dove, 'Hymnody and Liturgy in the Azusa Street Revival, 1906-1908',
Pneuma 31 (2009), pp. 248-49, calls singing in the Spirit 'the quintessential expression of the free liturgy of Azusa Street' as it 'appeared to be unplanned and un-
traceable to human origins'.

[56] D. Daniels, '"Gotta Moan Sometime": A Sonic Exploration of Earwitnesses
to Early Pentecostal Sound in North America', *Pneuma* 30 (2008), p. 17, explains
how important music and music-making was to the Azusa Revival but also how
debates arose over musical instruments. 'Sacred instruments included the piano
and organ; homemade instruments included washboards, bones, jugs, and kazoos;
and "worldly" or "the devil's" instruments included the violin (fiddle), banjo,
guitar, and drums'. He also documents how guitars, drums, and brass instruments
made their way into the Pentecostal soundscape (pp. 20-22).

of hymns, offering the 'Amen', presenting prayers to God, and prostration – the elders and living creatures instruct the hearers in appropriate worship. Prostration demonstrates that the worshiper recognizes the presence of the Divine, as evidenced in John's 'falling as though dead' at the feet of Jesus as he worshiped on the Lord's Day (1.17). Such recognition demands a response not only of mind but of body. If the heavenly residents who dwell continuously in the presence of God respond in such a way, how much more should the hearers respond to the presence of God in their midst with an act of bodily worship. In the Apocalypse, it is this singular act of kinesthetic *worship* that gives full expression to the experience of being overwhelmed by God.[57] Early Pentecostals looked to the Apocalypse for verification for their experience of being 'slain in the Spirit', and contemporary Pentecostals continue this ritual act, often in special times of prayer at the altar. In the Apocalypse, however, prostration is a liturgical act of worship offered in worship. This suggests that worship *in the Spirit* is embodied worship. Pentecostals worship with their whole bodies; thus, falling prostrate should be affirmed as an embodied response of being so overwhelmed by the presence of God that standing is no longer possible.

A final liturgical activity to mention is prayer. In Rev. 5.8 and 8.3-4, the prayers of the saints are depicted as incense offered up in golden bowls to God and the Lamb. The significance of the prayers of the saints is in their location – the throne room of God – and in the symbolism of the golden bowls, suggestive of the value and worth of the prayers. The prayers of the saints are part of the ongoing worship in heaven (5.8-10). In the unsealing of the fifth seal, the souls under the altar lift up a prayer of lament for justice (6.9-10). The answer to this prayer for justice begins to unfold with the sounding of the seven trumpets. The message for the hearers is clear: God hears and responds to the prayers of the people of God. Prayer constitutes a liturgical act that is pleasing to God – like the fragrance of incense.[58] In addition to prayers for justice, the Apoca-

---

[57] The rebuke that John receives when attempting to prostrate himself before the heavenly messengers reinforces that prostration is an act of worship reserved for God alone.

[58] Thomas, *The Apocalypse*, p. 230, writes, 'The prayers of the saints are not simply a ritual to be rendered in a perfunctory way, but are reflected in the activi-

lypse instructs that the people of God should pray for the return of Christ (22.20b). Such a prayer reminds the community that this world is not their home, that though they reside in Babylon, Babylon does not reside in them. The prayer for Jesus' return is not to be prayed lightly but fervently with the full knowledge of what his return entails, for it is the return of Jesus (Revelation 19) which then gives way to eternal destinies for all (Revelation 20). Finally, prayers for healing are supported by the Apocalypse, for Jesus himself counsels the Laodicean church to buy from him salve to put on their eyes so that they can see (3.18) – an image that suggests healing. Further, it is in New Jerusalem that, among other things, pain will cease (Rev. 21.4) and the leaves of the tree of life will be for the healing of the nations (Rev. 22.2). Healings in the present are proleptic experiences of complete healings in the future. All of this, of course, has application for Pentecostals for whom prayer is a significant theological activity.[59] Pentecostals expect God to answer their prayers.[60] From the Apocalypse, Pentecostals should find encouragement to offer prayers of lament and cries for justice. Prayers all too often collapse into self-centered wish lists that reflect personal wants and needs, yet in the Apocalypse, the cries of lament reflect the realities of an oppressed people – a people for whom God is their only source of help. Pentecostals must learn the language of lament and engage in it, for 'in doing so, Pentecostals do not escape from reality. Rather they take hold of reality and bring it to the One who reveals to them victory'.[61] Fervent prayers for the return of Jesus, once a staple of Pentecostal worship, must be sounded forth again to remind Pentecostals that Jesus is the King of kings and Lord of lords *soon* to come. Similarly, prayers for healing need not be neglected in Pentecostal worship for Jesus is the healer. Pentecostal worship should include times of corporate prayer where be-

---

ty around the throne of God himself. If the prayers of the saints on earth enable them to participate in heavenly worship, surely the same would be true of other forms of worship.'

[59] Land, *Pentecostal Spirituality*, p. 166.

[60] Warrington, *Pentecostal Theology*, p. 216. Boone, 'Community and Worship', p. 140, identifies prayer as 'a rite performed with the expectation of results'.

[61] C. Bridges Johns, 'The Adolescence of Pentecostalism: In Search of a Legitimate Sectarian Identity', *Pneuma* 17.1 (Spring 1995), p. 15. See also S.A. Ellington, 'The Costly Loss of Testimony', *Journal of Pentecostal Theology* 16 (2000), pp. 48-59.

lievers pray in expectation, knowing that God silences all of heaven (8.1) to hear and respond to prayer.

The Apocalypse conceives of witness as an act of worship. The language of witness or testimony is found throughout the Apocalypse.[62] What the churches read and hear in the Apocalypse is what they are called to proclaim to the world around them through their witness. The churches' witness is not separate from their worship. In their witness, the churches look outward to the inhabitants of the earth, and like John, submit to the prophetic task to prophesy again (10.11). Like the two witnesses (Revelation 11), the churches give their testimony without fear of the beast because they have already overcome through the blood of the Lamb and the word of their testimony (12.10-12). Thus, even death – which *will* come to the witnesses – does not keep them from their witness; rather, losing their lives because of their testimony (11.7; 13.15) is their final act of worship while on earth! Further, they will continue their witness to the Lamb through their worship in heaven (11.9-17; 14.1-5; 15.1-8). Thus, the people of God are to follow their Lord in giving their lives in witness in hopes that the world will repent and give glory to God (11.13). The churches give witness to a God who offers water without cost (21.6), and they call the world to come and receive this free gift (22.17). They give witness to Jesus' love (1.5), to redemption through his sacrifice (1.5b-6; 5.9-10), to his soon return, and to their own anticipation of the wedding of the Lamb (19.7-8; 21.2). All of this takes place by means of the Spirit of God who empowers the witness of the church.

Pentecostals maintain that the Spirit is the 'empowering resource' for mission.[63] To claim to be people of the Spirit means Pentecostals should follow the Spirit in testifying to the world. To recognize witness *as* worship rather than distinct from it is to suggest a more holistic and integrative understanding of both witness *and* worship than is currently found in many Pentecostal circles. Witness as worship calls for a conscious evaluation of daily activities to ensure that all of life is lived as worship before God and in behalf of the world. Witness as worship should lead Pentecostals to

---

[62] Μαρτυρέω appears in 1.2; 22.16; μαρτυρία is used in 1.2, 9; 6.9; 11.7; 12.11, 17; 19.10 (2x); 20.4; μαρτύριον is used in 15.5; μάρτυς is used in 1.5; 2.13; 3.14, and 11.3.

[63] Warrington, *Pentecostal Theology*, p. 249.

renewed prophetic critique or even activism against the evil structures of Babylon by standing in solidarity with the oppressed even
while continuing to call both oppressed and oppressor to God.
Pentecostals can gain from the Apocalypse the courage needed to
be the prophetic counter-witness to the dominant culture in which
they exist. Like early Pentecostals, contemporary Pentecostals might
consider the revival of the testimony as an important liturgical activity. Testimonies give witness both to the people of God *and* to the
inhabitants of the world of the 'power and reality of God'.[64] Often
in testimony, the witness to the community is about witness to a
hostile world not unlike that depicted in the Apocalypse. Hearing
such testimony can strengthen the community in their resolve to
witness even in the face of the Dragon. Testimonies carry 'a sense
of participation in the future' and become a way to express 'the dis-
sonance of living in the kingdom of God while waiting on the full
reign of God'.[65] Just as the Spirit as the eyes of the Lamb is sent out
into all the earth (5.6), so too are the Spirit-empowered followers of
the Lamb. Pentecostals can integrate Spirit-empowered worship and
witness: *Spirit*ed worship *is* witness; *Spirit*ed witness *is* worship.

This essay has endeavored to demonstrate what the Apocalypse
reveals about worship and has offered initial suggestions as to ways
in which Pentecostals can make profitable use of the Apocalypse in
constructing a Pentecostal theology of worship. It is hoped that this
essay will encourage Pentecostals to rediscover the richness of the
Apocalypse and seek to hear what the Spirit is saying about worship.

---

[64] Ellington, *The Costly Loss of Testimony*, p. 48.
[65] Bridges Johns, *Pentecostal Formation*, p. 132.

6

THE NATURE AND PATTERN OF BIBLICAL WORSHIP

R. Hollis Gause[*]

Introduction

Worship is an end in itself, not the means to an end. Worship is essential to the satisfaction of God and a necessity for the fulfillment of the nature of humankind. It is, therefore, a moral obligation on the part of humanity – failure to worship is morally culpable. It is not simply a forfeiture of an optional privilege.

When Satan tempted Jesus to worship him, he used the following words: 'These things [i.e. the kingdoms of this world order] I will give you if when you have bowed down you will worship me' (Mt. 4.9). Jesus responded with a citation of Deut. 6.13: 'Depart, Satan, for it is written, "The Lord thy God you shall worship, and him alone you shall serve"'. In the Deuteronomic text two significant words appear: יָרֵא and עָבַד. Their meaning is 'fear' and 'serve', respectively. Both of these are words of worship. Deuteronomy 6.13 uses three expressions in this commandment: 1. Fear only Yahweh (and fear no other in this sense). 2. Serve him as master; serve him ahead of and above all masters. 3. Bind yourself to his

* R. Hollis Gause (1925-2015, PhD, Emory University) was founding Dean and Director of the Church of God Graduate School of Christian Ministries (now the Pentecostal Theological Seminary), where he later served as Professor of Theology.

name. The truth of his name is the measure of your speech; this is the dictate for the truth of your speech. All of these go into what we mean by the word 'worship'. It is all pervasive. No quarter of life is left untouched.

There are three texts that are critically important to this inquiry: Jn 4.23; 4.24 and Heb. 9.14. The first two are from Christ's conversation with the Samaritan woman at the well outside the city of Samaria (Jn 4.7-26). The third text is from the Hebrews writer in his explanation of the crucifixion of Jesus. This writer explains Jesus' death as a sacrifice offered by Jesus as the priest after the order of Melchizedek. Jesus is worshiper and he is the officiating priest in the sacrifice. These are all essential to our understanding of biblical worship. This understanding will enable us to make the applications of worship to a lifetime of service to God.

In order to interpret these texts and to understand the nature of worship, we will direct our attention to these texts in this order: Heb. 9.13-14 and Jn 4.23-24.

There are some fundamental presuppositions of our study. Worship is always the worship of the creator by the creature. Any other arrangement is idolatry and abominable.

When we say that worship is not a means to an end, we are insisting that worship has its own purpose, and that is to provide union of the creature with God. It is the avenue of communion between creature and God. It is the realization of a common 'language' between the two. It is the unifying event between them.

Since the first human sin, people have engaged in two forms of idolatry. The first is the most obvious: the creation of physical and visual objects that represent the person and presence of God. These are visible projections of the human imagination of the form of God. They are always exploratory, local, tentative, changeable, and creature centered. This is the height of their excellence and it is also the lowest depth of their short comings. The second is conceptual and is manifested in idealized concepts of human perfection. It attempts to answer the question what is the perfect realization of human perfection; this humanly created concept becomes the image of God. These are also exploratory, tentative, local, changeable, and creature centered.

The fact is that each of these is idolatry, which is prohibited by the first two commandments of the Decalogue. The first commandment prohibits any conceptualization of deity other than Yahweh. The second prohibits the fashioning of any visual representation of divine person and presence.

In the light of the supremacy of God, he alone determines the nature and terms of worship. We are dependent on him to reveal these things to us. This does not allow for experimentation and discovery. As revelation is essential to our knowledge of God, it is also essential to our practice(s) of worship.

Biblically ordered worship satisfies the love of God and fulfills the nature of humankind. This is an appropriate representation of union between God and humanity and of the provision of communion between them.

The Provision for Worship

As we stated in the introduction, the provision for worship and the terms of worship come to the creature by revelation. In the light of the supremacy and infinity of God, he alone determines the nature and terms of worship. We are dependent on him to make these known. Hence we are dependent on his Word for our knowledge of appropriate terms and actions that describe and prescribe worship.

This prohibits creature-centered definitions and practices of worship. This does not allow for experimentation and discovery as means of defining worship. God determines and reveals the nature, terms and manner in which he is to be worshiped. The arrogance of fallen human nature finds this hard to accept (as Satan and his followers did – Jude 6). The king of Babylon mimicked Satan in the same way (Isa. 14.9-15). Humankind must dethrone itself and enthrone God.

The sacrifice of Christ is the supreme moment of worship for time and eternity. Hear this paraphrase of the text of Heb. 9.13-14.

> For if the blood of goats and bulls and the ashes of a heifer sprinkling the unclean to the purifying of the flesh, how much more the blood of Jesus, who through the eternal Spirit offered himself to God as a spotless sacrifice purge our consciences from dead works [in order that we may] serve the living God?

This is the perfect example of worship, and it defines the character of worship.

This text tells us the following things about the death of Jesus on the cross:

1. The death of Jesus is a sacrifice of worship that provides atonement for sins. It is the climaxing event in which Jesus offers the perfection of his life to the Father as a sacrifice of worship.
2. This sacrifice is offered by Christ as the officiating priest. He is the officiating eternal priest because he is priest forever after the order of Melchizedek (Ps. 110.4; Heb. 8.17).
3. The sacrifice is offered to God; so this is an act of divine worship. This is the act of worship that legitimizes and fulfills all other biblically prescribed practices of worship. Conversely, this prohibits any other form of worship[1].
4. The agent who provokes and inspires this act of worship is the eternal Spirit (i.e. the Holy Spirit)).
5. The purpose of this sacrifice is to make it possible for us to serve the living God.

When we have said these things about the cross, we have defined the cross as the supreme event of worship for both time and eternity. As such it is the defining sacrifice for all acts of worship on the part of the human race. It is the sacrifice that judges all worship offered to God. The judgment is for acceptance of the offering or for the rejection of the offering: in other words, for salvation or damnation.

In the remarks that follow, we will explain and apply these points more fully. First, the cross of our Lord Jesus Christ is the worship event of eternity. It is the sacrifice that is offered on the heavenly altar and provides access for believers to follow Christ into the heavenly 'most holy place' (i.e. to go with him through the torn veil). He is our 'forerunner' not the substitute runner. We follow him into the most holy place and take our position with him within the veil as priests.

We observe that this event fulfills all worship that has been provided by God for access to him. It catches up all of their promise

---

[1] There is considerable evidence that liturgical forms of worship were used in the early Christian community; the New Testament gives us glimpses into these practices (1 Cor. 15.1-3; 1 Tim. 3.16 and other texts. Liturgy must come under the proscription of Scripture, but it is a useful and edifying mode of worship.

and supersedes them by fulfillment. We observe also that it is the archetype of all biblically prescribed events of worship. It provides eternal salvation (as distinct from the year by year reprieves of the Aaronic priestly order). It is the paradigm of all worship. The eternal God is being worshiped. He is being worshiped by the eternal Son and high priest. The sacrifice of worship that is being offered here is the eternal Lamb that takes away the sin of the world (Jn 1.29, 36). The officiating priest of this sacrifice is the eternal Son, the priest forever after the order of Melchizedek (Ps. 110.4; Heb. 7.17). The agent who inspires and provokes this event of worship is the eternal Spirit (i.e. the Holy Spirit). This event is the perfect union between worshiper and the triune God.

Furthermore, the cross is the temporal (i.e. historical) center/climax of the life of Christ while he was among us in the flesh. Each step from Bethlehem to Calvary was his participation in the end. Every day the cross of Jesus was being proleptically fulfilled. By this we mean that each day of his life was a day on the cross. It is day-by-day crucifixion. The words of Simeon to Mary are prophetic and existential for Mary, for Israel, and for Jesus: 'Behold, this Child is set for the falling and rising again for many in Israel, and for a sign to be spoken against' (Lk. 2.34). Then, Simeon speaks directly to Mary: 'And a sword shall pierce your soul also' (Lk. 2.35). The devotion of Mary is represented in these words, 'And Mary kept all these things as treasures in her heart' (Lk. 2.51).[2] The shadow of the cross fell across this holy scene, for Jesus had been born to Calvary. Everyday thereafter was a fulfillment of the crucifixion. This burden never left him, neither did the glory. This combination makes the cross the greatest oxymoron of human history. It is a union of abject humiliation and supreme glory. It is his suffering and rejection (Phil. 2.8; Jn 12.31). It is his exaltation and glory (Jn 12.32-34; Phil. 2.9-11; 1 Tim. 3.16).

This contradiction is on display in the transfiguration. The transfiguration occurred while Jesus was praying (Lk. 9.29). The glory of the transfiguration was enhanced by the conversation between Jesus, Moses, and Elijah. The subject of conversation was Jesus' coming exodus which he must fulfill in Jerusalem (Lk. 9.31). This is a

---

[2] On this translation of διατηρέω, see Frederick W. Danker, *The Concise Greek-English Lexicon of the New Testament* (Chicago, IL: The University of Chicago Press, 2009), p. 93.

scene of agony because his exodus includes his crucifixion. It is also a scene of exhilaration. This is the nature of worship.

This is a paradigm of worship. If we have experienced only the joy of worship (without its agony), we have not known the fullness of worship. If we have not wept as we go out to plant the seed, we will not return with rejoicing bearing precious sheaves with us (Ps. 126.6).

Jesus made this a pattern of discipleship: 'And he said to all, "If any person would come after me, let him deny himself and take up his cross and follow me"' (Lk. 9.23). As Jesus lived his life in anticipation and fulfillment of the cross, the disciples of Jesus must fulfill their own crosses on a day-by-day basis. As Jesus was born to the crucifixion, believers are born again to their own crucifixion. For the believer, as it was for Jesus, each moment of existence is a participation in the cross. There is never a reprieve; it must end in death or there is no glory: no resurrection.

At the same time, the glory is always present in the agony. The marks of the suffering become the 'stigmata of Jesus which [we] carry in our bodies' (Gal. 6.17). The 'stigmata of Jesus' (the marks in our own bodies of suffering with and for him) are the signs of our identity with Jesus in the wounds of his crucifixion.

It is this understanding that is the heart of worship. Worship is cross-bearing and participation with Christ in the fellowship of his sufferings and the glory of his resurrection (Phil. 3.10). This is the essence of worship in the fulfillment of life. However, this is not asceticism. Asceticism treats the body as the enemy of the soul and a deterrent to the richness of spiritual life. This treats the body as worthy of being destroyed. If this is the case its destruction is no sacrifice; it is something that needs to be done.

This is participation in the cross on our journey to the cross. This is worship throughout life as Jesus exemplified it and taught it by example and by exhortation. If we are experiencing crucifixion day-by-day, the final moment of crucifixion is not strange. It is the spiritual outcome of the manner in which we have lived. It was so for Jesus; it is so for us.

The Nature of Worship

In his conversation with the Samaritan woman, Jesus describes to her (and by application to us) the nature of worship. In Jn 4.23-24, he makes two statements about the nature of worship. We will examine each of these in the material to follow.

In verse 23, Jesus says, 'The hour is coming and it is now upon us when true worshipers will worship the Father in [the] Spirit and in [the] Truth'. This is an eschatological statement. The formula 'the hour is coming and now is' is for John an eschatological formula. In these words of Jesus to this woman he indicates that her questions of the 'place' of worship are irrelevant. Place of worship has nothing to do with its correctness. In essence he is saying to her, 'There is no point in answering your question'. The only thing that matters is that we recognize the dignity of the Father, the Son and the Holy Spirit in our worship: that we recognize that each one has personal dignity worthy of worship.

Each of the nouns in this statement represents a divine person: namely, the Father, the Holy Spirit, and the Son. In consistency with the theology of John the terms 'Spirit' and 'Truth' are personal references to the person of the Holy Spirit and the person of the divine Son. The Spirit is the paraclete whom Christ promised to come after his ascension; hence we translate 'the Spirit'. The truth is the person of the *Logos* (Jn 1.1-18), Jesus himself. Hence we translate, 'the Truth'. 'Just as Jesus himself was "the Truth" (14.6; compare his self-designation as "the true Bread", "the true Vine," and so on), so the Paraclete who comes after his exaltation is the "Spirit of truth" (14.17; 15.26; 16.13)'.[3]

In the Gospel of John, the Spirit is the one who descended on Jesus after his water baptism (1.32), who is the origin of the birth from above (3.5), who is the source of living waters that flow out of the hearts of those who believe on Jesus (7.38, 39), who is the 'other paraclete' whom Christ will send after his ascension (14.16-17), who is the Spirit of truth who will guide into all truth (14.16-17), who is the one whom the world cannot receive because it does not know him (14.16), who will dwell in the believers (14.17), who will bring all things to the memory of the disciples (14.26), who will be

---

[3] Geoffrey Wainwright, *Doxology* (New York: Oxford University Press, 1980), p. 89.

witness to the Son (15.26-27), who will convict the world of sin, righteousness, and judgment to come (16.13-14).

The Truth is the *Logos* who is with the Father eternally (Jn 1.1-2), who made all things that were made (1.3, 10), who has the power to make the children of men and women the children of God (1.12), who was made flesh and dwelt among us (1.14), who is the origin of grace (1.14-16), who is the only 'begotten God' (1.18),[4] who is in the bosom of the Father while he is among us in the flesh (1.18), and who provides and pours out the Holy Spirit on his believers (15.26; 16.7).

With this understanding of Spirit and Truth it is not necessary to supply the definite article in the Greek text. So John records this conversation as it is given here. There are other personal references in Scripture to the divine agents of worship: the Holy Spirit by whom we cry 'Abba, Father' (Rom. 8.15), who reveals the deep thing of God (1 Cor. 2.10-16), and by whom we confess that Jesus is Lord (1 Cor. 12.3). The fundamental truth of this text is that true worship is always through the inspiration of the Holy Spirit and by the redemptive intercession of the Son of God the incarnation of Truth. A willful denial of the ontological existence and the distinct personhood of these two divine persons is not in the pattern of biblical worship. To deny the personal distinct existence, nature, and work of the Holy Spirit is to deny his role as the revealer of God and agent of communion. To deny the personal distinct existence, nature, and work of the incarnate Truth – Jesus Christ – is to deny his role as mediator and sacrifice for sin.

There are two other important messages here. First, worship is commanded by God. The first part of Deut. 6.13-14 is the command to worship Yahweh. We often focus on the latter half of this commandment which is the prohibition of false gods: 'You shall not pursue other gods'. Notice, however, that the first part of this commandment is, 'You shall worship Yahweh, thy God'. Worship is a moral and spiritual obligation, not simply the loss of privilege.

The second message is that you are to worship God in accordance with his nature. This provides a transition to the saying of Jesus in Jn 4.24. 'God is Spirit, and it is required that those who wor-

---

[4] Almost overwhelmingly manuscript evidence favors this reading over the *Textus Receptus*.

ship him worship him in the Spirit and in the Truth. In the material above we focused on the essential agents of worship. Here we focus on the character of worship.

The character of worship is dictated by the character of God. The fact is that our notions about the nature of God always show in the form of worship that we offer him. Witness the material nature, grotesque forms and ceremonies, and the vulgarity of pagan worship. These forms of worship are also marked by the tentativeness of such worship. This is what Paul noted in Athens concerning their many altars, and the one altar to the 'unknown god' (Acts 17.23).

The one aspect of divine nature is that he is spirit. This means that we are to worship him in a manner consistent with his spirituality. God is spirit and not material. Material things (such as animal sacrifices, human sacrifices, the ascetic punishment of the body, ceremonial practices which are temporal and physical) cannot provide union with God. These things not only deny the spiritual nature of God; they also violate the holiness of God.

This is the message of Psalm 50 – God needs nothing from the creature. He is not enriched by our sacrifices; they add nothing to his being or to the fulfillment of his nature:

> I will take no bullock out of thy house, nor he goats out of thy folds. For every beast of the forest is mine, and the cattle upon a thousand hills. I know all the fowls of the mountains; and the wild beasts of field are mine. If I were hungry, I would not ask you: for the world is mine and the fullness thereof (Ps. 50.9-12).

To imagine that we enrich God through any act of worship is to imagine that a pauper can give to a millionaire.

God has provided a bridge of union and communion between human beings and himself. It is his Spirit. For this understanding we are informed by the Apostle Paul in 1 Cor. 2.10-16. We cannot know the things that God has provided for us, but God has given them to us his Spirit. The Spirit of God knows the deep things of the nature of God (v. 10). The Spirit has revealed these things to us (v, 10). 'Now we have received, not the spirit of the world, but the Spirit which is of God; that we might know the things that are freely given to us of God' (v. 12). The Holy Spirit teaches us to use the evaluation of spiritual things to understand spiritual things (v.

13). Spiritual issues are resolved by understanding that is imparted by the Holy Spirit. The Holy Spirit has equipped us with the mind of Christ in order that we may perceive spiritual things (v. 16).

The Old Testament Patterns of Worship

In the Old Testament there was a category of sacrifices that were offered to God for a 'sweet smelling savor'. In many of these sacrifices the question of expiation was not a factor. No blood was shed. These were sacrifices offered at the will of worshipers who wanted to offer to the Lord a sacrifice of fellowship for any occasion of gratitude or for a sense of intimacy with God. The symbolism of such sacrifices was that the aroma from the burning of the sacrifice would please God. It would the believer's wish to commune with God in such a way as to give the believer spiritual pleasure and would present to God a sacrifice that would give him pleasure. It is a metaphor in action. As the odors of the burning incense waft out from the altar to the tabernacle and into the air around the tabernacle, they also rise into the 'nostrils' of God; and they give him pleasure.

These sacrifices were no less worship than such sacrifices as passover and atonement. God is pleased to forgive sins, and he is also pleased when the forgiven returns to offer him sacrifices that give him the sensation of a sweet smell. We cannot talk about the Old Testament orders of worship without taking this component of sacrificial worship into account. Note the following examples. Noah and his family had come out of the ark having been saved from the flood. He offered burnt sacrifices to the Lord, and we are told two things about this event. First, the Lord smelled the pleasing odor of the sacrifice, and it gave him pleasure. God had already saved Noah, the preacher of righteousness, and his family from the flood (2 Pet. 2.5). Second, God responded to this sacrifice with the giving of a covenant to Noah and the whole earth. God promised that he would not ever again judge the earth in this manner – i.e. by universal flood. God also promised that he would provide for the earth and its inhabitants by giving seed time and harvest (v. 22). This description of God's pleasure in sacrifice is pre-Mosaic. So, the law in prescribing such sacrifices is adapting a mode of worship that was already in use.

In the Aaronic order of worship prescribed in the Torah, God made provision for this kind of offering. A good example is the description of the morning and evening sacrifices in the Tabernacle. They are described as perpetual sacrifices of a sweet smell unto God. Such sacrifices as this recall the sacrifices of atonement. They keep alive in the memory of the worshipers what God had done in the passover and the atonement. They are a way for the people to give thanks to God for what he had done in the forgiveness of sins. They also remind the people of the approaching passover and atonement in which God would 'repeat' the forgiveness of sins. The believer need not be burdened with a sense of doom even though he/she knew that he/she had committed sins since the last passover and atonement. This sacrifice reminded them that passover and atonement are coming again.

To God the odor of these sacrifices (and other sacrifices as well) 'smelled good'. They gave him pleasure. The worshiper and God become one in each other in their mutual joy in worship: the worshiper in taking pleasure in God, and the worshiped in taking pleasure in his people.

The same metaphor is used in the New Testament to describe the worship and service of believers in Jesus Christ. In 2 Cor. 2.14-16 the Apostle Paul applies this understanding of worship in the following ways. God makes manifest in the world the savor of his knowledge of us. The knowledge of Christ by believers spreads out into all the world as evidence of God's pleasure (v. 14). Believers are the sweet aroma of Christ in the nostrils of God (v. 15). This affects all the world: both believers and unbelievers. To those who believe the gospel with us, we are the 'savor of life unto life'. But there is the opposite effect; to those who do not believe the gospel, we are a noxious odor: the savor of death unto death. Believers become to the world what the gospel is: either salvation or damnation (v. 16). The important thing about this text is that it shows that by their existence in the world believers are an odor of a sweet smell either for the salvation of others or the judgment of others. This is not something that is sporadic; it is the character of believers to be worshipers of God through the priesthood of Christ. They are this simply by their life and existence in the world. Gifts offered in the support of the ministry of the Word and the wellbeing of those who

minister are treated as 'an odor of a sweet smell, a sacrifice acceptable and well pleasing to God' (Phil. 4.18).

The prayers of the saints are held in censers on the heavenly altar
(Rev. 5.8; 8.3). This follows in the pattern of the sacrifices in the
tabernacle and temple in the Old Testament. The odor of their
burning is the sweet smell of divine worship: a sweet smell to those
who worship in the tabernacle or the temple, and a sweet smell in
the nostrils of God who is being worshiped. This is a powerful image. The prayers of believers are their participation in the kingdom,
their participation in the blessings of the kingdom, their participation in God's judgments in the fulfillment of the kingdom on the
impenitent world, and their participation in God's pleasure. Similar
language is used in Rom. 12.1-2:

> I am urging you, brothers and sisters, through the mercies that
> reside in the heart of God, that you offer your bodies as living
> sacrifice [a sacrifice that is to be kept alive even as it is being of-
> fered on the altar] holy and delightful to God, [which] is your
> reasonable service. And that you not become indistinguishable
> from the world, but [ἀλλά, a strong adversative] that you should
> keep on being transfigured [μεταμορφόω, the same word that is
> used to describe the transfiguration of Jesus in Mt. 17.2 and Mk
> 9.2], by the making of your minds new that you may manifest
> the will of God [which] is good, and pleasing and perfect.

This text tells us the following things. The origin of the exhortation is God in his mercy. Your body is holy and is a worthy sacrifice
to God. The body is not the 'despised enemy' of the soul. The
body, though destined for death (Heb. 9.27) by sacrifice, may be
offered to God as living sacrifice. This is nothing more than what is
reasonable that we are to render to God. We must remain distinct
from the world and incapable of being confused with the world. In
this act of worship, we are to be transfigured into a glory appropriate to divine worship. The manner in which this transfiguration occurs is by the renewing of the mind. The mind is made new and
continues to grow in that renewed state. This is the fulfillment of
the will of God which is good, pleasing and perfect.

Conclusion

The subject of worship is vital to all of life. We are affected by this issue in every breath we take and in every step that we walk, whether in work or recreation, weeping or laughter, rejoicing or mourning, in the house of God or in the field of labor, Sabbath or days of labor. Our very way of life must be a sacrifice of a sweet smelling savor to God.

7

SIGNS OF GRACE: TOWARDS A CHARISMATIC THEOLOGY OF WORSHIP

Frank D. Macchia[*]

Introduction: Diversely Gifted Worship

It is no accident that Jesus' first miracle according to the Gospel of John was done at a wedding feast (John 2). He seemed to use the occasion to show that the Kingdom of God is not primarily a moral duty or ethical obligation. It is that, but it is primarily a *celebration*. The Kingdom was first like that wedding banquet, a wonderful celebration in which the tables are open to all and God sets them with a celebratory meal, saving the absolute best wine for last. I see worship as analogous to that celebration so basic to the life of the Kingdom, as a place where we as a people exalt the heavenly Father through Christ and in the power of the Spirit (or exalt Christ to the glory of the Father, in the power of the Spirit). In so doing, we celebrate the grace poured out upon and through us, that grace that sustains us, causes us to flourish, and reaches out beyond us to a world that is far too graceless.

Worship is arguably at the very core of the gifted church's life. Geoffrey Wainwright noted that the praise of God is given forth in

* Frank D. Macchia (DTheol, University of Basel; DD, Pentecostal Theological Seminary) is Professor of Systematic Theology at Vanguard University in Costa Mesa, CA, USA and Associate Director of the Centre for Pentecostal and Charismatic Studies at Bangor University, Bangor, Wales, UK.

all that we do: belief, worship, and life witness, and that worship is at the core of it all. It is in the worship of the church that the vision of Christian identity in Christ is fundamentally formed. Doctrine and Scripture exposition guides and feeds this formation, and life witness proceeds out from it. But it is in worship itself that the identity is formed at its core.[1] Simon Chan has similarly supported the centrality of worship with regard to the Christian life. He seeks to remedy the ecclesiological deficit of evangelicalism by pointing to the historic worship of the church as the central locus of divine-human encounter.[2] Steven J. Land has noted that spirituality is vital to the church's theological thinking and life witness. Right affection is therefore just as important as right belief and right praxis.[3]

Worship may be said to bridge the practice of doctrine and the practice of life witness and ministry. Indeed, worship brings right belief into life so that it might then nourish and support life witness. Worship is the context in which the church lives the biblical story in resistance to the world and in witness to an alternative reality. Worship is thus downright countercultural. In a world convinced that it has its own lords of power, the church celebrates Jesus as Lord of all. In the midst of a world dominated by a grab for power and influence, guided by the illusion of autonomy and self-sufficiency, the church yields in thanksgiving and praise to God as creator, redeemer, and giver of life. In the midst of a world dominated by systems of exchange (in which one allegedly gets what one deserves), the worship-driven church celebrates grace in celebrating the presence of the gracious God among us. In celebrating grace, the church finds the fulfillment of its humanity, for we were made 'to glorify God, and to enjoy him forever', as the Westminster Catechism notes.[4] In a world in which diversity is sometimes confused with autonomous individuality or corporate identity, the worshiping church points to a diverse reception and expression of grace. The

---

[1] Geoffrey Wainwright, *Doxology: The Praise of God in Worship, Doctrine, and Life* (New York, NY: Oxford University Press, 1980).

[2] Simon Chan, *Liturgical Theology: The Church as Worshiping Community* (Lombard, IL: InterVarsity Press, 2006).

[3] Steven J. Land, *Pentecostal Spirituality: A Passion for the Kingdom* (Cleveland, TN: CPT Press, 2010).

[4] S.W. Carruthers, *The Shorter Catechism of the Westminster Assembly of the Divines* (London: Presbyterian Church of England, 1897), p. 1; available online at https://archive.org/stream/shortercatechis00west#page/n3/mode/2up.

diversity that comes to expression in worship does not leave behind the richly diverse cultural and biological diversity that God has created; to the contrary, worship brings this diversity to fulfillment. In the heavenly city, the kings will bring the diversely rich splendor of the nations into the city in honor of the Lamb (Rev. 21.24).

Within this diversely-gifted worship, natural human capacities and talents are enhanced and flourish in the Spirit. Extraordinary gifts burst forth and grant the people of God signs of a coming fulfillment that goes way beyond the natural capacities that we creatively bring to expression in various avenues of thanksgiving and praise. The expressions that come forth in the church's worship do not represent an indistinguishable, monolithic voice. The praise goes forth in many 'tongues' and in an increasingly-diverse and interactive gifted expressions. Tongues may respond to intercessory prayer, interpretation responds to tongues, prophecy may respond to singing, and discernment responds to prophecy. Faith may respond to preaching, and scholarship responds to faith (etc.). The gifts are interactive, for, being filled with the Spirit, we speak to one another with psalms, hymns, and songs from the Spirit (Eph. 5.18). Worship responds to God and to one another in response to God. All of it flows diversely in celebration of grace.

Spiritual gifts can thus be viewed as 'individuations of grace'.[5] The term 'charismata' (χαρίσματα), Paul's favored term for spiritual gifts, harbors that word for grace, 'charis' (χάρις). This term can thus be literally translated as diverse 'manifestations' or 'embodiments' of grace.[6] Grace is indeed rooted in God's gracious self-giving, but it is not therefore a generic experience of power that moves us to worship in exactly the same ways. Grace is uniquely experienced and expressed for '[w]e have different gifts', writes Paul, 'according to the grace given to each of us' (Rom. 12.6). In a world that is increasingly graceless, the church's gifted worship offers richly diverse signs of grace.

---

[5] Ernst Käsemann, *Commentary on Romans* (Grand Rapids, MI: Eerdmans, 1994), p. 334.

[6] James Dunn, 'Ministry and the Ministry: The Charismatic Renewal's Challenge to Traditional Ecclesiology', in Cecil M. Robeck (ed.), *Charismatic Experiences in History* (Peabody, MA: Hendrickson, 1985), pp. 81-101 (p. 87).

The Church's Charismatic Structure

Worship is not simply the expression of a leader backed by a mono-lithic 'amen'. Worship is an orchestra of colorfully diverse expres-sions. Essential to the church's worship, therefore, is the church's *charismatic structure*. What is this 'charismatic structure' precisely? Hans Küng popularized the notion of the 'charismatic structure of the church' in his classic, *The Church*, where he made it the overall context in which the church's gifts of oversight are to be discussed.[7] He noted that juridical thinking is mistrustful of movements of the free Spirit of God for fear of a non-regimented enthusiasm. The tendency has been to 'sacramentalize or make uniform the charism, and hence the workings of the Spirit'.[8] The result is a clericalism in which the notion of charism is overwhelmingly discussed in the context of ordained ministry. Neglected are the richness, variety, and exuberance of spiritual gifts in the context of worship as pic-tured in such texts as 1 Corinthians 12–14 and Ephesians 4, and exercised throughout the lives of 'ordinary' Christians.

Küng wished to reverse the historic trend toward clericalism. Ra-ther than subsume charism under church office, Küng wished to do the opposite, namely, subsume office beneath charism.[9] Since char-isms are universally exercised by all as everyone in the church is called and commissioned to worship and serve as bearers of the Spirit, the charisms are not peripheral but are rather essential and central elements of the church. Küng does not deny the unique role played by those who exercise the charism of oversight (or pastoral leadership), but he places both gifts of oversight and other giftings within an overarching concept of the church as a fellowship of faith in which all members (including ordained clergy) as bearers of the Spirit are gifted to glorify God. For Küng, 'the church must be seen first as a fellowship of faith and only in this light can ecclesiastical office be properly understood'.[10]

---

[7] Hans Küng, *The Church* (New York: Sheed & Ward, 1967). This concept is developed by Miroslav Volf, *After our Likeness: The Church as the Image of the Trinity* (Grand Rapids: Eerdmans, 1997), esp. p. 231; and Veli-Matti Kärkkäinen, 'Pente-costalism and the Claim for Apostolicity: An Essay in Ecumenical Ecclesiology', *Ecumenical Review of Theology* 25 (2001), pp. 323-26.

[8] Küng, *The Church*, p. 184.

[9] Küng, *The Church*, p. 187.

[10] Küng, *The Church*, p. 363. More recently, Volf has expanded on this idea in his, *After our Likeness*, esp. p. 231.

The Pentecostal and Charismatic churches that are becoming so visible globally and are arguably changing the face of Christendom in the world have traditionally stressed the charismatic structure of the church as essential to the strength of the church's worship and witness. In fact, James Dunn proposed that the gifted nature of the entire church may be viewed as one of Pentecostalism's most distinctive doctrines.[11] David Lim maintained also that the Reformation doctrine of the universal priesthood of believers was never adequately brought to bear on the local church worship service. The Pentecostal stress on the charismatic church helps to bring this idea to fulfillment.[12] The practical result of elevating the church's charismatic structure to prominence is the strong admonition that the people of God not fall short of any gift while waiting for the Lord's return (1 Cor. 1.9).

Walter Hollenweger added that the emphasis on the charismatic participation of the entire people of God in worship gave Pentecostal worship certain distinctive features. First, there tends to be the dominance of oral rather than written communication, expanding participation among those not trained in written communication. Second, preference is typically granted narrativity of theology and witness. The story and the testimony will tend to take precedence over abstract or rational systems of doctrine. Third, maximum participation is granted at the levels of prayer, reflection, and decision making. All believers are viewed as gifted of the Spirit to contribute to all facets of the church's worship. Fourth, visions, and dreams (and other gifts that involve the depths of the human spirit) are commonly allowed in all forms of the church's private and public worship. This feature points to experiences in worship that transcend the limits of rationality, experiences which might include speaking in tongues also. Lastly, Pentecostalism typically fosters experiences of interaction between body and mind, for example in healing or liturgical dance.[13] Of course such accents are not restricted to Pentecostalism, but Hollenweger would point out that Pentecostalism is flourishing within those locations where such features

---

[11] Dunn, 'Ministry and the Ministry', pp. 81-101.
[12] David Lim, *Spiritual Gifts: A Fresh Look* (Springfield, MO: Gospel Publishing House, 1991), pp. 34-38.
[13] Walter J. Hollenweger, *Pentecostalism* (Grand Rapids, MI: Baker Academic, 2005), pp. 17-18.

are prominent. It may still be maintained, therefore, that they are all typically Pentecostal. For Pentecostalism, all believers are to participate in line with their own unique gifting in the manifold worship of the church.

Hollenweger's research points to a charismatic diversity in Pentecostal worship that may be waning among white Pentecostal churches in the US but is still flourishing in the global south, even among non-Pentecostal churches. Orality, narrativity, visions, dreams, healing, and bodily movement imply a charismatically-diverse worship service that is holistic (involving the subconscious mind as well as rationality, story as well as confession of beliefs, body as well as spirit). At its best, Pentecostals are urging other church families to be more intentional about charismatically expanding their worship services so as to cherish a greater variety of gifted expressions. It is increasingly becoming the case that there are members of non-Pentecostal churches that (perhaps only intuitively) sense that their giftings are analogous to typically 'Pentecostal' gifts. In discouraging these gifted expressions, other church families could end up marginalizing a significant minority of their own members. Charismatic worship is no longer merely a Pentecostal/non-Pentecostal issue. Of course, non-Pentecostals can remind Pentecostals of certain neglected gifts. For example, the Reformed tradition has historically done a better job of cherishing the input of scholarship in the substance of worship than have Pentecostals.

What all churches have in common is the fact that Spiritual gifts participate in worship in harmony with the ways of the Spirit. Looking more carefully at 1 Corinthians, one notes that Paul seeks from the start to resist the idea that the church exists for one's own self-aggrandizement. Rather, the Spirit urges us from the start to exalt Jesus as Lord (12.1-3). All of the church's diverse celebration of grace points in this direction. This worship is obviously personal and individual, but it is not by any means individualistic. One worships in a way that builds up the others and enhances them in their own capacity to exalt the Lord. Notice in chapter 14 how speaking in tongues 'gives thanks well' but does not edify the other (14.18). It is thus not fitting as an audible expression within the public assembly unless followed by an interpretation (14.14-15). The various and diverse expressions of praise within the church's charismatic structure directs everyone to the Lord and enhances their capacity to uplift him along with others. We worship in unity through the unique contribution of each and every gifted person, for the body of Christ is 'joined and held together by every supporting ligament'. (Eph. 4.16). It is indeed fitting also that the self-offering of praise to God is immediately followed by a discussion of how the diverse gifts of the church bind together to aid one another in this process (Rom. 12.1-8).

In the process, each gift is valued equally, for the end result of the working of every gift is ultimately not measureable; indeed, the Lord is glorified. The exaltation of Jesus as Lord thus sets the stage for the entire discussion of 1 Corinthians 12. In fact, the less honorable gifts (in terms of temporal outcome) are granted even more honor so as to make clear the fact that the Lord is glorified equally in them all (1 Cor. 12.21-26). All of the gifts are thus needed to edify the church and enhance its corporate worship. The ear and the eye need the little finger, for all of the members please the Head who is Christ. The degree to which the Lord is pleased cannot be limited to temporal importance but is rather tied to the intention of the heart and the love shown to God and others. Without worship as a context for spiritual gifts, the special attention showed to temporally less honorable gifts slips into patronizing sentimentality.

Preaching and Sacrament

Within the diversely gifted church (and not apart from it) are the important ministries of word and sacrament. Luke in particular tells us that Jesus was made known to the two disciples on the Road to Emmaus through the breaking open of the scriptures (their hearts 'burned' when he 'opened' the Scriptures to them, 24.32) and the breaking open of the bread (24.35). This text foreshadows how the community of faith would recognize and commune with its Lord, exalting him together through these two important means of grace.

The proclamation of the word is indeed to be viewed as a means of opening us up to exalting Christ or God in the Spirit:

> If anyone speaks, they should do so as one who speaks the very words of God. If anyone serves, they should do so with the strength God provides, so that in all things God may be praised through Jesus Christ (1 Pet. 4.11 NIV).

The word of God in proclamation/teaching and in multiple gifts of love open up the church to exalt the Lord together in greater depth and with greater clarity. The Word of God has a doxological as well as ethical function. Its effect is not only in knowledge but in the affections, as well as the will to act righteously. The Word is a means of new creation and not only new knowledge. Discussing the ministry of the Word in the context of spiritual gifts makes it impossible to overemphasize the rational dimension of understanding. Spiritual gifts reach deep into the soul and far out into the world. One speaks in tongues, gains greater rational comprehension, and lives more ethically in the world, bearing witness also through acts of love and words of healing. Indeed, we all speak the word in love (Eph. 4.15), though there are those especially gifted to minister the word.

So also the table of the Lord, which is open to all who genuinely call upon the name of the Lord to be saved. The Lord's Supper is the meal of 'thanksgiving' by which we 'participate' in the body and blood of Christ (1 Cor. 10.16-17). To participate in the meal is a communal reality that we do with our fellow believers. It is experienced in communion with the Lord. As we praise and give thanks during this meal, all the while remembering what he did for us, we experience the Lord embrace and admonish us. The invocation of the Spirit, which should accompany the words of institution, recognizes a diversely gifted body drinking of the cup of thanksgiving together in unity, for we 'who are many, are one body' (v. 17). We all participate in this meal each in our own way but we do so as one body, reconciled and reconciling.

Signs of Grace in a Graceless World

Gifted worship reaches out to the world. Indeed, we live in an increasingly graceless world. This statement is one-sided but true nonetheless. Though natural life is graced by God and lives from God (e.g. Acts 17.24-25), it also confronts us as ambiguous, especially when grace seems eclipsed by gracelessness. This ambiguity is especially evident in the realm of social relationships. As Christopher Lasch has noted in, *Haven in a Heartless World*, the structures of capitalist society have come increasingly to dominate even the life of the family, which has served traditionally and ideally as a 'haven' in the midst of a heartless world. Families are losing their role as 'haven' and are becoming less and less influential in imparting values, caring for their young and elderly, and upholding human dignity and worth. Family members share little in common, since they spend most of their time serving different institutional interests. Moreover, familial relationships often seem as graceless as the institutions that have influenced them.[14] For example, seemingly ungrateful children are sometimes reminded of the need to obey in return for the shelter, food, clothing, and other 'services' granted by parents as providers, as though parenting can be reduced to the provision of various goods and services!

And the media is quick to sell the illusion that a haven may yet be found through increased purchasing power. Marketing experts have done sufficient research to know what kind of consumers to make of us and how to instruct us effectively in the task of measuring one's attainment of personal worth by the level of consumption achieved. Socialist societies have not historically been more liberating, since one in such contexts was generally judged by how well he or she could 'produce' for the state or, ideally, the 'common good'. Indeed, the principalities and powers of human social life have sought to make us into one-dimensional beings fit for a particular social function and disposable if shown to be unfit for use. A certain social worth is only granted to those who benefit most from a complex interplay of values shaped by the dominant culture and connected to such factors as race, gender, class, and physical or mental capabilities.

Connected to these social dynamics is that to which Paul Tillich referred as a universal 'Angst' or dread that takes many forms, spanning such concerns as death, guilt, and meaninglessness.[15] Perhaps 'gracelessness' should be added to this list in the light of our discussion above. We live in an increasingly 'graceless' world.[16] Throughout the myriad of relationships that extend our sense of self into the world, we teeter between threats of ruthless domination and cowardly assimilation. People, even entire peoples, are treated as means to some social end. We seem bound by flesh in the sense of being bound by this 'fallen' situation. Language, culture,

---

[14] Christopher Lasch, *Haven in a Heartless World* (New York: Basic Books, 1977), pp. 12-21.

[15] Paul Tillich, *The Courage to Be* (New Haven: Yale University Press, 2000).

[16] This notion of the church giving forth signs of grace in an increasingly graceless world was used often in lectures and discussions by my doctoral mentor, Jan Lochman, at the University of Basel. More recently, Volf has used this idea effectively in his, *Free of Charge: Giving and Forgiving in a Culture Stripped of Grace* (Grand Rapids: Zondervan, 2006).

and social structures shape and maintain our alienation from self and others. In such a situation, flesh cries for the Spirit and liberty, to taste that to which the New Testament refers under the loaded term, 'grace'. Where can this grace be found? It should be found centrally in the church as the place where in the Spirit grace is celebrated and practiced in the midst of the world. This affirmation of the church as the chief context of the celebration of grace is not meant to eclipse the nature of the church as a fallen reality. Martin Luther once called the church the 'infirmary of the sick'.[17] This is true, however, not only because we are wounded sinners, but also because we are wounded healers, gifted to heal and to strengthen one another by helping each other in unique ways to be receptive to the grace of God and to express that grace in worship. The church should pulsate with ever-increasing gifts of helps and edification toward this end.

A Call for Discernment

So what makes a spiritual gift fitting for worship? There are four criteria given for us in 1 Corinthians 12–14. First, and foremost, Christ is exalted as Lord (12.1-3). We are all utterly dependent on the Lord for all that we have to give to him in worship. We are all baptized into one body by the Spirit and are made to drink from the one Spirit. Only by being incorporated in the Lord's body and drinking together in him can we all find unity and the capacity to give of ourselves diversely for the Lord's glory (1 Cor. 12.13). We thus fittingly recognize his Lordship as the beginning and end of our celebration of grace (12.1-3).

Secondly, the gifts must be exercised in a way that is consistent with love to be a fitting part of the church's worship (1 Corinthians 13). God revealed his love for us by coming into flesh and dying for us while we were yet sinners (Rom. 5.5). Indeed, Jesus is himself the ultimate offering that is pleasing to the Father (Heb. 10.5). We offer ourselves diversely by the Spirit and through Christ's perfect self-offering. Our self-offering to God in worship thus follows the path of divine love (12.1-2). In this light, how can gifted worship have any credibility if it arises from a context of hate and division? For Paul, the church's diversely gifted worship is not merely fulfilled by

---

[17] Martin Luther, *Lectures on Romans* (trans. Wilhelm Pauck; Philadelphia: Westminster Press, 1961), p. 130.

love, for without love, this worship is itself discredited. Speaking in tongues, for example, becomes mere noise. This love is not mere emotion. It is an attitude, a life orientation; indeed, a way of acting. This must be the context from which worship arises. 'Have the same mindset as Christ Jesus …' must be the constant admonition for worship (Phil. 2.5).

Thirdly, closely related to the point given above, the gifts must be oriented towards building up others rather than merely the self (1 Cor. 14.26). Though we build up ourselves as well (1 Cor. 14.4), our priority in worship is building up others. Strength and guidance in worship does not only come from the preaching of the word or the open table of the Lord's Supper. It certainly comes from these primarily clerical ministries. But it also comes from the encouragement of all spiritual gifts: 'Speaking the truth in love, we will grow to become in every respect the mature body of him who is the head, that is, Christ' (Eph. 4.15). We all revere one another in revering the Lord, for we see the Lord in one another and are edified thereby (Eph. 5.21). We are all living letters of grace written by the Lord (2 Cor. 3.3). The glory of the Lord shines from us all, causing everyone to be transformed into the image of that glory (3.18).

Fourthly, the spiritual gifts legitimately participate in worship according to scriptural order and guidance. Everything should be done in a 'fitting and orderly way' (1 Cor. 14.40). For example, two or at most three prophets can address the church, but the others who are gifted with discernment should 'weigh carefully' what is said (v. 29). The spirits of the prophets (speaking) should be 'subject' to the prophets (discerning) (v. 32). This surely means that the prophets must be humble enough to accept the evaluations or those other prophets exercising prophetic discernment. In this way, those bearing prophetic gifts glorify God and open the church to greater worship by engaging in the loving practice of self-correction. But notice how Paul's tone changes when it comes to his apostolic authority in writing his letter to a church:

> Or did the word of God originate with you? Or are you the only people it has reached? If anyone thinks they are a prophet or otherwise gifted by the Spirit, let them acknowledge that what I am writing to you is the Lord's command. But if anyone ignores this, they will themselves be ignored (1 Cor. 14.36-38 NIV).

In other words, the fact that the word originated at Corinth through Paul's apostolic witness, his proclamation is a notch above the words of the Corinthian prophets when it comes to authority. Paul does not submit to the discernment of the prophets; they must submit to him. His word of instruction sets the standard by which the diversely gifted life of the Corinthian church is to be kept in order. So also today, the words of Scripture guide and nourish the gifted life of the church, including that of the preacher! If the gifts of the Spirit, all of them, including those of the pastor and bishop, are to function fittingly within the worship of the church, they must function in harmony with the words of Scripture. Scripture is the privileged voice of the Spirit in the churches. The Scriptures are thus the living measure of the church's diversely-gifted worship.

Conclusion

Clark Pinnock summarizes best the diversely-gifted worship of the church:

> As well as receiving the sacraments from the Spirit, we need to cultivate openness to the gifts of the Spirit. The Spirit is present beyond liturgy in a wider circle. There is a flowing that manifests itself as power to bear witness, heal the sick, prophesy, praise God enthusiastically, perform miracles and more. There is a liberty to celebrate, an ability to dream and see visions, a release of Easter life.[18]

Indeed, without the diversely-gifted church, the worship of the church would be rather drab and lifeless: a single voice, an overwhelmingly dominant medium, a solitary artistic expression, rather than a richly diverse orchestra of expressions. The gifted church is reminded of the fact that the worship of the church is not primarily a duty or a work but rather a gift, signs of grace before an increasingly graceless world.

---

[18] Clark Pinnock, *Flame of Love: A Theology of the Holy Spirit* (Downer's Grove, IL: 1996), p. 129.

8

LITURGY, *THEOSIS,* AND THE RENEWAL OF THE WORLD

Daniela C. Augustine[*]

Introduction

The liturgy of the Church is the cradle of her theology. Indeed, the ancient theological assertion *lex orandi, lex credendi* is consistent with the spirituality and theological development of the just over a century old Pentecostal movement. Pentecostals 'believe as they pray',[1] and their communal worship is the *theologia prima*[2] (choreographed, enacted theology in songs and hymns, prayers and sermons, symbolic gestures and congregational movements) from which dogmatics receive their form and content. Yet, worship is the liturgical anamnesis of the Church's transformational/transfiguring encounter with the divine presence, and as such is witness to, as well as proc-

---

[*] Daniela C. Augustine (DTh, University of South Africa) is Associate Professor of Theological Ethics at Lee University in Cleveland, TN, USA.

[1] *Lex orandi, lex credendi* is often translated as 'the rule of prayer (is) the rule of faith', in other words, 'we believe as we pray'.

[2] For the essence of liturgy as the first and fundamental theology see Dorothea Haspelmath-Finatti, *'Theologia Prima* – Liturgical Theology as an Ecumenical Challenge to Lutheran Worship Practice', *Dialog: A Journal of Theology* 48.4 (Winter 2009), pp. 374-79. Also, David W. Fagerberg, *Theologia Prima. What is Liturgical Theology?* (Chicago, IL: Hillenbrand Books, 2004). Both authors engage the thought of the Eastern Orthodox liturgist, Alexander Schmemann in relation to their own faith tradition.

lamation and depiction of God's ongoing redemptive and renewing action upon and on behalf of His people and the rest of creation. The trans-generational memory of the Church is the foundation of her faith not as a dogmatic ascent but as a living relationship with Jesus – the incarnate, crucified and resurrected God; a relationship saturated in the Pentecost *kenosis* of the Holy Spirit which constitutes the community of faith as Christ's body on earth according to the will of the Father. Therefore, in her worship the Church embodies/lives and proclaims 'What was from the beginning, what we have heard, what we have seen with our eyes, what we beheld and our hands handled, concerning the Word of Life' (1 Jn 1.1).[3]

Because liturgy is anemnetic it is also doxological and eucharistic[4] – expressing both glorification of God for who He is and thanksgiving for what He has done (while understanding His action as proceeding from, and thus being inseparable from, His identity). However, remembrance as liturgical anamnesis is not just a mental recollection of past events, but both their enacted likeness as well as the re-experiencing anew of what is being remembered. In worship, the liberating and transformative power of the recollected encounter (of the past event) is (in the words of Don E. Saliers) 'here and now, made actual among the community of memory and hope'.[5] Through the Holy Spirit, the living memory of the faith community becomes a mystical, trans-generational, pneumatic participation in the remembered events. As Alexander Schmemann points out, the Church's faith 'is not only not detachable from her experience – but is indeed that experience itself'. She is nothing less than 'the very epiphany of these events'.[6] Therefore, embodying the redemptive encounter with the divine presence, the Church and her entire liturgy are manifested as a sacrament for the life of the world, for where two or three are gathered together in Christ's name, He – the crea-

---

[3] Quotations of Scripture are taken from the New American Standard Version unless noted otherwise.

[4] Henry H. Knight III, 'Worship and Sanctification', *Wesleyan Theological Journal* 32.2 (Fall 1997), pp. 5-14 (p. 7).

[5] Don E. Saliers, *Worship as Theology: Foretaste of Glory Divine* (Nashville, TN: Abingdon Press, 1994), p. 96.

[6] Alexander Schmemann, 'Liturgy and Theology', in Thomas Fisch (ed.), *Liturgy and Tradition: Theological Reflections of Alexander Schmemann* (Crestwood, NY: St. Vladimir's Seminary Press, 2003), pp. 49-68 (pp. 54-55).

tor – himself is in their midst (Mt. 18.20), redeeming, sanctifying, healing, and renewing the world.

In light of this, the anamnesis of the Pentecostal Church transforms each worship service into intensified anticipation (and re-living) of Pentecost. The longing for *revival*, so emblematic for Pentecostal spirituality and its liturgical expression, is a longing for the coming of the Holy Spirit. Therefore, 'from beginning to end', Pentecostal worship is 'an *epiclesis*' – an invocation of the Holy Spirit 'who transfigures everything done in it … into that which it manifests and reveals to us'.[7] Indeed, the Pentecost *kenosis* of the Spirit transfigures the present into the future of the world, the human community into the Kingdom of God. Therefore, the thirsting for the Holy Spirit (and for a fresh experience of Pentecost) is longing for the coming of God and the advent of the *eschaton*. 'The Spirit and the bride say "Come"' (Rev. 22.17), and in the deep mystical union with her Lord, this cry of the Church becomes groaning in and with the Spirit for the renewal of the cosmos (Romans 8). Therefore, revival is taking the world into God's future (in and through the Holy Spirit) where all of creation stands wholesome and healed – an ontological renewal (a reviving) that starts with the gathering of the faithful (as the new, renewed humanity), the priesthood of all believers, anointed to intercede on behalf of the world and to carry it into its own being before the throne of God. It is not accidental, then, that the Pentecostal spiritual intuition has a distinctly eschatological orientation. The day of Pentecost is the beginning of the *eschata* and 'the first day of the new creation'[8] that manifests the Church 'as the gift and presence' of a new, never-ending 'eighth day' that frames the gates of eternity, where the cosmos experiences 'the gathering together and transformation of matter into spirit',[9] in other words, becomes pneumatized.

The Church's sacramental essence proceeds from and points to the 'sacramentality of creation itself'.[10] It unveils the liturgical character of the world's *beginning* and its eucharistic reality (being created

---

[7] Alexander Schmemann, *The Eucharist* (Crestwood, NY: St. Vladimir's Seminary Press, 1987), p. 222.

[8] Schmemann, *The Eucharist*, p. 36.

[9] Dimitru Staniloae, *The Experience of God: Orthodox Dogmatic Theology, Volume 2, The World: Creation and Deification* (Brookline, MA: Holy Cross Orthodox Press, 2005), p. 6.

[10] Schmemann, *The Eucharist*, p. 33.

– sang into existence – by God and given to humanity as means of communion with the creator and the fellow human), and depicts its *telos* in the joining of heaven and earth, of the visible and invisible, of the material and the spiritual, gathering *all* of creation in Christ who is to be *all in all*. This very *telos*, in the words of Schmemann, 'constitutes the essence and the purpose of the Church'.[11] Therefore, the community of faith is the 'manifestation and presence of the new and transfigured creation',[12] the inbreaking of the age to come and the adventing of God's Kingdom on earth. This is why the Church in its essence and vocation is both 'cosmic and eschatological',[13] and so is her liturgy. In light of this assertion, redemption could be understood as renewal of the sacramental reality of creation (and life itself). As Schmemann states,

> Precisely in this *sacramental* understanding of the world is the essence and gift of that *light of the world* that permeates the entire life of the Church, the entire liturgical and spiritual tradition … Sin is itself perceived here as a *falling away* of man, and in him of all creation, from this sacramentality, from the 'paradise of delight', and into 'this world', which lives no longer according to God, but according to itself and in itself and is therefore corrupt and mortal. And if this is so, then Christ accomplishes the salvation of the world by renewing the world and life itself as sacrament.[14]

In the midst of the sacramental/liturgical reality of the world, the human being is created not only as *homo sapiens* or *homo faber* but first and foremost as '*homo adorans*',[15] as a priest standing in the center of the world in order to unify it with the fulfillment of its destiny. As a worshiping creature, humanity is created with an inherent longing for a union with God – for its actualization in *theosis*.[16] The peculiar-

---

[11] Schmemann, *The Eucharist*, p. 19.
[12] Schmemann, *The Eucharist*, p. 21.
[13] Schmemann, 'Liturgy and Theology', pp. 57-58.
[14] Schmemann, *The Eucharist*, p. 34 (emphasis original).
[15] Alexander Schmemann, *For the Life of the World* (Crestwood, NY: St Vladimir's Seminary Press, 1983), p. 15.
[16] The term '*theosis*' refers both to the process and the *telos* of the Christian's transformation 'from glory to glory' (2 Cor. 3.18) towards attaining the likeness of God (understood fundamentally as Christ-likeness) by becoming partaker of the divine nature (2 Pet. 1.4). The goal of *theosis* is to be united with God – a difficult to articulate mystical notion of participation in the divine communal life while

ity of the dialectic of worship, however, is that we worship what we love and we become what we worship. Indeed, worship is a transfiguring pedagogy on becoming like God that accomplishes its aim through the intentional *askesis* of fasting from one's own misdirected desires, turned from the creator to the created (from God to the world, thus making it an end in itself). Therefore, right worship (*orthodoxy*) is disciplining and re-ordering the affections so that the worshipers may learn to love and be loved rightly (*orthopathy*) until they themselves (their entire lives) become love – God's love for all of His creation (*orthopraxy*). This is why humanity is instructed to love God with the entirety of one's being (Deut. 6.5; Mt. 22.37; Mk 12.30; Lk. 10.27) so that it may worship Him alone and therefore, be transformed into His likeness – experience *theosis*. Thus, idolatry endangers humanity's destiny by forming it into the likeness of something else (something less) than God – of something created rather than of the creator.

In light of this, the present chapter offers a theological reflection on the Judeo-Christian understanding of the liturgical and sacramental essence of cosmic and human ontology in their transfiguring journey toward *theosis*. This reflection begins by exploring the reality of creation as a divinely built temple and of the Jewish tabernacle/temple (and its worship) as a liturgical replica of creation (and the divine creative act). Further, the chapter discusses the particularity of human ontology as a living temple of the divine presence and an imaged revelation of the invisible Triune life within the visible materiality of the cosmos. The text concludes with a view towards the *eschaton*, where the Church (the New Jerusalem – the City of God) encompasses the world as the new temple full to its limits

---

retaining one's distinct creaturely identity. While the term does not have a clear analogue in Protestant theology, the closest parallel to it would be John Wesley's idea of both the process of sanctification and the stage of 'entire sanctification'. This parallel is not accidental since, as recent scholarship has established, Wesley's doctrine of sanctification was inspired by and developed in dialogue with the Eastern Church's understanding of *theosis*, as articulated in the writings of the Church Fathers. Yet, in the Eastern Orthodox vision of salvation, *theosis* eventually is experienced by all of creation and as such could be understood as the stage of complete ontological renewal and healing of the cosmos in a mystical union with the creator – a transformation initiated by the coming of the Holy Spirit on the day of Pentecost and the inauguration of the Church as Christ's body on earth, as the beginning of the new creation and the embodied future of the world in the midst of the present.

with the divine presence, radiating the glory of God in her *theosis*. There creation experiences its *telos* of partaking in the divine nature and the world stands unveiled in its transfigured form as a cosmic, ecclesial *macro-anthropos* (a destiny actualized in the cosmic Christ as the last Adam).[17]

Creation as a Temple and the Temple as Creation

The Judeo-Christian theological imagination has long hermeneutically linked the creation of the cosmos with the building of a temple. According to Jewish tradition (e.g. as articulated in the *Book of Jubilees*),[18] when Moses was summoned to Mt. Sinai by the creator he was given a vision 'of everything that had happened before he lived' ('of what was in the beginning and what will be' [*Jubilees* 1.2-4]) including the act of creation – a vision that he recorded in the opening chapters of Genesis.[19] Reminiscent of this assertion is

---

[17] For Vladimir Lossky, *The Mystical Theology of the Eastern Church* (Crestwood, NY: St. Vladimir's Seminary Press, 1976), the Church (as the communal body of Christ) is destined to engulf the cosmos, reuniting it with God. Lossky states,

> The church is the center of the Universe, the sphere in which its destinies are determined. All are called to enter into the church, for if man is a microcosm, the church is a *macro-anthropos*, as Maximus says. It increases and is compounded in history, bringing the elect into its bosom and uniting them to God. The world grows old and falls into decay, while the church is constantly rejuvenated and renewed by the Holy Spirit who is the source of its life. At a given moment, when the church has attained to the fullness of growth determined by the will of God, the external world, having used up its vital resources, will perish. As for the church, it will appear in its eternal glory as the Kingdom of God (p. 178).

Dimitru Staniloae, also utilizing the language of St. Maximus the Confessor (*Mystagogy*, ch. 7, PG 91.684C-685A) depicts the human being as a microcosm and the world as a *macro-anthropos*, and emphasizes human agency in the process of gathering all creation into union with God. See Dimitru Staniloae, *Experience of God: Orthodox Dogmatic Theology, volume 1, Revelation and Knowledge of the Triune God, The Experience of God* (Brookline, MA: Holy Cross Orthodox Press, 2005), pp. 4-6.

[18] The *Book of Jubilees* offers a parallel version of Genesis. It was preserved by the Ethiopian Church; however, fragments of the text were also found among the Dead Sea Scrolls.

[19] Margaret Barker, *Creation: A Biblical Vision for the Environment* (New York, NY and London, UK: T&T Clark, 2010), p. 36. I am truly indebted to Barker's enchanting book for the development of this particular section in the present paper. See also John H. Walton, *The Lost World of Genesis One: Ancient Cosmology and the Origins Debate* (Downers Grove, IL: Inter-Varsity Press, 2009), especially chapters 7, 8, and 9. Walton argues that the ancient readers saw the narrative of Genesis one as an account of temple-building and that the presence of day seven

Philo's famous depiction of the moment of revelatory impartation/illumination experienced by Moses in the mystical encounter with the divine presence. He is described as entering 'the darkness where God was, that is to say, into the invisible, and shapeless, and incorporeal world, the essence, which is the model of all existing things, where he beheld things invisible to mortal nature'.[20] On Mt. Sinai, Moses enters the Holy of Holies.[21] There he is engulfed beyond the opacity of the veil partitioning the material and the spiritual realms into the place where time and space become obsolete within the infinite, immutable omnipresence of the One Who is eternity itself. In a dramatic tension that merges together the limitations of human language with the monumentality of experience, Exod. 24.15-18 builds a textual memorial of this event. Moses ascends up the mountain where

> ... the glory of the Lord rested and the cloud covered it for six days; and on the seventh day He called to Moses from the midst of the cloud. And to the eyes of the sons of Israel the appearance of the glory of the Lord was like a consuming fire on the mountain top. And Moses entered the midst of the cloud as he went up to the mountain; and Moses was on the mountain forty days and forty nights.

For the nation of Israel, the cloud and the fire on the mountain top are the two familiar manifestations of the *shekinah* as visual theophany of the divine presence associated with God's redemptive, liberating, and renewing activity in the cosmos. Moses enters the

---

(the Sabbath of God) in that account would have been understood by the Near Easterners not in terms of cessation of divine creative activity but as a depiction of the moment in which, after the temple is built, the deity enters in it and occupies it as its dwelling place from which it governs the world. The author asserts that 'in the ancient world rest is what results when a crisis has been resolved or when stability has been achieved ... Consequently normal routines can be established and enjoyed'. Therefore, the seventh day does not describe God's 'disengagement from the cares, worries and tasks of life'. 'This is more a matter of engagement without obstacles rather than disengagement without responsibilities' (p. 73).

[20] Philo, *Life of Moses* I, p. 158, *The Works of Philo, Early Jewish Writings* (http://www.earlyjewishwritings.com/text/philo/book24.html).

[21] As Margaret Barker, points out, 'Scholars realized long ago that memories of Sinai had fused with memories of the holy of holies, and so what Moses "saw" on Sinai was what the ancient royal high priest "saw" in the holy of holies' (*Creation*, p. 37).

fearsome darkness of the cloud where he sees the unseen and is given knowledge of the unknown. There, where his natural eyesight fails amidst the surrounding darkness, he receives spiritual illumination. Immersed in the immediacy of the divine presence, Moses is given a two-fold vision of both the creation of the world and the creation of the tabernacle – a vision that unveils the divine creative act as a cosmic temple-building and presents the architectural plans for its sacred replica in the human-made sanctuary as a home for the divine presence. Both sanctuary-building and the daily liturgy within it become an embodied echo of the act of creation (vibrating in the fibers of communal life) and its perpetual sustaining and renewal by the creator; for worship could be viewed as reordering the human community and the cosmos (as its habitat) – according to God's will, spoken forward as His Word and made visible through the agency of the Spirit in its embodiment as (harmoniously-ordered) cosmic matter. Therefore, as Margaret Barker remarks, it was 'the creation that Moses had to replicate in the tabernacle, and so both the tabernacle, and later, the temple, represented the creation, and the worship there both preserved and renewed the creation of human society'.[22]

---

[22] Barker, *Creation*, p. 38. Barker also engages the thought of Rabbi Tanhuma bar Abba's assertion that 'the tabernacle is equal to the creation of the world itself' (*Midrash Tanhuma-Yelammedenu*, [trans. S.A. Berman; Jersey City, NJ: KTAV Publishing, 1996], pp. 648-49). Thus, Gen. 1.1 ('In the beginning God created the heaven and the earth') was linked with Exod. 26.7 ('Thou shalt make curtains of goats hair' and Moses erecting the outer structure of the tabernacle on the first day of the new year marked by the celebration of the Day of Atonement); the veil separating the Holy of Holies (Exod. 26.33) was linked to the creation of the firmament (Gen 1.6); the brass laver (Exod. 30.18) represented the gathering of the waters (Gen 1.9); the lights in the sky (sun, moon, and the five planets known at that time) were depicted by the menorah (Exod. 25.31); the birds created on the fifth day (and flying before the firmament) were linked to the winged cherubim standing before the veil (Exod. 25.20); 'and the creation of the human was linked to anointing the high priest (Exod. 29.1-7)'. Barker adds to these associations between the creation and the making of the tabernacle also the ones between the table of the 'Bread of the Presence' (Exod. 25.30), ornamented by exquisite depictions of lavish plants bearing forth abundance of fruit on which bread, wine, and incense were placed (all produced from the fruit of the earth's vegetation) and which reflected the third stage (day) of creation (Gen. 1.12), as well as the altar of burnt offerings (Exod. 40.28-29), 'which would have represented the creation of animals and birds' (Barker, *Creation*, pp. 41-42). See also John H. Walton, *The Lost World of Genesis One*, pp. 81-82.

The tabernacle depicted both the visible and invisible creation (heaven and earth) separated by the veil as by a divinely constituted boundary between the place of human habitation and the comprehension of the immediacy of the divine presence (with the entire heavenly hosts). As Josephus writes, each one of its furnishings was 'intended to recall and represent the universe'.[23] Indeed, the Jewish temple is a sacral microcosm depicting the divine cathedral of the cosmos filled to its limits by God's omnipresence,[24] in which the sense of vertical progression from earth to heaven is translated into the horizontal movement from the outer courtyard towards the Holy of Holies. This shift in the axis of relationship between heaven and earth depicted in Exodus' detailed instruction for the building of the tabernacle has also a revelatory significance. The dominant Near Eastern sacral imagination maintained the verticality of association between the realm of humanity and that of the gods (witnessed both by the architecture and function of ancient temples as well as by worship taking place on hills and mountain tops) articulating a notion of worship as ascent to a distant realm occupied by the deity. In contrast to that, Israel's ethos (and its undergirding cosmology) was to be formed by the creator who chooses to dwell with and among His creatures. From that position of indwelling nearness within the covenantal communion with His people, God rules the universe, sustaining its existence with His very presence. He is nearer to His creatures than their very breath. In fact, He is their very breath and life, for life itself is an expression of unconditional divine hospitality to the other since if He withdraws His Spirit everything will perish (Job 34.14-15).

This radical cosmogonic shift within Israel's sacramental imagination, however, is presented within Moses' revelatory vision on Mt. Sinai as being as old as the world itself – as a reality depicted from the beginning within the fibers of creation that now has been illuminated by the divine light of revelation, becoming transparent and visible through the symbolism of the tabernacle. This dual vision of creation and its sacred reproduction in Israel's worship could be seen as a parallel between general and specific revelation in

---

[23] Josephus, *The Jewish War* 3, 7.7, *Loeb Classical Library* (trans. H. St. J. Thackeray; Cambridge, MA: Harvard University Press, 1957), p. 403.
[24] Jan Assmann, *The Search for God in Ancient Egypt* (Ithaca, NY: Cornell University Press, 2001), p. 37.

which the second interprets/illuminates the first. Indeed, all of creation is an act of revelation, of God's self-sharing with the other.
The inaugural creative speech recorded in Gen. 1.3 – 'Let there be
light' – could be understood as a vocalization of the divine intent to
unveil the mystery of the invisible presence by pouring it forth into
visible, tangible materiality – it could be seen as 'let there be illumi-
nation/unveiling/revelation'. Since the sun, moon, and stars were
not created until the fourth day (Gen. 1.16-19), this verse could be
understood as referring to the 'heavenly light'[25] – a stage of being
within the progression of creation where the divine light holds all
things together in an undivided wholeness. Perhaps we can think of
it as a stage of full illumination, of unlimited disclosure, of rapturous unveiling of the divine essence in its splendor, beauty, and
goodness. A stage in which one knows fully just as they have been
known (1 Cor. 13.12).

God affirms that this light – revelation itself – is good (Gen. 1.4)
and He proceeds by separating it from darkness – revelation as illuminated mystery is separated from the opaqueness of concealed
mystery surrounded by the depths of silence. Within the realm of
illumination, creation comes forward as the substance of general
revelation. It unfolds before the eyes of its witness – heaven itself
with its entire host, also a creation of the Only Uncreated One.
Heaven hears and sees the birth of the cosmos amidst the unceasing
worship of the angels who sing from joy at the unveiling of the divine mystery (Job 38.4-7) understanding that they themselves are an
outcome of God's kenotic self-sharing in Word and Spirit. Creation
unfolds as a divine liturgy performed by God himself before heav-
en's worshiping host. It is a sacrament enacted by the creator. Its

---

[25] Barker, *Creation*, p. 39, states also that the Talmud, reflecting on Gen. 1.3,
asserts that the seven pillars in Wisdom's house (as depicted by Prov. 9.1) were
the seven books of the Torah of which only five were have come to us today.
One of the two missing books contained the teaching concealed in the opening
four verses of Genesis. The text to which she refers is found in the Babylonian
Talmud, *Tractate Shabbath*, 116a. It contains the following lines: 'Rabbi said: It is
not on that account, but because it ranks as a separate Book. With whom does
the following dictum of R. Samuel b. Nahmani in R. Jonathan's name agree: She
[Wisdom] hath hewn out her seven pillars: this refers to the seven Books of the
Law? With whom? With Rabbi'. The notations to the text, however, indicate that
'Since that section [discussed by the Rabbi] is a separate Book, the portions of
Numbers preceding and following it are also separate Books; hence there are
seven in all'.

cultic replica within the building (and worship) of the tabernacle is to become an embodiment of God's Word as the very source of life for the universe. Thus, the liturgy performed by the High Priest in the earthly sanctuary is not conducted only on behalf of Israel, but for the life of the world. It further transcends the limits of material creation joining together heaven and earth, the visible and the invisible realm (from the outer courtyard to the interiority of the Holy of Holies) in a singular all-engulfing movement of worship to the creator.

The liturgy in the tabernacle (and later in the temple) is an enactment of God's Word according to the revelation articulated to Moses through the divine vision and its instruction. That Word written on tablets of stone (as a depiction of unchangeable/intransient essence engraved upon the transient creation) stands at the very heart of the sanctuary, holding everything together as the inner structure and substance of the cosmos – as its source of life, meaning, harmony, and future. Thus, the tabernacle manifests itself as both a 'mini cosmos'[26] revealing the universe's essence as a grandiose temple filled with the divine presence (Isa. 6.1-5), as well as a portable Mt. Sinai[27] and a lasting memorial of Moses' encounter with God on behalf of Israel, being paradigmatic for the covenantal communion between Him and all of humanity.[28]

Indeed, the horizontal integration of heaven and earth within the structure of the tabernacle and the centrality of the divine Word for worship and communion with God has its precedent in Genesis' primordial memory of paradise. The Garden of Eden can be viewed as the first sacred structure built by God himself in the very fabric of the cosmos – or more precisely, it can be understood as the proto-holy-of-holies within the created order. Eden stands out in the

---

[26] Walton, *The Lost World of Genesis One*, p. 83.

[27] On the parallels between the tabernacle and Mt. Sinai, see Rabbi Jonathan Sacks, *To Heal a Fractured World: The Ethics of Responsibility* (New York, NY: Schocken Books, 2005), p. 151.

[28] The rabbinic tradition eventually developed the belief that when the law was given on Mt Sinai, it was heard not only by Israel but by the 72 nations listed in Gen. 10.2-31. The voice of God circumscribed the earth and all humanity heard it. As the Talmud states, 'For when the Torah was given to Israel the sound thereof travelled from one end of the earth to the other' (*Mas. Zevachim*, 116a). See also *Schemoth Rabba*, 70 d and *Midrash Tanchuma*, 26 C.

narrative of Genesis as 'archetypal sanctuary'[29] where God dwells within creation and where humanity's fundamental form of worship is life according to His Word. Indeed, through the lenses of Genesis 1 and 2, we see creation as a living, breathing temple, animated by the Spirit, in which all of God's creatures are organically connected with one another and their environment in the wonder-inspiring beauty of the cosmic liturgy. In this divinely-instituted and exquisitely choreographed worship, the Word and the Spirit vibrate within and throughout the materiality of creation in an embodied self-expression depicting the divine communal life as all-engulfing, unconditional love.

The formless, void, and dark earth described in Gen 1.2 is primed by the Spirit before being seeded by the Word, for apart of the Spirit's creative agency the Word does not accomplish its embodiment either in the first or in the last/the new creation. The Spirit translates the Word from the realm of the invisible into the visible, from the incorporeal to the embodied, making it tangible and comprehensive within the fibers of creation. The Spirit as the unveiler of the eternal Logos makes its meaning transparent in the opaqueness of the cosmos as revealed Word, and in the midst of this embodied revelation stands humanity – itself a part of the revelatory essence of creation.

Human Ontology and Divine Liturgy

The ontology of humanity, embodied in the first Adam (male-and-female [Gen. 1.27]) before the fall, is that of a community of priests in the cathedral of the cosmos, bearing the image and growing into the likeness of the communal Trinity amidst the material world. As a priest before God, Adam stands as the embodiment of the cosmic communion of matter and Spirit, representing in his very being a sacrament in which the icon of the cosmos and the icon of God are united together as an evocation of the destiny of the world where God is to be all in all (Eph. 1.21). Thus, human ontology is to be the materialization of the sacred story of the world, joining together the primordial memory of its beginning with the anticipation of its

---

[29] Gordon J. Wenham, 'Sanctuary Symbolism in the Garden of Eden Story', in *Proceedings of the Ninth World Congress of Jewish Studies* (Jerusalem, Israel: World Union of Jewish Studies, 1986), p. 19.

eschatological unfolding. In the words of St. Gregory the Theologian,

> The Word of God wanted to reveal that humanity participates in both worlds, namely in invisible as well as in visible nature … Therefore, Adam was placed on this earth as a second world, a large world within a small world, like an angel that worships God while participating in the spiritual and material worlds alike. Adam was created to protect and preserve the visible world, while at the same time being initiated into the spiritual world.[30]

Therefore, Adam's priestly function as a mediator between heaven and earth is engraved in his very being. He is created to abide both in the Holy of Holies and in the rest of the cosmos, seeing the Word and mirroring its image in the world so that the world may live life more abundant – life according to the Word that has spoken it into existence. Adam is a Word made flesh through the agency of the Spirit – formed from the earth as spoken-forth Word and animated by the divine breath – but also as an enacted Word within the universe that preserves its harmony and wholeness. Thus, his priestly function is to keep the cosmos (gathered and abiding) in the Word – it is the mission of keeping the Word (and the boundaries placed by God within the structure of the world) and passing that calling and sacred knowledge from generation to generation for the life of the world. That knowledge proceeds directly from the Holy of Holies – from the very presence of God in the midst of creation. In a sense, Adam is the keeper of the right measurements, architectural plans, and proper function of the cosmic temple, so that its structure may remain uncorrupted and it may not be condemned to demolition. For as Philo states, the Word of God is 'the first beginning of all things, the original species or the archetypal idea, the first measure of the universe'.[31] Later, in the conditions of a fallen/broken world, the Word shared itself with Moses in the giving of the Torah, which was to be kept in the Holy of Holies within the Ark of the Covenant. The Ark marked the place where God descended and spoke to His people, the place from where His Word,

---

[30] H.A.H. Bartholomew I, Archbishop of Constantinople and Ecumenical Patriarch, *Encountering the Mystery* (New York, NY: Doubleday, 2008), p. 96.

[31] Philo, *Questions and Answers on Genesis 1.4, The Works of Philo, Early Jewish Writings* (http://www.earlychristianwritings.com/yonge/book41.html).

as the true measurement of the cosmic sanctuary and all in it, meas-
ured humanity and exposed its shortcomings, but also shared itself
as the means for the mending of the fractured human community
and the rest of the world. Thus, the priest stood in the tabernacle
(the sacred replica of the cosmos) as a renewed/re-consecrated Adam, as the sanctified image of God in the universe.[32] The priestly
garments testified to that assertion: the inner garment made of
white linen depicted the uncreated, heavenly aspect of Adam's essence, invisible for human sight and thus covered with the outer
garment, the appearance of which resembled the material of the veil
that separated the Holy of Holies and represented humanity's created, visible, earthly, essence. Similarly to the veil, the outer garment
both revealed and obscured the presence of heaven on earth, pointing to it, yet preserving its mystery. Its colors depicted the four
basic elements: earth, air, fire, and water.[33] Therefore, as Philo
states, the high priest stood in the presence of God as the cosmos
itself – the entire created world entering the Holy of Holies and
worshiping its creator. In a way, the priest also represented the
cosmic temple within the human-built temple. Further, in contrast
to the pagan priest who offered (in the words of Philo) 'prayers and
sacrifices solely for their own relations, and friends, and fellow citizens', the high priest of Israel interceded for all humanity and the
rest of creation and poured 'forth his prayers and thanksgivings for
them all, looking upon the world (as indeed it really is) as his country'.[34] This strikingly inclusive, cosmopolitan depiction of the high
priest's role confronts the destructive forces of ethnocentrism, alienation, fear, and violence against the other, offering a vision of the
world in its unbroken wholeness – a vision of comprehensive shalom in the presence of the creator. Thus, as through the first Adam,
so also through the high priest the whole of creation engaged in

---

[32] Barker, *Creation*, p. 202. Also, C.H.T. Fletcher-Louis, *All the Glory of Adam:
Liturgical Anthropology in the Dead Sea Scrolls* (Leiden: Brill, 2002), p. 71.

[33] Philo, *The Special Laws* 1.84-85, *The Works of Philo*, *Early Jewish Writings*
(http://www.earlyjewishwritings.com/text/philo/book27.html) Also see Josephus on the curtain of the temple in *The Jewish Wars* 5, 5.4, *Early Jewish Writings*
(http://www.earlyjewishwritings.com/text/josephus/war5.html)

[34] Philo, *The Special Laws* 1.95-97. He notes: 'For God intends that the high
priest should in the first place have a visible representation of the universe about
him, in order that from the continual sight of it he may be reminded to make his
own life worthy of the nature of the universe, and secondly, in order that the
whole world may co-operate with him in the performance of his sacred rites'.

performing the divine liturgy within the earthly temple for the renewal of the entire cosmos.

Indeed, ontologically, the first Adam represents the communion of heaven and earth, as the mystical unity of matter and spirit – of the visible and invisible, the created and uncreated. Thus, according to Dimitru Staniloae, the human being appears last within the divine creative act 'as a kind of natural link (*syndesmos*) between the extremities of the whole' so that on behalf of the cosmos he/she may maintain and fulfill 'the all-encompassing mystery that is the union of God with creation' and that may be 'the conscious and willing means through which God maintains and fulfills this union'.[35]

Yet, Adam is created not just as a priest and keeper of the cosmos, holding it together in the Word. He himself is to become a sacrament and a temple – a sacred replica of the origin and *telos* of the cosmos, designed to be perpetually filled with the divine presence – an embodied/materialized Word permeated by the *shekinah* of God, enacting His will within the universe as a visible icon of the invisible divine reality. Adam is to be a living temple within the temple, an embodied revelation within the revelation. Yet, in order to fulfill this destiny of incarnated likeness of God in and through union with Him, Adam has to choose to offer his very being as a temple for his Maker – the creature has to make place for God within itself, inviting the divine presence in and becoming its living home on earth. God creates the universe by building within himself a home for the other; now humanity is to become an imitator of God by building (out of its free choice) within itself a home for God – the ultimate other[36] – becoming a living sanctuary for the divine presence. Thus, life in Eden as well as (later in the conditions of the Fall) in the building of the tabernacle (and the ongoing divinely-ordained liturgy within it) could be viewed also as pedagogy on becoming like God depicted in one's (individual and corporate) kenotic, covenantal re-spacing in unconditional hospitality for the other. It is a process of divinely-sustained transfiguring of humanity

---

[35] Dimitru Staniloae, *The Experience of God. Orthodox Dogmatic Theology, volume 5, The Sanctifying Mysteries* (Brookline, MA: Holy Cross Orthodox Press, 2012), p. 4.

[36] Rabbi Jonathan Sacks points out the intentionality in the use of key words from Genesis 1 in describing the making of the tabernacle (*To Heal a Fractured World*, p. 151).

into a sanctuary built of the Word and saturated with the Spirit where the cosmos finds its actualization in *theosis*.

What the first Adam sees before the fall in the Holy of Holies of Eden, Moses sees in the Holy of Holies of Mt. Sinai and the descendants of Aaron see behind the veil of the tabernacle. They behold (and hear) the Word and translate/apply it into the cosmos so that it may live, so that God's sanctuary may stand. But even more than that, they are to be themselves an embodiment of its right measurements as a living temple – to be an incarnate, Spirit-filled Word. Undoubtedly, the fall of humanity, resulting in the fracturing of all creation, manifests this dimension of human ontology since the distortion of the entire cosmos starts with the corruption of the one who is its right measure, keeper, and priest. Adam transgresses the boundaries set by the Word (and no right embodied measurement is left to set the cosmic temple straight since all humanity stands corrupt in him). Expelled from the Holy of Holies he does not see the Word face to face, yet remains imprinted with its image and now hears its echo in the interiority of his being (in the resonance of his conscience) as an engrained memory of the lost paradise – as a twinkling knowledge of a once fully-illuminated, fully-alive, harmonious world. Adam exits Eden remaining forever a 'paradise-haunted'[37] creature searching for home in this world, not realizing that the only way to get home is by surrendering and consecrating him/herself as a home for the creator.

If Adam is created as the bond between the cosmos and God, uniting the creation to the creator in whom there is no separation but all things stand circumscribed and bonded 'tightly to one another and to himself through His providence',[38] then in its fallen stage humanity 'is capable of producing separation and alienation between all things'. Yet, in the words of Dimitru Staniloae, even further, the fallen Adam 'has likewise produced division between all things and God, their ultimate unifying principle'.[39]

Amidst this cosmic catastrophe, the healing of the broken world has to begin with the ontological renewal of humanity as embodied, Spirit-filled Word – it has to start with the birth of the renewed, last

---

[37] Peter Short, *Emmanuel College Newsletter* (Toronto, Canada: Emmanuel College, Autumn 2004).

[38] St. Maximus the Confessor, *Mystagogy*, PG 91.664.

[39] Staniloae, *The Sanctifying Mysteries*, p. 5.

Adam. In the first Adam, the icon of the uncreated image and created matter meet together in a communion destined to encapsulate the likeness of God's life within the embodied human communal essence amidst the created world. This is the human destiny of *theosis* realized and fulfilled in the last Adam – the One in Whom the fullness of deity dwells in bodily form (Col. 2.9), as the communion of heaven and earth, of matter and Spirit, of the uncreated eternal Word and enfleshed human existence (Jn 1.1, 14). The mission of the Word of God made flesh is 'to bring about a new union of all things in Himself' – 'an even closer union between creator and creature' in the mystery of the cosmic Christ[40] – a mission that is to be accomplished through His communal body on earth – the Church in the power of the Spirit. This is the new human community of priests whose *leitorgia* joins heaven and earth, the visible and the invisible, enfleshing within the present the future of the world (the life of the Kingdom that is to come) and, in intercession, carrying creation before the face of God in a proleptic anticipation of its eschatological renewal of which she – the Church as the body of the last Adam – is first fruit.

Instead of Conclusion … an Ascent to the *Eschaton*: The Church as the New Temple on Earth

Echoing St. Athanasius, Vladimir Lossky asserts that God became flesh so that humanity may receive the Holy Spirit[41] – become pneumatized. Therefore, Pentecost is not merely a continuation of the Incarnation or its sequel. It is its result and purpose. Through the redeeming ontological renewal of creation in Christ, the 'creature has become fit to receive the Holy Spirit'[42] and be the dwelling place and in-fleshed reality of the Trinitarian *koinonia* in the cosmos. Indeed, Pentecost marks the event of the transformation of the community of faith into the Body of Christ,[43] empowered by the

---

[40] Staniloae, *The Sanctifying Mysteries*, p. 5.
[41] Lossky, *The Mystical Theology of the Eastern Church*, p, 179.
[42] Lossky, *The Mystical Theology of the Eastern Church*, p. 159.
[43] The event of Pentecost could be viewed as the incarnation of Christ in the community of faith, a moment brought about through the agency of the Holy Spirit. As the third person of the Trinity pours himself over the one hundred twenty in the upper room, they become both Christ-bearers and a living extension of His resurrected Body on earth. Sergius Bulgakov, 'The Virgin and the

Holy Spirit to do the will of the Father. Therefore, this is the event in which the Church is established as the image of the Trinity on earth,[44] becoming a visible, embodied communal theophany of the invisible divine proto-community. Thus, in her mystical union with God in the Spirit-saturated human community, the Church becomes the *telos* of all of creation and stands within the present as the embodiment of the world's future in which God is all in all (1 Cor. 15.28). The Pentecost's *kenosis* of the Spirit transforms the corporate Body of Christ into the communally-embodied temple of the divine presence amidst the cosmos (2 Cor. 6.16, Eph. 2.19-22), destined to be the vehicle through which God extends His redemptive hospitality to all of creation. The Spirit births forth the Church so that the entire cosmos may become a Church – a Eucharistic communion of heaven and earth in the union of God and His world.

The sacramental anamnesis of the Church as the corporate body of Christ – the new temple on earth – celebrates the all engulfing mystery of this union of God 'with the whole of creation'[45] as its very essence and self-expression. The liturgical worship of the community of faith is not only a portal to heaven but a merging of the celestial and earthly celebration of God's presence. There is one altar, one sacrifice, one presence, and all the invisible host of heaven joins the redeemed humanity around that altar – the table of the Lord. We worship surrounded by 'the great cloud of witnesses' (Heb. 12.1), our spiritual eyes open to the nearness of the angels and the saints from all generations standing with us around the throne of God Who meets us in the familiar face of Christ – the

---

Saints in Orthodoxy', in Daniel B. Clendenin (ed.), *Eastern Orthodox Theology: A Contemporary Reader* (Grand Rapids, MI: Baker Books, 1995), pp. 65-75 (p. 67), has given us the image of Jesus' conception as being 'the Pentecost of the Virgin'. As the Holy Spirit descends upon Mary in response to her willingness and readiness for service (Lk. 1.38), she is transformed into an instrument of God's Word becoming flesh amidst humanity (Jn 1.14). For Bulgakov, it takes a willing human instrument to authenticate the humanness of Christ in the incarnation. In a similar manner, as the Spirit descends upon the disciples, Christ is conceived in them and they are empowered (Acts 1.8). Individually and corporately, they become Christ-bearers and bear forth an embodied Gospel as a hope realized in the midst of a destitute humanity. See Daniela C. Augustine, *Pentecost, Hospitality, and Transfiguration: Toward a Spirit-inspired Vision of Social Transformation* (Cleveland, TN: CPT Press, 2012), pp. 23-27.

[44] For more on the Church as the image of the Trinity on earth see Augustine, *Pentecost, Hospitality, and Transfiguration*, pp. 27-30.

[45] Staniloae, *The Sanctifying Mysteries*, p. 3.

incarnated eternal Word, the Lamb of God, the *Pantokrator* of all (Rev. 1.8). Thus, the worship of the Church arises within the present as an evocation and embodiment of the *eschaton*, in which the ontological renewal of cosmos is complete in its transfiguration into a temple of God, saturated with the divine glory.

Remembering amidst the brokenness of the world the primordial recollection of the all-engulfing and permeating heavenly light, depicted in Gen. 1.3, mystic Judaism longingly anticipated its eschatological restoration in the messianic age.[46] For the Christian, however, this stage of illumination has already manifested itself in Christ (the culmination of the divine self-sharing) as the light of the world (Jn 8.12, 9.5) but also in the Church as the corporate living extension of the Incarnate Word from where the divine light shines in the darkness as a city on a hill that cannot be hidden (Mt. 5.14). The embodiment of the eternal Logos in both cosmic matter during the first creation as well as in human flesh and ecclesial communal life in the last enlightens the world about its origin and *telos* – being primed for and gathered by the Spirit in the Cosmic Christ, joining heaven and earth, matter and spirit in the mystical union of the creator and the creation – in the *theosis* of the cosmos. Therefore, John's vision of the New Jerusalem recorded in Revelation 21 could be viewed as the eschatological counterpart (the divinely ordained *telos*) of Gen 1.3, depicting Moses' vision of the world's beginning. 'And I saw no temple in it, for the Lord God, the Almighty, and the Lamb, are its temple. And the city has no need of the sun or of the moon to shine upon it, for the glory of God has illumined it, and its lamp is the Lamb' (vv. 22-23) The omnipresent heavenly light has gathered creation into itself – into the full disclosure and transparency of God's glory.

Indeed, the vision of the transformation of the world into a sanctuary through the sacramental agency of the Spirit-filled Church is nowhere better articulated than in the book of Revelation and its depiction of the City of God (Revelation 21). The City descends on earth as the bride of the Lamb, the community of the saints – the church of the redeemed (Rev. 21.2). As John Christopher Thomas observes in his marvelous commentary on the book of Revelation,

---

[46] Barker, *Creation*, p. 39.

'The holy city and the holy people are one and the same'.[47] The Church is the City of God and she is filled with His glory (vv. 10-11) – His glory shines through her into the world. Therefore, the walls of the City are transparent so that nothing can obstruct the all-permeating light of the divine presence (v. 18). She is luminous with it, for the believers have become like their God and He is all in all within them (v. 23).

The city has no temple (v. 22), in fact, as Thomas asserts, the entire city is a temple.[48] This is why the text describes its gates beginning with the Eastern one, according to the orientation of the city which is identical with the orientation of the temple in the old Jerusalem (1 Kgs 6.20). In fact, its length, width, and height are the same (v. 16) – the city is in the form of a cube like the Holy of Holies in the Jerusalem temple. The entire city is Holy of Holies.[49] It is a sanctuary in the very presence of God where unceasing worship takes place joining heaven and earth as the life of the proto-community of the Trinity in-fleshed in the redeemed human society.

The magnitude of the city is breathtaking. Its size is unprecedented. It is beyond human comprehension – a mega-polis that, in the words of Thomas, stretches 'across the known world and into the heavens itself, perhaps indicating that the New Heaven and the New Earth unite in the New Jerusalem!'[50] The city of God has become the global village. The glory of God has covered the earth as the waters cover the sea.

The earth has been transformed into a sanctuary for all of God's creatures so that they may truly live. The believers as the temple of God on earth are now the very content of the heavenly city. God has become one with His people; Christ has become all in all, and the Church herself has become the Holy of Holies of the world as an embodiment of absolute divine hospitality in the very presence of God. A sanctuary that has covered the globe – this is the Church in her *theosis*. This transfiguring journey that started on the day of Pentecost has brought her to the summation of all existence into

---

[47] John Christopher Thomas, *The Apocalypse: A Literary and Theological Commentary* (Cleveland, TN: CPT Press, 2012), p. 645.
[48] Thomas, *The Apocalypse*, p. 646.
[49] Thomas, *The Apocalypse*, p. 646.
[50] Thomas, *The Apocalypse*, p. 645.

the likeness of Christ – it has translated her beyond time into eternity where the beginning and the end of all things stand joined together in the glorious beauty of the creator. This is the eternal eighth day in which the cosmos stands healed and whole – the day enacted and revealed in the liturgy of the Church for the life and the renewal of the world.

9

'IN YOUR PRESENCE IS FULLNESS OF JOY': EXPERIENCING GOD AS TRINITY

Chris E.W. Green*

Introduction

What do we experience when we experience God? What do we desire when we long for God's presence? Whom are we inviting to be there with us and for us, to act savingly on us? How does this desired, welcomed God make himself present to us? And why do we need God to be present in these ways? For a long time now, these questions and others like them have been troubling me toward reflection, and what I have written here is an attempt to give voice to the reflections born of that troubledness. I hope at least some of what I say here somehow stimulates further conversation about how we can speak more faithfully – or at least less *un*faithfully – of God's presence to and in us, and our experience of that presence.

Pentecostal Experience of God's Presence

Pentecostals talk often and at length about experiencing God. But because no pressing need is felt to work out a precise theological idiom for describing *how* God is present, talk about the experience

* Chris E.W. Green (PhD, Bangor University, Wales; DMin, Oral Roberts University) is Associate Professor of Theology at Pentecostal Theological Seminary in Cleveland, TN, USA.

remains by and large a first-order unreflective habit.[1] A remarkably labile range of terms – including 'heaven', 'glory', and 'power', as well as 'Lord', 'God', and 'King', and the more intimate names, 'Father', 'Jesus', and 'Spirit'[2] – are used to identify the presence encountered at 'the altar', and the emphasis remains on the experience itself rather than on the ways that experience is explained.[3] When Pentecostals *do* take pains to describe God's presence theologically in trinitarian terms, the second-order descriptions often suggest that the Spirit has replaced the once-present and soon-returning Jesus or that 'Spirit' is simply another name for Jesus in his post-ascension heavenly glory.[4] But even these descriptions[5] are used, if at all, only

---

[1] According to Daniel Albrecht and Evan Howard, 'Pentecostal Spirituality', in Cecil M. Robeck Jr. and Amos Yong (eds.), *The Cambridge Companion to Pentecostalism* (New York: Cambridge University Press, 2014), 'Pentecostalism is a renewal movement that emphasizes the experience of God' (p. 235). See also Keith Warrington, *Pentecostal Theology: A Theology of Encounter* (London: T&T Clark, 2008), pp. 20-27, and Daniel Albrecht, *Rites in the Spirit: A Ritual Approach to Pentecostal/Charismatic Spirituality* (JPTSup 17; Sheffield: Sheffield Academic Press, 1999), pp. 237-51.
Of course, we do not want to draw the difference between first- and second-order theological speech too sharply, or play one off against the other. See Kathryn Tanner, *Theories of Culture: A New Agenda for Theology* (Minneapolis: Fortress Press, 1997), pp. 71-79.

[2] The fact that this language seems to work for at least many Oneness and Trinitarian Pentecostals alike witnesses to the fact that their disagreements play out by and large only at the second order of theological reflection and speech. Perhaps, then, we need to bring our disagreements, so to speak, into the altar, reflecting together, as brothers and sister in Christ, directly on our shared experience of God. No doubt, re-contextualizing the disagreements in worship is sure to generate conflict, but hopefully they are the kinds of conflict that open us sanctifyingly toward one another and toward God. For more on what is at stake in Oneness- and Trinitarian-Pentecostal dialog, see Wolfgang Vondey, *Beyond Pentecostalism: The Crisis of Global Christianity and the Renewal of the Theological Agenda* (Grand Rapids: Eerdmans, 2010), pp. 89-98.

[3] In certain ways, Pentecostals often sound like Schleiermacher: when we experience God, we experience a unified and unifying presence, a oneness upon which we absolutely depend, and because all primary utterance of God speaks to this unity, Trinitarian talk is of secondary importance and at best marginal benefit. For more on Schleiermacher's understanding of experience, see Ted Peters, *God as Trinity: Relationality and Temporality in Divine Life* (Louisville: Westminster John Knox Press, 1993), p. 38. See also Jürgen Moltmann, *The Trinity and the Kingdom: The Doctrine of God* (Minneapolis: Fortress Press, 1993), pp. 2-3.

[4] In the words of one early Pentecostal (*Latter Rain Evangel* [Jan 1915], p. 4), '[Jesus] has gone into the heavens but the executive agent of the Trinity is here and He is subjecting hearts and lives and bringing them under the dominion of the Lord Jesus'. I am primarily concerned here with popular Pentecostal ministry, but some Pentecostal scholars make the argument in their own terms. For exam-

ad hoc, without much concern for consistency or coherence. We are left, then, with many witnesses affirming *that* God is present, but without any agreed-upon sense of how we are to speak of that presence.

What are we to make of this? One might argue that the inexactness and disorderliness of our descriptions should not be challenged or changed in any way because they testify to the unsearchable riches and indescribable glories of God's presence within and among us. Truth be told, Scripture itself seems sometimes to speak in this way – think, for example of the account of Yahweh's appearance to Abraham in Genesis 18 and the unpicturable images of the throne-room in the Apocalypse (4.1-5.14; 22.1-5).[6] And it does so for good reason: rightly understood, this strange way of speaking works apophatically, impressing on our imaginations the excess, the uncircumscribability, of the life encountered in the experience of God.

But as the church, we are called to bear witness faithfully to the God of the gospel. And this means that our experiences of God are never ends in themselves but belong to the Spirit's work of revealing Christ to the world as the revelation of the Father. We are bound not only to testify but also to *teach;*[7] therefore, we strive always to discern more theologically appropriate ways of identifying what happens in God's coming near to us. What is more, the way we describe our experiences of God is as formative as the experiences themselves, both for us and for others.[8] What we say about

---

ple, Simon Chan, 'The Liturgy as the Work of the Spirit: A Theological Perspective', in Teresa Berger and Bryan D. Spinks (eds.), *The Spirit in Worship – Worship in the Spirit* (Collegeville, MN: Liturgical Press, 2009), pp. 41-57, seems to affirm pneumatic replacement in classical theological terms.

[5] Usually, in my experience, these lines of thought are triggered by texts like Jn 16.7 and 2 Cor. 3.17. For an outsider's perspective on the issue, see Oliver Davies, *Theology of Transformation: Faith, Freedom, and the Christian Act* (Oxford: Oxford University Press, 2013), pp. 88-93.

[6] See John Christopher Thomas, *The Apocalypse: A Literary and Theological Commentary* (Cleveland, TN: CPT Press, 2012), pp. 201-37.

[7] Unlike the man healed by Jesus, we cannot simply say, 'I do not know whether he is a sinner. One thing I do know, that though I was blind, now I see' (Jn 9.25). We have to confess what the Spirit teaches us: that Jesus is God come in the flesh for us (see 1 Jn 4.1-3).

[8] Raimundo Panikkar, *The Experience of God: Icons of Mystery* (Minneapolis: Augsburg Fortress Press, 2006), pp. 25-26, describes the experience of God as constituted by four 'distinct but inseparable moments': (a) 'the pure experience, the instant of pure life, of immediate experience'; (b) 'the memory of that moment, which permits us to speak of it ...'; (c) 'the interpretation we develop of

what is happening to us is part of the happening itself. As Augustine insisted, if we are given a sign (*signum*) and we do not know the reality (*res*) it signifies, we learn nothing.[9] The reverse holds true as well. There can be no faithful believing where there is no push for faithful understanding.[10] If we hope to speak rightly to, for, and of the God we experience in worship, and if we hope to be formed together rightly by that experience, we cannot avoid the work of critical theological reflection and discerning theological construction.

Experience and the Triune God

The God of the gospel has made himself known to us as Trinity.[11] It follows then that as we strive to speak rightly about our experience of this God, we have to be learning to 'read' our experiences trinitarianly.[12] The problem is, we have to a large degree lost touch

---

this [remembered experience], which leads us to describe it as painful, sensitive, spiritual, loving, the experience of Being, of God, of Beauty, and so on'; (d) 'its reception in the cultural world that we have not created but which has been given to us and which bestows on experience a spiritual resonance'.

[9] Augustine, *De trinitate* 10.1.2.

[10] I agree with Steven Studebaker, *From Pentecost to the Triune God: A Pentecostal Trinitarian Theology* (Grand Rapids: Eerdmans, 2012), p. 191:

the options for Pentecostals do not reduce to the false alternatives of defining the movement in terms of either charismatic experience or theology and doctrine. The Pentecostal movement is about being caught up in an experience of God's Spirit that transforms lives and empowers them to serve God in this world. Yet that experience of the Spirit points the way toward a Pentecostal theology. Not a theology that fractures the Christian communities, but a theological 'tongue' of the Spirit of Pentecost that contributes to the richness of the Christian community.

[11] In the words of S.D. Kinne, an early Pentecostal (*Latter Rain Evangel* 2.10 [July 1910], p. 23): 'the revelation of the personal Trinity is the center of Christian experience'. This holds true, I believe, for Oneness and Trinitarian Pentecostals alike. The disagreements come when we begin to work out what it *means* to speak of God's tri-unity.

[12] From the beginning of the movement, at least some Pentecostals have sensed the need for this kind of reading. Take, for example, this account from Fannie Winn, a missionary to Jerusalem and Palestine (*The Bridegroom's Messenger* 2.26 [Nov 15, 1908], p. 4):

There were times ... when God poured out His Spirit upon us in the presence of the people. We could not do much but sing and shout God's praises and bear witness to the love and joy which can only come through Jesus Christ our Lord. They are Moslems and do not believe that Jesus is the Son of

with the 'grammar' of trinitarian dogma.[13] And without the ordering of that grammar, our speech about God, however well-intentioned, drifts toward unfaithfulness – even when it arises from authentic experience of God. To cite but one example: if we do not understand the Spirit as fully God – if we think of the Spirit not as person in the same sense as Father and Son, but merely as raw divine power – then we cannot appreciate what it means to be 'baptized' in the Spirit because only God can know God fully and make God fully known. We will instead wrongly imagine Spirit baptism as granting us possession of that raw power, putting it at our disposal. This, it seems to, is exactly the mistake of Simon Magus (Acts 8.9-25).

It is well known that the early Pentecostal movement was convulsed by arguments about the doctrine of the Trinity. But what is less often recognized is how those arguments were made necessary because the movement inherited from the Wesleyan-holiness traditions a theologically frail account of the doctrine. Jason Vickers has traced the demise of trinitarian theology in English Protestantism by identifying the process of theological and practical shifts that over time altered fundamentally how salvation was understood and how theology was practiced.[14] The collapse, Vickers shows, resulted from three interdetermining factors: 'the appeal to Scripture as the rule of faith; the shift in the understanding of faith from "trust" to "assent"; and the assumption about language and the necessity of "clear and intelligible" propositions'.[15] As Peter Leithart explains,

> The result was that the Trinity gradually slipped from its position of central significance in the life of the church. Instead of disclosing the name of the God who saves, along with identifying descriptions, Trinitarian formulae became simply propositions to which believers were to assent. Detached from baptism and

---

God and the Savior of the world. They say that God is One not Three; but during our stay they saw the power of the Third Person of the Trinity mightily manifested and heard His voice speaking in the unknown tongues.

[13] For the ways that anti-creedalism shaped early Pentecostal theology, and in particular the Oneness debates, see Aaron T. Friesen, 'Pentecostal Antitraditionalism and the Pursuit of Holiness', *JPT* 23.2 (October, 2014), pp. 191-215.

[14] Jason Vickers, *The Making and Remaking of Trinitarian Theology* (Grand Rapids: Eerdmans, 2008).

[15] Peter Leithart, 'Invocation to Assent'; available online: http://www.leithart.com/2012/09/03/invocation-to-assent/# more-15138; accessed: 15 November 2014.

worship, it had little practical use. Further, the fact that orthodox theologians had to expend so much space and energy to defending and explaining the Trinity proved that it failed to meet one of the basic Protestant criteria of 'essential' knowledge: It was obviously not obvious, and since it wasn't obvious it could not be understood – even if true – as a truth necessary to salvation.[16]

The Wesleys labored to return the doctrine to central significance, primarily through their hymns, prayers, and sermons. But the Wesleys's trinitarianism did not fully overcome the problems embedded in the English Protestant theological frames of reference, and those problems returned with a vengeance in the restorationist, biblicist theologies of the holiness movements. This is why Pentecostals, as heirs of those movements, have from the beginning of the movement struggled to appreciate how the doctrine of the Trinity matters for them.[17] If it is true that Pentecostals/charismatics have done more 'to recover an active doctrine of the Holy Spirit' than any other Western ecclesial tradition,[18] the same cannot be said (at least not yet) of the doctrine of the Trinity. While most Pentecostal denominations have retained a formal affirmation of the Trinity in their statements of faith and many Pentecostal scholars affirm the doctrine and work creatively with it, the doctrine continues to have little if any *formative* influence on how Pentecostals make sense of their churchly experiences of God.[19]

---

[16] Leithart, 'Invocation to Assent', n.p.

[17] See William P. Atkinson, *Trinity after Pentecost* (Cambridge: Lutterworth Press, 2014), pp. 3-11. This lack of formative influence is evidenced in a number of ways, including, perhaps most telling, in our songs. Very few contemporary Christian worship songs are recognizably trinitarian. See Lester Ruth, '*Lex Amandi, Lex Orandi*: The Trinity in the Most-Used Contemporary Christian Worship Songs', in Bryan D. Spinks (ed.), *The Place of Christ in Liturgical Prayer* (Collegeville: The Liturgical Press, 2008), pp. 342-59, and *idem*, 'How Great is Our God: The Trinity in Contemporary Christian Worship Music', in Robert H. Woods, Jr. and Brian D. Walrath (eds.), *The Message in the Music: Studying Contemporary Praise and Worship* (Nashville: Abingdon Press, 2007), pp. 29-38.

[18] Robert Davis Hughes III, 'The Holy Spirit in Christian Spirituality', in Arthur Holder (ed.), *The Blackwell Companion to Christian Spirituality* (Malden, MA: Blackwell Publishing, 2011), pp. 207-22 (p. 220).

[19] The history of doctrine shows that the churches, Catholic and Protestant, are always in danger of making the doctrine of the Trinity, as Robert Jenson says, 'a conceptual puzzle, rather than a saving mystery ... a liturgical flourish rather than the enabling structure of our worship' ('A Decision Tree of Colin Gunton's Thinking', in Lincoln Harvey [ed.], *The Theology of Colin Gunton* [London: T&T Clark, 2010], pp. 8-16 [p. 11]).

Experiencing God as Trinity

Assuming for the moment that we should seek to recover the formational use of trinitarian doctrine, how are we going to go about it? What can be done to remake what has been unmade? Some have suggested that we should begin with liturgical changes that suffuse our worship with trinitarian language.[20] I am sympathetic to this suggestion, but arguably it makes more sense to begin with our experience of God in prayer. Yes, it is necessary, but it is still not *sufficient* to flood our worship with trinitarian language. We need means of recognizing God's threeness as it happens to us in the moment of divine encounter.[21]

This recognition begins to become possible for us, I believe, at the altar. Praying together, we find ourselves *communing* with God.[22] And as our imaginations are faithfully shaped in and for that communion, we begin to discern that all forms of faithfully Christian prayer are 'inherently trinitarian'.[23] In prayer, we are experiencing the triune God who acts triunely on us. Of course, we do not sense three presences or even the difference between the Spirit's presence and the Son's. But we *do* sense that we are being joined in Christ to God's conversation with God. We find that we are not just speak-

---

[20] Such changes might involve setting aside times for preaching on the doctrine of the Trinity (perhaps, for example, on Trinity Sunday) and purposefully selected and performed songs that celebrate God's tri-unity. See Mark Cartledge, *Testimony in the Spirit: Rescripting Ordinary Pentecostal Theology* (Burlington, VA: Ashgate, 2010), p. 52.

[21] We need a way to make sense of how God is triunely present to us without suggesting either that the Trinity is merely an elaborate metaphor for three kinds of human experiences (one of God beyond us as 'Father', one of God with us as 'Son', and another of God within us as 'Spirit') or that we should be able to feel the distinct activity of the divine 'persons'.

[22] This underscores the fact that the Eucharist is the heart of our prayer. Attending to the Eucharistic liturgy, and especially the *epiclesis*, we learn how our salvation depends on our being taken into the mutuality of God's own perichoretic life. Frank D. Macchia, *Justified in the Spirit: Creation, Redemption, and the Triune God* (Grand Rapids, MI: Eerdmans, 2010), p. 289, is right: the Eucharist is 'communion with the risen Christ', a 'mutual indwelling in which we are in Christ and Christ is in us as Christ is in the Father and the Father is in Christ'. So, as we gather at his table in prayer to the Father, as 'we sup with him [and] he sups with us', we are filled with the same Spirit the risen Christ enjoys and gives. Within that communion and mutual indwelling, we become the people of the Father, the temple of the Spirit, and the body of Christ.

[23] Sarah Coakley, 'Living into the Mystery of the Holy Trinity: Trinity, Prayer, and Sexuality', *Anglican Theological Review* 80 (1998), pp. 223-32 (p. 223).

ing *to* God, but are speaking *with* and *for* God, who is also speaking with and for us. We are, as Sarah Coakley explains, 'caught up' into the 'ceaseless divine dialogue between Spirit and "Father"'.[24] We are taken into the intra-Trinitarian 'place' of the Son. We pray Jesus' prayer with him as the Spirit pressures us into him, freeing us for co-operation.[25]

Ralph Del Colle provides what I take to be a breakthrough insight: 'with respect to the notion of presence, the *Christus praesens* and the *Spiritus praesens* cannot be simply identical'.[26] What, then, is the difference? The Spirit's presence is 'a presence that directs one to another, provid[ing] the possibility for the *Christus praesens* to be actualized'.[27] Following Del Colle's insight, we can perhaps finally risk a blunt answer to the question that launched these reflections. What we *experience* in worship is neither several presences nor the presence of one of the divine 'persons'. What we experience is one presence of threeness. And because that triplicity is the being of the one God revealed to us savingly in the gospel, we can speak of that presence as the presence of the Father in Jesus Christ who is made experienceable for us by the Holy Spirit, *or* as the presence of the Holy Spirit, drawing us into the Father's embrace of the Son, *or* as the presence of Jesus, baptizing us in the Spirit who reveals to us the Father's heart.

John Wesley was open to the possibility of experiencing the three 'persons' distinctly.[28] But I think Sarah Coakley is right: there are not 'three distinguishable types of "experience" (in the sense of emotional tonality), each experience relating to a different point of identity – "Father", "Son" and "Holy Spirit"'.[29] In her judgment, 'the *homoousion* principle disallows that the different "persons"

---

[24] Coakley, 'Living in the Mystery of the Holy Trinity', p. 225.

[25] Rowan Williams, *On Christian Theology* (Malden, MA: Blackwell, 2000), p. 124.

[26] Ralph Del Colle, *Christ and the Spirit: Spirit-Christology in Trinitarian Perspective* (New York: Oxford University Press, 1994), p. 177.

[27] Del Colle, *Christ and the Spirit*, p. 177. Of course, the Spirit is not more *humble* than the Son or the Father. But the Spirit, like the Father, is not embodied, and so can not be experienced in the same way as the Son.

[28] See Fred Sanders, 'John Wesley on Experiencing the Trinity'; available online: http://seedbed.com/feed/john-wesley-experiencing-trinity/; accessed: 16 December 2014.

[29] Coakley, 'Living into the Mystery', p. 226.

should be experientially separate, or do different things'.[30] Instead, the experience of God in prayer is 'ineluctably, though obscurely, triadic':

> It is *one* experience of God, but God as simultaneously (i) doing the praying in me, (ii) receiving that prayer, and (iii) in that exchange, consented to in me, inviting me into the Christic life of redeemed sonship. Or to put it another way: the 'Father' (so-called here) is both source and ultimate object of divine longing in us; the 'Spirit' is that irreducibly – though obscurely – distinct enabler and incorporator of that longing in creation – that which *makes* the creation divine; and the 'Son' *is* that divine and perfect creation, into whose life I, as pray-er, am caught up.[31]

Coakley is very near the truth, I believe. But her account is, in the final analysis, just a bit too static and too linear because it privileges the one nature in a way that stratifies the hypostatic relations. She is right to say that the Three act inseparably. We experience in prayer not just one or another of the 'persons' but the *Trinity* personally. Nonetheless, and against her reading of 'the *homoousion* principle', I believe each of the 'persons' does act distinctly. To encounter God is to be drawn into contact with the event that is God's perichoretically-mutual life.

We catch a revealing glimpse of this perichoretic mutuality when we read 1 Cor. 2.9-16 alongside Rom. 8.26-27. First, the Romans passage:

> Likewise the Spirit helps us in our weakness; for we do not know how to pray as we ought, but that very Spirit intercedes with sighs too deep for words. And God, who searches the heart, knows what is the mind of the Spirit, because the Spirit intercedes for the saints according to the will of God (vv. 26-27).[32]

Here, the Spirit is described as interceding for us to the Father, according to the Father's will. The Father is identified as the one who searches our hearts, and is described as discovering his will for us in the 'mind of the Spirit' (that is, Jesus) – the very will that we know

---

[30] Coakley, 'Living into the Mystery', p. 226.
[31] Coakley, 'Living into the Mystery', p. 226.
[32] Scripture quotations are from the New Revised Standard Version unless noted otherwise.

determines the shape of the Spirit's intercession. We can be sure, then, that God is working all things together for our good, drawing us along toward glorification (Rom. 8.28-30), because we are caught up in the Spirit's intercession for us to receive all that the Father desires for us, a fullness that is revealed and given with and within Christ.

Now compare that logic of intercession with what Paul says in 1 Cor. 2.9-16:

> But, as it is written, 'What no eye has seen, nor ear heard, nor the human heart conceived, what God has prepared for those who love him' – these things God has revealed to us through the Spirit; for the Spirit searches everything, even the depths of God. For what human being knows what is truly human except the human spirit that is within? So also no one comprehends what is truly God's except the Spirit of God. Now we have received not the spirit of the world, but the Spirit that is from God, so that we may understand the gifts bestowed on us by God. And we speak of these things in words not taught by human wisdom but taught by the Spirit, interpreting spiritual things to those who are spiritual. Those who are unspiritual do not receive the gifts of God's Spirit, for they are foolishness to them, and they are unable to understand them because they are spiritually discerned. Those who are spiritual discern all things, and they are themselves subject to no one else's scrutiny. 'For who has known the mind of the Lord so as to instruct him?' But we have the mind of Christ.

In Romans, the Spirit was described as interceding for us to the Father who knows us and knows the Son, Jesus, as his will for us. Here, the Father is the one being searched, rather than the one searching. And instead of the Spirit taking the lead in intercession, as in Romans, it is the Father who gives us the all-knowing Spirit so that we might share in 'the mind of Christ' and share in his reign. Taken together, these texts image for us a perfectly, infinitely mutual life that opens itself for our participation. And it is that life, in its fullness, that makes itself available to us in the moment of divine-human encounter.

Scripture promises that God's presence is for us the 'fullness of joy' (Ps. 16.11). But why should that be so? The answer, I believe, comes when we see what Peter saw on Pentecost: before the word is spoken to us as promise it is spoken by Jesus in testimony.[33] In other words, the promise of eternal joy in God's presence is ours at all only because it is first *Jesus' experience* – an experience into which we have been incorporated by the Spirit at the Father's mercy. Jesus knows, divinely and humanly, eternally and temporally, the delighted and delighting intimacy of knowing and being known perfectly. As our lives are conformed to his, his experience becomes ours, and we are rapt into the joy he shares with the Father in the Spirit.

Conformed to the Image of the Triune God

Experiencing God, we experience the 'subsisting relations'[34] that are the divine life. And experiencing God as God is, we become *like* God. In trinitarian terms, that means we are not only conformed to Christ (as Rom. 8.29 promises), but also in being conformed to him we take on the likeness of the Father and the Spirit as well – and just so image forth the triune God truly.

To be made like Christ is to partake in his character and (to say the same thing another way) to participate in his intimacy with the Father and Spirit. But what does it mean to take on the likeness of the Spirit distinctly from the likeness of the Son? Bruce Marshall has it right, I believe:

The Holy Spirit does not impress himself upon us, shed the love he is abroad in our hearts, in order that we may love *him*, the Spirit, but in order that we may love Jesus. Precisely by impressing his own form upon us, we could say, the Spirit conforms us to Jesus Christ. Because he himself is love, in other words, he does not impress his own form upon us *instead of* the form of Jesus, but rather the Spirit impresses the form of Jesus upon us *by*

---

[33] In the midst of his sermon (Acts 2.22-28), Peter reads the final verses of Psalm 16 as a prayer of Jesus to the Father.

[34] Following Thomas Aquinas (*Summa Theologica* I.30.1), 'this word "person" signifies in God a relation as subsisting in the divine nature. It was also established that there are several real relations in God; and hence it follows that there are also several realities subsistent in the divine nature; which means that there are several persons in God'.

giving us a likeness to his own modest, self-disregarding person.[35]

What, then, of the Father's likeness? If the Son is the 'exact imprint of God's being' (Heb. 1.3), then how can we be made like the Father in any sense different from being made like the Son? How is the Father's uniqueness perfected in us? Borrowing Marshall's phrasing, we can perhaps say it like this: just as the Spirit creates in us a likeness to Jesus precisely by engendering in us the Spirit's own humility, Jesus creates in us a likeness to the Father just by marking us with his own delight in the Father's goodness. Or, we can say it like this: the Spirit creates Father-likeness in us by awakening in us the divine urgency to give ourselves joyfully and without reserve in love for our neighbor and our enemy.

Conclusion

In conclusion, a few words about how these reflections matter for the praxis and theology of Pentecostal worship. First, we have to make room for second-order theological reflection as integral to our worship and not merely an addendum to it. If, as I have argued, our experience of God is inseparably bound up with our theological accounts of that experience, then we are compelled to devote ourselves to discerning together the most faithful words possible, trusting that God is at work for good no less in our struggle for words than in the moment of divine encounter. Second, assuming that what I have just said is true, we can perhaps renew Oneness–Trinitarian Pentecostal conversations, to say nothing of other ecumenical ventures, if we insist on this truth: the shared experience of God in prayer is the crucible in which faithful theological language can be discerned. And, as Rowan Williams has said, if God's life is in fact the perichoretic mutuality of three 'persons' in one 'nature', then we should expect that 'the actual conduct of Christian theology, in its movement between Word and Spirit, confession and debate, image and negation' would draw us together into the same kind of freedom-in-dependence.[36] Third, bearing the hope of rec-

---

[35] Bruce D. Marshall, 'A Brief Anatomy of Holiness', *Wesleyan Theological Journal* 49.1 (Spring 2014), pp. 7-18 (p. 16, emphasis original).
[36] Williams, *On Christian Theology*, p. 147.

onciliation in mind, we need to fill our worship with prayers and songs, sermons and testimonies that attune us to the dynamics of God's triune presence by attending carefully to the trinitarian grammar witnessed in the Scriptures and affirmed in the Christian tradition. Because we know the faithfulness of God, we can be confident that over time, these habits will (trans)form our imaginations and our affections so that our lives, personally and corporately, are indelibly marked by 'the grace of the Lord Jesus Christ, the love of God, and the communion of the Holy Spirit' (2 Cor. 13.13).

10

'SINGING HEAVENLY MUSIC': R. HOLLIS GAUSE'S THEOLOGY OF WORSHIP AND PENTECOSTAL EXPERIENCE

Kimberly Ervin Alexander[*]

If you have never attended a Pentecostal camp meeting, you will not regret spending a few days where God's people meet to worship Him and He pours out the Holy Ghost and baptizes His honest hearted people. This is where we can sit together in heavenly places in Christ Jesus. Praise God for the fellowship of His saints.[1]

To be justified produces waves of glory. To repent is to be smitten in conscience with the terrible heinousness of sin – its repulsiveness to God and man. To be born again is to have a radical change of nature with an appropriate change of thinking and behavior. To be sanctified is to be set free from the law of sin and death and to be purged of the root of bitterness. To be filled with the Spirit is to be overwhelmed with joy and the power of love and witness. The marvel is not that these men and women shout, laugh, weep, leap and run. It would be a greater marvel if they did not.[2]

---

[*] Kimberly Ervin Alexander (PhD, The Open University/St. John's College, Nottingham, UK) is Associate Professor of Church History at Regent University, Virginia Beach, VA, USA.
[1] 'Camp Meeting in Florida', *The Bridegroom's Messenger* 1.14 (May 15, 1908), p. 2.
[2] R. Hollis Gause, 'Distinctives of a Pentecostal Theology' (unpublished paper), p. 32.

In 1998, at a conference sponsored by the Department of Ministerial Development of the Church of God (Cleveland, TN), hosted by Lee University, R. Hollis Gause, in a response to Harvey Cox and his study of the world Pentecostal movement, noted that in the book of Acts reception of baptism with the Holy Spirit was always in 'situations of divine worship'.[3] In his response to Gause and other respondents, Cox remarked that this insight by Gause had made his trip worthwhile.

That the experience of Spirit baptism would be associated with worship should come as no surprise to Pentecostals but, surprisingly, little reflection has been made on the relationship. Further, little has been written to develop a Pentecostal theology or spirituality that sees worship as *prolegomenon*. Worship may be discussed by Pentecostal theologians as a *practice*, and rightly so. However, this categorization may too easily fall into the trap of seeing worship (and witness or any other practice deemed constitutive of Pentecostal spirituality) as an activity that is second order at best or a style at worst.

In this chapter, I hope to broaden the conversation by bringing the important, but unpublished, reflections of R. Hollis Gause to the table. In his reflection, worship serves as *prolegomenon*, and not simply as an extension of experience. Indeed, worship is identified with Pentecostal experience. With an exploration of Gause's 'theology of worship' as a starting point, I will explore early Pentecostal discussions of worship in the Spirit, especially the practice of spiritual singing, and will move to examine the similar expressions, congruent with Gause's theology of worship, found in contemporary centers of worship and revival.[4]

R. Hollis Gause's 'Theology of Worship'
Guarding against the tendency toward rationalism of a so-called 'theology of the Word' and the subjugation of the Word to experience that may be found in some extreme versions of a pietistic the-

---

[3] R. Hollis Gause, *Living in the Spirit: The Way of Salvation* (Cleveland, TN: CPT Press, 2009), p. 133. Here, Gause states that this is 'normative'.

[4] For a comprehensive discussion of Gause's body of work see Kimberly Ervin Alexander, 'Under the Authority of the Word and In Response to the Spirit: The Written Work and Worship of R. Hollis Gause', in Steven Jack Land, Rickie D. Moore, and John Christopher Thomas (eds.), *Passover, Pentecost, and Parousia: Studies in Celebration of the Life and Ministry of R. Hollis Gause* (JPTSup 36; Blandford Forum, UK: Deo Publishing, 2010), pp. 1-32.

ology, Gause opts for a hermeneutic of a theology of worship citing three reasons for his contention that it is most suitable to Pentecostalism:

> First, it takes appropriate notice of the word of God and is indeed a theology of the Word. Second, it takes seriously the validity of religious experience in our knowing God and being known by Him (Galatians 4:9). Third, it is endemic to the Pentecostal movement. Worship provides the format in which the cleavage between clergy and laity may be bridged.[5]

This synthesis, then, supports, or is perhaps driven by, the democratizing tendencies of the Pentecostal movement and its emphasis on diversity as well as charismatic gifts.

Gause's theology of worship is dependent upon his view of the church of Pentecost as being a recapitulation of the church in the wilderness, both constituted by the presence of God and the responsive worship of the people of God. Influenced by the work of early Pentecostal bishop Joseph Hillery King, Gause writes:

> Pentecost is the fulfillment of the prophetic significance of Mt. Sinai and the giving of the law. The New Testament believers became this spiritual house on the day of Pentecost as Israel had become the people of God at Sinai. The church in the wilderness and the church in the New Testament are one as the kingdom of God is one in all ages. The distinction is that the church in the wilderness lived in promise; the church in the New Testament lives in fulfillment.[6]

Traces of Gause's theology of worship may be seen in his work as early as his 1975 dissertation, 'The Lukan Transfiguration Account: Luke's Pre-Crucifixion Account of the Exalted Lord in the Glory of the Kingdom of God'[7] and is continually developed throughout his life's work, culminating in the 2009 revision of *Living in the Spirit: The Way of Salvation*, an exposition of a Wesleyan-Pentecostal soteriology that situates Spirit baptism in the *via salutis*.[8]

---

[5] Gause, 'Distinctives', p. 27.

[6] Gause, 'Distinctives', p. 23.

[7] R. Hollis Gause, 'The Lukan Transfiguration Account: Luke's Pre-Crucifixion Presentation of the Exalted Lord in the Glory of the Kingdom of God' (PhD dissertation, Emory University, 1975).

[8] Gause, *Living in the Spirit*, back cover.

In the earliest glimpse of this theology (his dissertation), rather than seeing the transfiguration event in Luke as episodic, unique, or singular, he posits it as being paradigmatic of the worship of the Christian community to whom Luke writes (and therefore the Pentecostal community). Gause explains,

> One of the theses of this paper is that the Transfiguration account in Luke is a proleptic presentation of the kingdom of God in the experience of Jesus and His three intimate disciples, and that this account is used in a similar manner in worship in the Christian community.[9]

He discusses early Christian worship's eschatological outlook: 'This outlook combines present eschatological realization and future eschatological expectation'.[10]

Gause later developed this 'theology of worship' by delineating its three integral elements: *rapture, rapport,* and *proleptic*. The first term, *rapture,* describes the quality of ecstasy that is inherent to Pentecostal worship: 'overwhelming surges of praise and petition that cannot be suppressed without quenching, even grieving the Holy Spirit'.[11] Included in these ecstatic expressions are forms of prophetic speech, including glossolalia, prayer, and, importantly for this essay, song. Gause is careful to distinguish this ecstasy, or *rapture,* from a hypnotic state, citing biblical examples in which the worshiper is fully aware but lacking full comprehension. He goes on to argue that the worshiper actually has a heightened sense of the presence of the Spirit. She experiences the priesthood of believers with utter clarity and is in the immediate presence of God through the Spirit. Experiencing equally the prophethood of believers, she listens to the voice of God and speaks to God, mediated only by the Spirit and then boldly declares 'the whole counsel of God by the Inscripturated Word and by the gifts of the Holy Spirit'. Further, she may receive direction, cleansing, healing, or empowerment while seeing a vision or while in a trance, sometimes with full recollection of the transformative experience.[12]

---

[9] Gause, 'The Lukan Transfiguration Account', p. 133.
[10] Gause, 'The Lukan Transfiguration Account', p. 213.
[11] Gause, 'Distinctives', p. 28.
[12] Gause, 'Distinctives', p. 30.

The second element included by Gause is that of *rapport*, defined in relational terms: 'a union of love between the worshiper and God, and between all those who worship Him'.[13] In worship there is *koinonia* through the Spirit with God and with the people of God. In this intimacy, the worshiper and worshiping congregation respond and 'move and speak with one voice'. But this *rapport* may also be experienced in private worship as it knows no geographic boundary. It is a communion of the saints and, I would add, as such this *rapport* also knows no temporal boundaries. Gause sees the Pentecostal experience and practice of speaking in tongues as particularly exemplary. While maintaining an origination 'in the movement of the Holy Spirit and not in the will or action of believers' he does not hold that the believer is passive in the experience.[14] Rather, this is 'a profound rapport between two persons: the divine Person, the Holy Spirit, and the human person, the believer. These two persons meet together through kinship and affection in such intimacy that the believer becomes fully responsive to the Holy Spirit'.[15]

The final element in Gause's triad is *proleptic*. There are two aspects to this descriptor. First, it is a spiritual return to the historic events of redemption, including Passover and Sinai, the descent of the Spirit in the wilderness, or the *Shekinah*, Jesus' incarnate birth, life and ministry, Gethsemane, his death and resurrection, his ascension, and Pentecost.[16] In this return, the worshipers experience them in unity with the church, again transcending space and time.

The second aspect of *proleptic* may be described as anticipation in which the believer is transported via the Spirit in the final glory of the kingdom of God. Beyond merely looking forward, however, the worshiper is participating in 'the consummate glory of the King in His kingdom'.[17] Building on Paul's contention that the Holy Spirit has been given as '"earnest of our inheritance until the redemption of the purchased possession unto the praise of His glory" (Ephesians 1:14; cf., II Corinthians 5:5)', Gause emphasizes that the earnest is a part of the whole, a foretaste of what is to come. *Already* we experience, in part, what we will experience in full. This is real

---

[13] Gause, 'Distinctives', p. 30.
[14] Gause, *Living in the Spirit*, p. 135.
[15] Gause, *Living in the Spirit*, p. 135.
[16] Gause, 'Distinctives', p. 31.
[17] Gause, 'Distinctives', p. 31.

and not virtual experience of the glory of the kingdom. Spiritual blessings *in Christ*, in the Ephesian letter are 'in heavenly places' (Eph. 1.3).

The practice of prayer, specifically praying in the Spirit may be examined as a way of illustrating this anticipation and participation. In his commentary on Revelation, in discussing the prayers of the saints in chapter 8, Gause interprets the text through his particular Wesleyan-Pentecostal lens:

> Though they are always heard immediately by God, they are also reserved until this moment in the fulfillment of God's plan. The reservation of these prayers for this time and for this sacrifice and for this purpose makes the saints in their praying participants in God's eternal plan (Ephesians 1:9-12). The believer not only serves men for their good when he prays; he serves God and affects eternity.[18]

Praying in the Spirit is anticipatory and participatory. The fact that these prayers are depicted in the Apocalypse as being offered on the altar in heaven, with incense, and rising 'before God' – a description of the place and goal of worship – indicates that there is a real value assigned to them. They are transformed, in the fire of God, as instruments of judgment, making the praying worshiper a participant in the coming glory of God.

Worship in Early Pentecostalism

The examination of periodical literature from the early Pentecostal movement reveals a treasure trove of descriptions of the worship experience of women and men who became participants in what was understood to be a 'latter rain' outpouring of the Holy Spirit. Elsewhere I have shown the value of this historiographical approach that provides what may be akin to 'participant observation' in this dynamic and inclusive movement.[19] These records provide hundreds of accounts of worship services and testimonies of Pente-

---

[18] Gause, *Revelation: God's Stamp of Sovereignty on History* (Cleveland, TN: Pathway Press, 1983), p. 129.

[19] See Kimberly Ervin Alexander, *Pentecostal Healing: Models of Theology and Practice* (JPTSup 29; Blandford Forum, UK: Deo, 2006), and *idem*, 'O Boundless Love Divine: A Re-Evaluation of Pentecostal Experiences of Spirit Baptism', in Steven Jack Land, Rickie D. Moore, and John Christopher Thomas (eds.), *Passover, Pentecost, and Parousia: Studies in Celebration of the Life and Ministry of R. Hollis Gause* (JPTSup 36; Blandford Forum, UK: Deo, 2010), pp. 145-70.

costal experience in addition to more discursive and sermonic material.

This description from a worship service at The Stone Church in Chicago on 24 November 1908 is a case in point and an appropriate segue from Gause's discussion of the prayers of the saints:

> As the incense of prayer and worship arose to God, His glory came down and filled our hearts, some with a quiet peace, others with a joy which overflowed in praise.

> While we were singing 'I need Thee every hour,' the one sitting at the instrument struck up a strain of heavenly music, the Holy Spirit guiding the fingers into a harmonious accompaniment.

> Strain after strain of inspired music floated out over the audience. It was the wooing of the Spirit drawing us to God and filling our hearts with worship and deepest adoration to Him who purchased for us the right to enter into the Holy of Holies.[20]

This description of what is called an 'inspiring night's service' continues with a recollection of being led 'in the harmony of the Spirit' to sing, 'Oh come let us adore Him'. The article, apparently written by Lydia M. Piper,[21] continues by describing singing in 'the unknown tongue in a beautiful, impromptu melody, the song carrying the voice far above the natural range'. The writer describes the congregation, still led by the Spirit, as they 'soared up to the very gates of heaven, then back to earth again' while singing 'For He alone is worthy!' This alternating between singing in a known and unknown tongue lasted 'until the whole room was filled with the presence and glory of God'.[22] The remaining description includes a testimony of a dream by Mrs. Eugene Nix in which she is given a future glimpse into the suffering of those who have not yet heard the gospel, as well as a sermon by the pastor based on Jn 3.14.[23]

The writer's interpretation of that service, marked by a dynamic between the heavenly and earthly, 'the heights of glory with the dai-

---

[20] 'An Inspiring Night's Service – Jesus Must Be Lifted Up High – A Remarkable Dream. Singing in the Spirit', *The Latter Rain Evangel* 1.3 (December 1908), p. 21.

[21] The last section of the article titled 'Theme Continued', is written by Lydia M. Piper (p. 23).

[22] 'Inspiring Night's Service', p. 21.

[23] 'Inspiring Night's Service', pp. 21-24.

ly cares and crosses', was that it served a didactic function in that it showed the worshipers 'that the joys of the world to come would only be attained by our helping to alleviate the sorrows of a sin-cursed world, and by pointing the lost to the One who is mighty to save'.[24]

In this rather extensive description, Gause's triad of *rapture, rapport*, and *proleptic* are evident. As the congregants pray and their prayers go up as incense, the glory of God descends. This glory enraptures the worshipers bringing peace and joy as the musician is given a spiritual song through which the communion between worshipers is enhanced, as they return to the redemptive provision of Calvary. In this spiritual music, in both earthly and heavenly languages, they are carried *via* the Spirit up into heaven. Like the angels in Jacob's vision of the ladder between earth and heaven, the worshipers ascend and descend between the world to come and the present age. Through prophetic visions and speech they hear the voice of God urging them to lift Jesus up to those who have not yet been saved.

In the only extant copy of *The Whole Truth* (published by the Church of God in Christ) from this early period, brief 'reports' of the annual convocation fill the first page. The meeting convened in Lexington, Mississippi on July 23 and continued for twenty-nine days, ending on August 20. These reports indicate that the participants believed that as they worshiped, the Spirit of the Lord was present. The reporter, E.B. Williams, submitted notes on each of the services. Notable is the number of times the congregation is described as waiting for or before the Lord to move or speak (six references). More notable are the numerous mentions of the 'glory of the Lord', 'power of the Lord', or Spirit coming or being in the midst of the convocation. In only two of the twenty-nine entries is their no direct reference.[25]

Charles H. Mason, referred to in this issue as 'pastor', is reported to have sung songs in the Spirit to the congregation on at least six occasions during the convocation. The lyrics to these 'new songs' are printed. In two of the songs, Mason sings words of praise such

---

[24] 'Inspiring Night's Service', p. 21.
[25] E.B. Williams, 'Report of the Annual Convocation Held at Lexington, Miss, July 23–August 20, 1911', *The Whole Truth* 4.4 (October, 1911), pp. 1, 3.

as 'Oh, what a wonder!' or 'Glory and honor to the Lamb!'[26] The remaining songs are prophetic words: 'Hear ye the word of the Lord', 'Hear him while he calls', 'Wait on the Lord' and

> O repent, O sinner,
> Repent just now;
> The voice of the Lord is calling you;
> Repent of all thou hast done.
> The Spirit is calling now, repent tonight.[27]

In Mason's own testimony of Spirit baptism, printed in the Azusa St. Mission's *The Apostolic Faith*, he begins the account by describing his surrender to the Spirit followed by the Spirit singing through him. He then describes a transformative visionary experience:

> After that it seemed I was standing at the cross and heard Him as He groaned, the dying groans of Jesus, and I groaned. It was not my voice but the voice of my Beloved that I heard in me. When He got through with that, He started the singing again in unknown tongues. When the singing stopped, I felt that complete death. It was my life going out, but it was a complete death to me. When He had finished this, I let Him hold my hands up, and they rested just as easily up as down. Then He turned on the joy of it. He began to lift me up. I was passive in His hands. I was not going to do a thing. I could hear the people but did not let anything bother me. It came to me, 'I charge thee, O daughters of Jerusalem, that ye stir not up nor awake my Beloved until He please.' S. S. 8. 4. He lifted me to my feet and then the light of heaven fell upon me and burst into me filling me. Then God took charge of my tongue and I went to preaching in tongues. I could not change my tongue. The glory of God filled the temple. The gestures of my hands and movements of my body were His. O it was marvelous and I thank God for giving it to me in His way. Such an indescribable peace and quietness went all through my flesh and into my very brain and has been there ever since.[28]

---

[26] Williams, 'Report of the Annual Convocation Held at Lexington', p. 1.
[27] Williams, 'Report of the Annual Convocation Held at Lexington', pp. 1, 3.
[28] *The Apostolic Faith* 1.6 (February-March 1907), p. 7.

In this ecstatic experience (*rapture*), Mason is, as Gause has distinguished it, not unaware of others but is not hindered by them, as he is filled with joy and peace. As priest, he is in the immediate presence of God and is filled with the presence of God. As prophet, he hears the voice of God and preaches and sings the word of the Lord in known and unknown languages. He groans with the dying Jesus in *proleptic* participation that is 'trans-historical'.[29]

Far away from the Mississippi Delta and further still from Los Angeles, California, the Pentecostal movement's beginnings in Great Britain were documented in *Confidence* published in Sunderland, in the northeast of England. This periodical, like those published in North America, included testimonies and reports of worship services along with biblical exposition and doctrinal discourse. In the first issue (April 1908), a builder from Lancashire, H. Mogridge, reported on the work of the Spirit in Lytham, Lancashire. He describes nightly meetings: 'At times, great power has pervaded the meetings in a Holy hush, so that the dear people present feared to speak. At other times we were affected in quite a different way. All would be filled with joy, and many would break out in Holy laughter and songs of victory and praise, and be bowed down in Holy worship and adoration of the Lamb'.[30] For Mogridge, 'Holy worship' here was already a participation in the worship scenes of Revelation. The worshipers, overcome with awe or joy by the power of the Spirit, responded in manifestations interpreted as 'Holy'.

The testimony of Mrs. C. Beruldsen of Edinburgh reports coming to All Saints' in January of 1908. Entering the meeting in the vicarage at nine p.m., while it was already in progress, she describes the 'solemnity' and 'holy awe' she sensed upon arrival. The meeting, led by Mrs. Boddy, moved to a 'season of prayer' in which Mrs. Boddy laid hands on Mrs. Beruldsen in order that she might be baptized in the Spirit. She testifies to being healed of a six month illness as well as being filled. Several days later, at another meeting led by Mrs. Boddy in the vicarage dining room, during prayer, her tongue was 'loosened' and she 'spoke in New Tongues for about two hours', 'singing heavenly music' throughout the night. She goes on

---

[29] Gause, 'Distinctives', p. 31.

[30] H. Mogridge, 'Report from Lytham (Lancashire)', *Confidence* 1 (April 1908), p. 6.

to describe the Lord giving her an interpretation of her experience: she was to proclaim, teach, and preach Jesus. In her closing she notes that she held meetings in Edinburgh on 'Tuesdays, afternoon and evening'.[31]

The testimonies of Mogridge and Beruldsen indicate that, indeed, worship in the Pentecostal movement in Great Britain was attended by the same transformative and dynamic worship as in North America. This worship was filled with ecstatic manifestations, a unity of the Spirit, and the kind of eschatological anticipation posited by Gause in his theology of worship.

The first Pentecostal conference held in Sunderland occurred during Whitsuntide, the week following Pentecost Sunday, June 6-11 of 1908. The paper noted that the 'Evening Meeting' on the opening day of the conference was marked by a 'spirit of praise and prayer', and all prayed, on their knees, for one and a half hours, 'in the very presence of God'. The writer described it: 'Prayer and praise arose incense-like to His Throne. All Heaven surely was interested in that wonderful meeting'.[32] One observer and participant noted, 'The preliminary Prayer Meeting of Friday night will ever be stamped on our memory. It was the first touch we had felt in England of the united worship and adoration in the immediate Presence of God of those on whom the "Latter Rain" had fallen.' The writer observed: 'If these beginnings are so beautiful what will it be like when the Bridegroom comes for His Bride? The blessed Spirit is teaching, is brooding over us, and is even teaching us some of the music to be sung at the Wedding'.[33] Another observer described occasions during the conference when

'Heaven came down, redeemed spirits to greet,' as wave after wave of spontaneous praise and adoration swept through the audience, many speaking in 'other tongues' simultaneously, others in their own tongue, but all voicing with one accord the never-ceasing anthem, 'Worthy is the Lamb slain...' Truly, one be-

[31] C. Beruldsen, 'A Testimony from Edinburgh', *Confidence* 1 (April 1908), pp. 11-12.

[32] 'Opening Meetings of the Conference', *Confidence* 3 (June 30, 1908), p. 8.

[33] 'Notes by Two Visitors', *Confidence* 3 (June 30, 1908), p. 14.

gan to understand something of the 'sound of many waters,' in Revelation.[34]

This same observer noted that in the meeting there was a strong sense of the 'intense yearning of the Spirit' and the 'nearing fulfill-ment of our Lord's prayers, "That they all may be one."'[35]

Clearly at this meeting, where Pentecostal believers from North America, England, Norway, Holland, and other parts of Europe gathered there was a *rapport*, there were times of *rapture* and a sense of their participation in the coming Kingdom (*proleptic*).

Singing in the Spirit

It is difficult to read this early literature without being struck by the high incidence of singing as a manifestation of Pentecostal experi-ence and a dominant practice of Pentecostal worship. Singing in the Spirit, singing in tongues, the 'heavenly choir', the 'new songs' of Charles H. Mason, or spiritual songs were all understood to be signs of Pentecostal experience. Whether experienced in private or cor-porate worship there is no doubt that these expressions were freighted with significance for the participants. For the observer or hearer, they served as prophetic words or signs of assurance.

Cecil M. Robeck writes about this phenomenon at the Azusa St. revival and concludes that it 'received nearly unanimous praise from all who heard it'.[36] He goes on to point out the similarities of the descriptions of this singing at the Azusa St. revival and the descrip-tions one reads of the '"Negro Chant" prevalent in the African-American "praise houses" during and after the time of slavery', proposing that the roots of Pentecostal spiritual singing might be found in its African–American precedent.[37] While there are obvious connections, the presence and prevalence of this phenomenon in British Pentecostalism seems to indicate that the experience is something more than what Charles Parham, in rebuke, called 'a modification of the Negro chanting of the Southland'.[38]

This spiritual singing of the early Pentecostal movement is par-ticularly well-suited as a paradigm for Gause's theology of worship.

---

[34] 'Notes', p. 13.
[35] 'Notes', p. 13.
[36] Cecil M. Robeck, *The Azusa Street Mission and Revival: The Birth of the Global Pentecostal Movement* (Nashville, TN: Thomas Nelson, 2006), p. 149.
[37] Robeck, *The Azusa Street Mission and Revival*, p. 150.
[38] Robeck, *The Azusa Street Mission and Revival*, p. 150.

Like prayer, singing in the Spirit may be experienced by an entire body of worshipers or by the individual worshiper in a public or private setting. For purposes of this discussion, a closer examination of these corporate expressions, sometimes referred to in the early literature as the 'heavenly choir' or 'heavenly chorus', are most insightful.

On the first page of the first issue of *The Apostolic Faith*, where headlines boldly announce 'Pentecost Has Come', what is perhaps the first mention of this phenomenon is reported and described:

> Many have received the gift of singing as well as speaking in the inspiration of the Spirit. The Lord is giving new voices, he translates old songs into new tongues, he gives the music that is being sung by the angels and has a heavenly choir all singing the same heavenly song in harmony. It is beautiful music, no instruments are needed in the meetings.[39]

This earliest explanation of this sign indicates that the revival participants and leadership believed the songs to be the same as those sung by the angelic choirs of heaven. These songs were sung with 'new voices', and even 'old songs' were being sung now in other languages. In this single reference, Gause's three elements are salient. The experience is ecstatic. There is harmony. They are participating in the coming kingdom.

By this time a veteran evangelist, Maria Woodworth-Etter, in a lengthy article on the Pentecostal revival and its detractors, describes a meeting in 1913 in which the phenomenon was experienced. Her interpretation is insightful:

> At our last meeting at Long Hill, Connecticut, the heavenly choir surpassed anything I had ever heard. We had it two or three times a day and there wasn't a discord. It was the Holy Ghost making harmony through these bodies and the singing was no earthly tune but heavenly. Sometimes I would be a little late in getting to the meeting and as I came up the hill the sound of the heavenly choir was wafted down. It sounded as though it came from heaven; it was the song of the redeemed. God is getting His children ready to sing at the marriage supper of the Lamb. They sing a song no one can sing except the redeemed. No out-

---

[39] *The Apostolic Faith* 1.1 (September 1906), p. 1.

siders can join in. The Spirit has shown me the coming of the Lord is very near and I know it now more than ever.[40]

Woodworth-Etter's account indicates that this manifestation was still occurring seven years after the beginning of the Azusa St. revival. Further, she was quite familiar with it, indicating its prominence in the larger movement. In this particular meeting it was a frequent, even regular occurrence. The ecstatic phenomenon (*rapture*) originated in the Spirit and produced harmony (*rapport*) among the revival participants. For Woodworth-Etter it was equated with the 'song of the redeemed', a reference to the scene in Rev. 14.3 where those who have been redeemed sing a new song before the throne of God (*proleptic*). These experiences were a kind of preparation for an eschatological event, 'the marriage supper of the Lamb'. Importantly, for Woodworth-Etter, these events were prophetic, pointing her to the realization that the coming of the Lord was near.

Though the Pentecostal movement, as it developed over the century, was always noted for its music and singing, the concept of spiritual singing, and certainly the 'heavenly choir', seemed to dissipate. This study is not sufficient to examine this devolution in detail, but the discussions of two later classical Pentecostals and one early observer with regard to singing and music in the Pentecostal church are instructive. First, the work of Ray H. Hughes, a Church of God minister and leader of the classical Pentecostal movement in the late twentieth century provides a glimpse at a possible trajectory. In a discussion of the role of singing in Pentecostal worship, Hughes cites Paul's admonition to sing in Eph. 5.19 and comments,

> Therefore, singing in the Spirit is not an exhibition of talent, nor is it entertainment for the hearers. It is making melody in the heart to the Lord. This accounts for the apparent lack of inhibition of Pentecostal worshipers. They lift their souls to God, completely caught up in the ecstasy of the moment, wafted away on the wings of song. Often they are oblivious to fellow wor-

---

[40] Maria Woodworth-Etter, 'Blasphemy Against the Holy Ghost: God's Cyclone of Power a Great Leveler', *The Latter Rain Evangel* 5.11 (August 1913), p. 22.

shipers or to bystanders. This also accounts in part for their beaming, shining countenances as they are enraptured in song.[41]

Hughes goes on to state that 'songs of spiritual lyrics' have originated in worship, 'often sung spontaneously when the Spirit envelops a Pentecostal congregation', and this singing inspires the congregation and glorifies God.[42] This interpretation resonates with Gause's theology of worship. However, the final statement on singing is telling: 'This type of singing does not preclude training. Intellectual refinement when touched by the Spirit often makes the singing even more edifying.'[43] While not explicit, inherent in that statement is a kind of preference for more 'refined' less extemporaneous expressions of singing. Further, it is an indication of an approach implemented in later years of the movement and an apology for it.

The second insight comes from another COG minister and educator, Delton L. Alford, author of the entry on music in *The New International Dictionary of Pentecostal and Charismatic Movements*. Alford begins with a generalized summary of music in the early Pentecostal tradition, emphasizing the 'exuberant and spirited singing of gospel hymns'.[44] He states, 'Their singing was joyful in spirit and consisted primarily of congregational expressions of praise and testimony'.[45] Alford allows that it 'sometimes included "singing in tongues"' but makes no reference to the 'heavenly choir'. His entry is developed offering a chronology detailing the inclusion of gospel songs, choral arrangements, and music education. Alford offers a helpful discussion of the contributions of the Charismatic renewal, including the singing of Scripture songs and a 'return to emphasis on spirited congregational singing, featuring leaders rather than choirs', 'spontaneous and choreographed dance and pageantry', and 'emphasis on the prophetic role of the musician'.[46] The entry concludes with a projection about the future of music in the tradition:

---

[41] Ray H. Hughes, Sr., *Classical Pentecostal Sermon Library* (Cleveland, TN: Pathway Press, 2011), VI, p. 51.

[42] Hughes, *Classical Pentecostal Sermon Library*, VI, p. 51.

[43] Hughes, *Classical Pentecostal Sermon Library*, VI, p. 51.

[44] D.L. Alford, 'Music, Pentecostal and Charismatic', in Stanley Burgess and Eduard M. Van Der Maas (eds.), *The New International Dictionary of Pentecostal and Charismatic Movements* (Grand Rapids, MI: Zondervan, 2002), p. 912.

[45] Alford, 'Music, Pentecostal and Charismatic', p. 912.

[46] Alford, 'Music, Pentecostal and Charismatic', p. 918.

The time has come for development of a total music ministry that will serve the spiritual, emotional, aesthetic, and educational needs of the pentecostal-charismatic movement. Such a ministry concept will recognize contributions of the past while encouraging acceptance of new ideas and efforts. It will emphasize education and training in music both in preparation and performance and provide organized programs denominationally and locally. Finally, it will always recognize and promote excellent and proficient performance of religious music without lessening the importance of the spiritual dimension that must accompany music offered in praise and service to God.[47]

Alford's vision could not be further from that of Frank Bartleman, early Pentecostal leader and Azusa St. eyewitness. According to Robeck, Bartleman 'vehemently condemned any worship singing ordered by the intervention of some leader who would direct the "song service", because he believed such intervention resulted in worship that was forced or contrived'.[48] It was not innovation that Bartleman condemned as he was open to newer songs given by the Spirit; it was the imposition of 'designated leaders' who 'pre-selected songs'. This imposition of control was seen by him as 'attempts to control the Spirit' or, in his own words 'murdering the spirit'.[49] Bartleman reluctantly concluded, however, that the tide had turned.

There is much to explore and, elsewhere, sociologists may provide insight into this trajectory from spontaneous movement to more instituted approaches. Alford's discussion of later contributions of the Charismatic Renewal does provide a starting point for what may be seen as a revival of earlier spiritual forms of music but is probably better understood as a new movement(s) having significant influence on the Pentecostal tradition(s). His reference to a congregational singing and the prophetic role of the worship leader is helpful.

While the transition is by no means without difficulty, newer expressions of Spirit movements, at least in the Western world, not only include an emphasis on spiritual singing but that singing is ar-

---

[47] Alford, 'Music, Pentecostal and Charismatic', pp. 919-20.
[48] Robeck, *The Azusa Street Mission and Revival*, p. 148.
[49] Robeck, *The Azusa Street Mission and Revival*, p. 149.

guably the most salient feature and the dominant manifestation. Out of various centers in North America, the United Kingdom, and Australia, young musicians and singers lead thousands into spiritual experience that bears the Gausian marks of Pentecostal worship. These 'new songs', are captured in live recordings and disseminated almost immediately through video streaming and downloads.[50]

If one hears the lyrics of the songs, like the testimonies of early Pentecostals, as voices by which we hear the movement's heart and ethos, it is not difficult to draw the conclusion that a similar phenomenon is occurring. Worship song lyrics, as poetry, are expressive of the affective and interpretations of that affect, and analysis will reveal not only beliefs but also dispositions. Another advantage of this kind of approach is that the songs are often written and sung by women. Indeed, many of the worship leaders in these centers are women, even if the pastoral leadership is still dominated by men. In this kind of analysis, then, the worship experience is described by the female voice not always heard in sermons or doctrinal discourse.[51]

In 2012, on the album *Still Believe*, Kim Walker Smith (Bethel, Redding, California) recorded the song 'Spirit Break Out', written by Luke Hellebronth, Tim Hughes, Myles Dhillon, and Ben Bryant (Worship Central, Holy Trinity Brompton, London).[52] The song begins with Smith backed by keyboard alone. These lines are repeated two more times as she is joined by the full band:

Our Father, all of Heaven roars Your name;
Sing louder, let this place erupt with praise.

---

[50] For a more thoroughgoing treatment of the role of this music at Worship Central in the UK, see Chris Anthony, 'Spirit Break Out: Examining the Theological and Musical development of Worship Central' (unpublished paper presented at the Westminster Theological Centre conference on 21 June 2014). http://www.academia.edu/7214441/Spirit_Break_Out_Examining_the_theological_and_musical_development_of_Worship_Central. Accessed 22 December 2014.

[51] See Kimberly Ervin Alexander, 'Girl Talk: A Feminist Re-Imagination of Pentecostal Theological Discourse and Experience' (presented at the 43rd Annual Meeting of the Society for Pentecostal Studies, Springfield, MO, March 7, 2014).

[52] https://www.youtube.com/watch?v=7eTgseG9TGE.

> Can you hear it, the sound of Heaven touching earth,
> The sound of Heaven touching earth?[53]

The participation between earth and heaven (*proleptic*) is emphasized with repetition and crescendo. Smith continues, invoking the Holy Spirit,

> Spirit break out; Break our walls down
> Spirit break out; Heaven come down.[54]

The song pleads for an inbreaking of the Spirit that will bring harmony (*rapport*) between worshipers and between the worshipers and Heaven. Walker continues,

> King Jesus you're the name we're lifting high
> Your glory shaking up the earth and skies
> Revival we wanna see your kingdom here
> We wanna see your kingdom here.[55]

Throughout this song, and especially notable in this last verse, Walker's voice is prophetic (*rapture*) as she calls for revival and sees the glory of the Lord 'shaking up the earth and skies'. The lyrics call for a Transfiguration-like coming of the kingdom in the glory of the King in an interpretation similar to that of Gause in his dissertation (*proleptic*).

Catherine Mullins' (The Ramp, Hamilton, Alabama) 'All My Worship', from the album *Intimate Encounters Volume 2*,[56] reflects the *rapport* between the worshiper and the Spirit as well as the *rapture* of ecstatic worship. While the song is sung in the first person and seems to be the song of a woman in a private devotional act, the music video portrays the intimacy of a small group of worshipers in the setting of a home, devoted in practices of prayer, singing, playing musical instruments, and reading Scripture.[57] In the opening lyrics, Catherine speaks directly to Jesus,

---

[53] Luke Hellebronth *et al.*, 'Spirit Break Out', recorded by Kim Walker Smith, *Still Believe* (Jesus Culture Music, 2012). Lyrics accessed 1 June 2015, http://www.azlyrics.com/lyrics/kimwalker smith/spiritbreakout.html.

[54] Hellebronth, *et al.*, 'Spirit Break Out'.

[55] Hellebronth, *et al.*, 'Spirit Break Out'.

[56] http://catherinemullins.com/store/.

[57] https://www.youtube.com/watch?v=iekwIVqA8oI

I will stay here for a little while
Until I look like the one I behold
And I will pour out my vial
Until all of me is on the floor.

And at your feet, I will sing
At your feet, I will sing

Here the singer has *rapport* with those mystics throughout the history of Christianity who've made vows to devote themselves until they reach *theosis*, looking like the one they see in a beatific vision. In *proleptic* participation with the worship of the woman with the alabaster box in the gospels, she vows to worship in song,

Your name is sweet like honey
Your voice it sounds like the waters
Your eyes are full of fire
Fairer than the sons of men

Your name is pure and holy
For you alone are worthy
For there is none beside you
Lord of Lords and King of Kings

Evoking images of Jesus from Revelation, the singers (now in harmony) worship the King of heaven, not only the Jesus of the gospels. Passionately, with hands raised, they continue to sing,

I give you all my worship
I give you all my worship
I give you all my worship
For you alone are God

No one is as holy
No one is as worthy
No one is as righteous
A the precious Lamb of God

The worshiper moves into the intimacy singing,

I will pursue you
Even now
You're the one I want

In *rapport* with female mystics, particularly of the middle ages, the singer is transformed into lover. Reflecting her desire 'to see the church come forth in purity and holiness',[58] Mullins' lyrics and this recording conform to Gause's understanding of adoration that is overwhelming and transformative.

Conclusion

The worship of Pentecostals, whether from the earliest years of the movement or in its most recent incarnations, is not driven by doctrine or dependent upon first having correct theology.[59] Instead, Pentecostal worship, inclusive of singing in the Spirit, as Gause contends, is experiential and dynamic. In it, the worshiper and worshiping community are responsive to the Spirit's movement into the glory of God, realized already in part but not yet in fullness. It is communion with the Spirit and the people of God. As it is grace-filled, it transforms the community of worshipers 'from glory to glory' until that day they stand in the fully realized presence of the King.

A 1911 letter from an unnamed female aptly describes the experience of *rapture*, *rapport*, and *proleptic* that is Pentecostal worship:

First we all prayed for a sick woman, to whom Mr. Boddy was sending a handkerchief, that she might be healed in the name of Christ. Then we had hymns and the Word. Almost directly the prayer began [*sic*] Jesus was manifested amongst us. I was perfectly conscious of His presence, and, from the prayers, it was evident that others were, too, and later on, while we were singing 'Jesus is mighty to save', the room became full of heavenly music again. It was surpassingly beautiful. It seemed as though we must stay there all night to adore The 'Lamb for sinners slain'.[60]

---

[58] http://catherinemullins.com/store/.

[59] For instance, popular Reformed preacher John MacArthur describes proper Christian worship music: 'The music of the redeemed is different. It is reflective of the truth of God that never changes and I think it displays the elements that are true of God … order, design, intelligence. The music that is reflective of God is systematic, sequential, poetic, harmonic, rhythmic, possesses resolution. It expresses the unchangeable reality of God and His truth' ('Spirit-Filled Music'. http://www.gty.org/resources/pdf/sermons/90-377).

[60] 'Sunderland', *Confidence* 4.4 (April 1911), p. 88.

11

PENTECOSTAL WORSHIP AND THE CREATION OF MEANING

Johnathan E. Alvarado*

Introduction

Corporate worship is a central feature of Pentecostal spirituality. Pentecostal hermeneutics is a theological concept that relates to the way meaning is derived and the exegetical particularities of Pentecostals, which are often worked out within the context of the worshiping community. This chapter suggests that understanding Pentecostal worship is helpful to understanding the creative synergism between the worshiping community and the creation of meaning. Building upon the work of Martin Heidegger, Hans-Georg Gadamer, Charles Taylor, James K.A. Smith, Scott Ellington, and others, this chapter seeks to explicate a Pentecostal hermeneutical method through the lenses of worship, Pentecostal spirituality, and ecclesial community.

The chapter is divided into three sections. The intersection of these three sections forms the nexus out of which meaning is created. In the first section I will offer a way of understanding Pentecostal worship as theology and play. In the second section I will discuss the philosophical hermeneutics of Heidegger, Taylor, Gadamer, and

---
* Johnathan E. Alvarado (DMin, Regent University, Virginia Beach, VA) is Bishop and Senior Pastor of Grace Church International, Atlanta, GA, and is a PhD student at Bangor University, Wales.

Smith with a view to understanding created meaning through social imaginaries. Finally, I will construct a Pentecostal hermeneutical method of meaning creation that takes seriously the place of worship in the hermeneutical process. The scope of this work cannot be fully explicated within the limitations of one chapter. However, the overview presented here will serve as a guide to future thinking about Pentecostal worship and hermeneutics. I am writing this chapter to discover and to discuss how meaning is created within the context of Pentecostal worship. Therefore, this chapter will explicate a faithful Pentecostal hermeneutic that is couched in philosophical hermeneutics and Pentecostal worship. It is to this latter end that I now turn.

Pentecostal Worship as Theology and Play

Pentecostal worship has received little scholarly attention over the past one hundred years. Fewer persons have written and published scholarship about a Pentecostal theology of worship from an academic or constructive theological perspective than have written about various theologies of worship within other Christian traditions.[1] However, the faithful who have written about Pentecostal worship have bequeathed unto the readers historical data as well as a narrative theological approach. Their contributions thirty to forty years ago tended to be didactic, practical, and instructive for the facilitation of Pentecostal worship. It has only been within the last fifteen years that a creative and constructive theology of Pentecostal worship has begun to surface and that only in small bursts.

In 1974 Cecil B. Knight articulated a Pentecostal theology of worship that described many of the same elements that are practiced in other Christian worship traditions.[2] From its beginnings as a small, marginalized sect of Christendom, Pentecostals have co-opted worship practices from the main line denominations, bringing structure and order to what would otherwise be less structured wor-

---

[1] Keith Warrington, *Pentecostal Theology: A Theology of Encounter* (New York: T&T Clark, 2008), p. 219. See also Wolfgang Vondey, 'The Making of Black Liturgy: Pentecostal Worship and Spirituality from African Slave Narratives to American Cityscapes', *Black Theology: An International Journal* 10.2 (2012), pp. 147-68 (p. 147).

[2] Cecil B. Knight (ed.), *Pentecostal Worship* (Cleveland, TN: Pathway Press, 1974), p. 9.

ship. For Pentecostals, this 'borrowing' of some of the worship elements of the so-called 'main line' traditions afforded the Pentecostal worshiping community the opportunity to infuse play into what was, to many of them, dead ritual. This was all performed under the auspices of the Holy Spirit's superintendence. Knight asserts that the Holy Spirit is what makes the difference in Pentecostal worship.[3] He enunciates a theology of encounter, which he suggests, will radically alter a person's life. Keith Warrington agrees with this description of a theology of Pentecostal worship as a theology of encounter.[4] A divine encounter where the Spirit is the facilitator, the motivator, and through the Spirit, Jesus is the object of worship.

Knight sees the altar, the invitation to follow Christ, and prayers at the altar as essential to a Pentecostal theology of worship.[5] For him, the altar is the place of encounter, where the Spirit is at work in the lives of the repentant turning their hearts to God in seasons of worship and prayer. Without an invitation to the altar for a salvific encounter with Jesus, Knight believes the Pentecostal worship experience to be lacking, incomplete, or devoid of Pentecostal power.

Walter Hollenweger has contributed significantly to the church's understanding of Pentecostalism in general and Pentecostal worship specifically. He frames Pentecostal worship principally in terms of oral liturgy.[6] Hollenweger highlights its similarities with the liturgical structures of the early church in the first century and parallels its usage with the orality that Pentecostals have received from their African American Pentecostal progenitors and contemporaries.[7] Hollenweger accents the importance of total and active participation of every member of the worshiping community as characteristic of Pentecostal worship. In my opinion, that aspect of Pentecos-

---

[3] Cecil B. Knight, 'The Wonder of Worship', in Cecil B. Knight (ed.), *Pentecostal Worship* (Cleveland, TN: Pathway Press, 1974), pp. 7-16 (p. 12). See also Johnathan E. Alvarado, 'Worship in the Spirit: Pentecostal Perspectives on Liturgical Theology and Praxis', *Journal of Pentecostal Theology* 21.1 (Spring 2012), pp. 135-51.

[4] Keith Warrington, *Pentecostal Theology: A Theology of Encounter*, p. 219.

[5] Knight, *Pentecostal Worship*, p. 14.

[6] Walter J. Hollenweger, *Pentecostalism: Origins and Developments Worldwide* (Peabody, MA: Hendrickson Publishers, 1997), pp. 269-77.

[7] Walter J. Hollenweger, 'The Black Roots of Pentecostalism', in Allan H. Anderson and Walter J. Hollenweger (eds.), *Pentecostals after a Century: Global Perspectives on a Movement in Transition* (JPTSup 15; Sheffield, UK: Sheffield Academic Press, 1999), pp. 36-41.

tal worship in great part resembles child's play. This depiction of participatory worship is the theological underpinning of Pentecostal worship. The worship must be joined by the total worshiping community even if the order of the liturgy has to give way to the spontaneity of dancing feet, the disorder of prostrate bodies, the aleatoric cacophony of loud voices, and the (apparent) chaos of Spirit movement.[8]

Hollenweger recognized the genius in the way Pentecostals used music and song as liturgical markers.[9] He affirmed how Pentecostal liturgy was performed in contradistinction to the formal liturgical structures of the written liturgies of other Christian traditions. His comparative characterization of the flexible, oral tradition of Pentecostals to the improvisational performance of Jazz music offered an alternative view to liturgy that captures the gestalt of Pentecostal worship.[10] In so doing, he introduced the concept of Pentecostal worship as 'play', the interplay between structure and spontaneity, formalism and freedom, Rubrics and Nigrics.

Wolfgang Vondey and Nimi Wariboko have further explored this conceptualization of Pentecostal worship as play.[11] Their work builds upon Hollenweger's thesis and frames it within ever growing conceptualizations of pentecostalisms and robust pneumatology. Vondey's work reframes the worship life of Pentecostals in terms of imagination.[12] He then recapitulates Hollenweger's characterization of Pentecostal life and worship as Jazz performance. In it he characterizes the improvisational nature of Pentecostal worship as 'singing in the Spirit'. He depicts this action as 'spirit-forming' for the worshiping community, which through these exercises has been 'spirit-formed'.[13] Wariboko's work further expands Hollenweger's understanding of play to encompass the whole of Pentecostal life in the Spirit.[14] Though he is critical of Vondey's work, indicting him for

---

[8] Alvarado, *Worship in the Spirit*, pp. 140-42.

[9] Hollenweger, *Pentecostalism*, p. 271.

[10] Harvey Cox, *Fire From Heaven* (Boston, MA: Da Capo Press, 2001), summarizes Hollenweger's view (p. 148).

[11] Wolfgang Vondey, *Beyond Pentecostalism* (Grand Rapids, MI: Eerdmans, 2010), pp. 40-46. See also, Nimi Wariboko, *The Pentecostal Principle* (Grand Rapids, MI: Eerdmans, 2012) pp. 161-95.

[12] Vondey, *Beyond Pentecostalism*, pp. 40-46.

[13] Vondey, *Beyond Pentecostalism*, pp. 40, 44.

[14] Wariboko, *Pentecostal Principle*, pp. 149-51.

not going far enough, Wariboko builds upon Vondey's work characterizing it as the playful, imaginative, creative center of Pentecostal worship, spirituality, and life.[15]

The Concept of Play as a Theological Motif

There is much to be appreciated and written about the theological concept of play. Theological reflection on play is perhaps most appropriately framed within the context of corporate worship. Because worship is a defining characteristic of Pentecostal spirituality, the concept of play can be readily discerned and meticulously explored within the context of this spirituality. Some of that exploration should entail recognition of the nature of play as expressed in freedom, fantasy, spontaneity, creativity, and imagination. These characteristics are demonstrated in play as attributes of both God and humans.

There is within the construct of Pentecostal worship room for ritual and play, form and freedom, and these dyads should be seen as congruent and not oppositional. Ritualized play is still play indeed. Within the nexus of structure and play there is tremendous spiritual potential. To this point, Nimi Wariboko (quoting Giorgio Agamben) asserts, 'Thus we can think of the Pentecostal-Charismatic worship service as "a zone in which possibility and reality, potentiality and actuality, become indistinguishable"'.[16] This section of the study will argue that the potential that exists in Pentecostal worship is creative potential, and it offers much promise for Pentecostal hermeneutics, the creation of meaning.

Harvey Cox explores some of these concepts in an attempt to articulate life as festival and fantasy.[17] In so doing he proffers the idea that 'life as fantasy' is celebratory and transformative. He asserts that it offers those who fantasize the opportunity to envision a radically different life for themselves by reason of the celebration.[18] He couches this dialogue within the context of a theology of hope. This type of exploration is congruent with and often descriptive of Pentecostal worship. Deeply rooted in the liberation traditions of

---

[15] Wariboko, *Pentecostal Principle*, pp. 165-71.

[16] Wariboko, *Pentecostal Principle*, p. 100.

[17] Harvey Cox, *The Feast of Fools* (Cambridge, MA: Harvard University Press, 1969), pp. 7-12.

[18] Cox, *The Feast of Fools*, p. 22.

marginalized people,[19] Pentecostal worship fosters a liberating spirit that transforms the reality of the worshiper into something previously not envisioned.

Cox holds fantasy and religion in tension and sees the two as mutually informing realities. The former he sees relative to the individual and the latter as it relates to the community or what he calls the civilization.[20] Worship within the Pentecostal tradition as fantasy affords the worshiper the opportunity to experience alternate realities of life, even if those experiences are episodic and infrequent. That same axiom applies to religion and religious experience in that it transports communities out of their current state and gives them a new corporate identity, an identity that is shaped by their shared religious experience. This transmuting effect can be understood as the child-like substratum to many games involving role-playing. Role-playing is the realm of play in which new realities of life are forged and new identities are assumed. Through the fantasy, alternate realities are embraced and fresh possibilities emerge, thus transforming the players into new creatures with new possibilities.

Cox explores the phenomenon of ritual as important and necessary for the facilitation of fantasy. He dubs ritual as 'embodied fantasy', indicating that it is more than a mental ascent or cerebral notion.[21] For Cox, ritual necessitates embodiment for full expression. Though within the context of worship there is often a needless bifurcation made between play and ritual, this study affirms that even when play becomes ritualized it yet remains play. Just as school children on the playground repetitively play the same games in a ritualized way without losing their joy, spontaneity, or freedom, playful worship also maintains its verve and creative impulse and though ritualized, does not cease to be play.

Wolfgang Vondey has explored the roots of liturgical play and asserts that with respect to liturgical development within classical Pentecostalism, 'Pentecostal origins are deeply connected with African American spirituality'.[22] Though he insists that classical Pentecostalism is not as profoundly connected to a pure African spiritual-

---

[19] Cheryl Bridges Johns, *A Pedagogy Among the Oppressed* (JPTSup 2; Sheffield: Sheffield Academic Press, 1993).

[20] Cox, *Feast of Fools*, p. 68.

[21] Cox, *Feast of Fools*, p. 73.

[22] Vondey, *Beyond Pentecostalism*, p. 119.

ity, to which as some scholars have innocently defaulted, rather than attributing the whole of Pentecostal spirituality to African roots, he finds it more appropriate to connect African spirituality with Pentecostal liturgy.

Margaret Poloma expounds upon the theology of play and establishes its common usage among contemporary Pentecostals in Toronto, Canada.[23] She chronicles the way the worshipers at the Toronto Vineyard church understood what was happening in their revival during the late 1990's. Their descriptions of the events depicted God as, 'playing with His kids'.[24] They understood the spiritual and varied phenomena happening to them to be play. They appraised tears and laughter equally as the playfulness of God. They did so principally because no matter what the manifestation, it came as a surprise and an interruption to their prescribed liturgy. For the purposes of this essay, this speaks to the ways in which play is understood and a way in which play can be theologically categorized. It seems that God is at liberty to be playful and even spontaneous in His dealings with His children.

Though some would argue that in these settings God is *working*, I would like to suggest that this type of divine interruption and spontaneous intervention is indeed God at work, *playing*. Poloma encountered the same bifurcated attitude within the church that saw spiritual renovation as the works of God,[25] but for the purposes of this study I would like to proffer the notion that Pentecostal spirituality, which has influenced contemporary spirituality in many denominations, is a theology wherein worshipers work at playing. This spirituality is characterized by an openness to play, a readiness to play, and the desire for playful encounter with God that transforms the worlds of worshipers into one in which all things have become new.

---

[23] Margaret M. Poloma, *Main Street Mystics: The Toronto Blessing & Reviving Pentecostalism* (New York: AltaMira Press, 2003).

[24] Poloma, *Main Street Mystics*, p. 63.

[25] Poloma, *Main Street Mystics*, p. 69.

Philosophical Hermeneutics as a Backdrop to Meaning Creation

Worshiping communities in general and Pentecostal worshiping communities in particular are creative communities.[26] Their creativity is often expressed through their rituals, songs, prayers, and preaching. Therefore, the connection between worship and creativity as a general practice is a natural congruence. In this section, I argue that the philosophical hermeneutics of Heidegger, Gadamer, Taylor, and Smith provide a suitable framework for understanding the link between Pentecostal worship and the creation of meaning.

The term 'hermeneutics' in this essay harkens back to a premodern definition, which depicts the hermeneutical enterprise as conversation, communication, encounter, and embrace.[27] These tenets, when understood as hermeneutical method, evince a profound connection between the interpretive arts and Pentecostal spirituality. In writing this section I seek to repristinate the core identity of hermeneutics and liberate that core from the reductionist tendencies of modernist scholars like Humboldt, Schleiermacher, and Kierkegaard whose scientific approach to texts often only allowed for a unilateral monologue.

In contrast, Heidegger's hermeneutical approach primarily calls for a revision of one's self-understanding from 'being' to 'being there' or 'being in'.[28] This is a statement of ontological essence that depicts personhood as a philosophical and equiprimordial relationship of encounter with God in the world and for the purposes of this essay, an encounter through worship. In speaking of this phenomenon, David Lines comments on Heidegger's notion of what constitutes encounter thusly, 'All beings are revealed in events, each

---

[26] Teresa Berger, '*Veni Creator Spiritus*: The Elusive Real Presence of the Spirit in the Catholic Tradition', in Teresa Berger and Bryan D. Spinks (eds.), *The Spirit in Worship – Worship in the Spirit* (Collegeville, MN: Liturgical Press, 2009), pp. 141-43.

[27] Martin Heidegger, *Ontology – The Hermeneutics of Facticity* (Bloomington, IN: Indiana University Press, 1988), p. 11.

[28] Martin Heidegger, 'Phenomenology and Fundamental Ontology: The Disclosure of Meaning', in Kurt Mueller-Vollmer (ed.), *The Hermeneutics Reader* (New York: The Continuum Publishing Company, 1992), pp. 214-15.

fresh instance coming forth as a cycle of change'.[29] This Heidegger also calls 'Dasein'.

'Dasein is distinguished by the fact that it is the being that is concerned with its own being, its ability to be in the world'.[30] Heidegger asserts that it is human involvement in the world that frames and informs the hermeneutical enterprise, the creation of meaning. The interplay between the world, the shared presuppositions within a community, and the text being interpreted, forms the hermeneutical circle, which demonstrates the mutually informing character of his hermeneutics. I contend that it is through the awareness of being, and engagement of being within the worshiping community that meaning is created.

Hans-Georg Gadamer adds to this insight by positing 'the universality of hermeneutics'.[31] For him this means that all human knowing is mediated. That mediation of knowledge comes through texts and communities. Pentecostal biblical scholar Scott Ellington proffers a similar understanding of Pentecostal hermeneutics. He asserts, 'the truth-claims made by the Bible are not only conceptual but also experiential in nature. Pentecostals have always placed a particular emphasis on the direct experiencing of God and on application when practicing biblical interpretation'.[32] For Gadamer, this implies the fusion of text with reader(s). This fusion changes both the reader and the text into something that neither was before the encounter, through the acts of reading and for our purposes, 'hearing' texts in worship. This is both descriptive of and prescriptive for Pentecostals in worship. Pentecostal worship cultivates the heart's disposition to be open to the fusion of text with community thus creating meaning where before the encounter there was only sound and gesture.

The fusion of text with reader(s) through the experiential lenses of Pentecostals in worship has the potential to communicate transforming grace and can thus be seen as sacramental. While the scope

---

[29] David Lines, '"Working With" Music: A Heideggerian Perspective of Music Education', *Educational Philosophy and Theory* 37.1 (2005), p. 67.

[30] Jean Grondin, *Introduction to Philosophical Hermeneutics* (New Haven, CT: Yale University Press, 1994), p. 95.

[31] Jeannine K. Brown, *Introducing Biblical Hermeneutics: Scripture as Communication* (Grand Rapids: Baker Academic Publishing, 2007), p. 66.

[32] Scott A. Ellington, 'History, Story, and Testimony: Locating Truth in a Pentecostal Hermeneutic', *Pneuma* 21.2 (Fall 2001), p. 245.

of this essay does not permit me to fully expound the nuances and layers of these possibilities, the sacramental inclination that Gadamer's hermeneutical proposition affords the Pentecostal community is worthy of mention. One could describe the mediation of meaning through reading, hearing, and encountering God as sacramental because it transforms, even sanctifies.[33] The transforming effect of the fusion between text and community through worship and the mediation and creation of meaning that occurs as a result transforms the community and opens up fresh ways of understanding the texts encountered by the community through the Spirit.

In his seminal work on 'Social Imaginaries', Charles Taylor posits a psychosocial phenomenon that is germane to the human experience in which the collective whole is oriented into social existence.[34] Thus, meaning for life and social norms are created through the social dynamics and interactions of that community. Though he is writing specifically to explain the existence of multiple modernities, Taylor's insights into the public sphere as central to society rings true for ecclesial life and for postmodernity. It should be noted however that the supposed consistencies between postmodern epistemology and Pentecostal hermeneutics are not as congruent as some would affirm.[35] However, Taylor proffers at least three important axioms that buttress this chapter.

First, Taylor claims that *how* people imagine their social existence and *how* they fit together with others is an important though complex factor and reality.[36] The significance of this understanding cannot be understated when one considers the outworking of created meaning through social interaction (i.e. worship), normative notions, common images, and expectations that frame the community. Second, Taylor comments on the unconscious way in which humans embrace social imaginaries in this statement: 'Humans operated with a social imaginary well before they ever got into the busi-

---

[33] Hans-Georg Gadamer, 'On the Scope and Function of Hermeneutical Reflection', in David E. Linge (ed.), *Hans-Georg Gadamer: Philosophical Hermeneutics* (Los Angeles: The University of California Press, 1976), p. 38.

[34] Charles Taylor, *Modern Social Imaginaries* (Durham, NC: Duke University Press, 2004), pp. 83-85.

[35] Veli-Matti Kärkkäinen, 'Pentecostal Hermeneutics in the Making: On the Way From Fundamentalism to Postmodernism', *The Journal of the European Pentecostal Theological Association* 18 (1998), p. 97.

[36] Taylor, *Modern Social Imaginaries*, pp. 23-24.

ness of theorizing about themselves'.[37] This notion is consistent with a Pentecostal understanding of worship that operates in hidden catechesis, shaping the understanding and the affections of worshipers toward a created meaning of experiences, Christian life, and texts.

Finally, Taylor's assertion that social imaginaries are living dynamisms interacting with, informing, and being informed by the collective practices of the community rings true in this statement: 'The relation between practices and the background understanding behind them is therefore not one-sided. If the understanding makes the practice possible, it is also true that it is the practice that largely carries the understanding.'[38] When applied to Pentecostal hermeneutics, the message becomes clear. Pentecostals bridge hermeneutical gulfs through their practices of worship, and Pentecostal practices of worship are informed by the hermeneutical gulfs that they bridge.

A Pentecostal Theology of Worship and Meaning Creation

As I bring this chapter to end, there are three axioms that feature prominently as it pertains to Pentecostal worship and the creation of meaning. First, Pentecostal worship cultivates the disposition and affections of the worshiper converting her into a sensitive reader. Jamie Smith affirms this thusly, 'The core claim of this book is that liturgies – whether "sacred" or "secular" – shape and constitute our identities by forming our most fundamental desires and our most basic attunement to the world'.[39] It is through the cultivation of identity and the attunement of Christian sensibilities to the world that lenses and reading of texts is shaped and thus meaning is created. The transformative experience of Pentecostal worship is not only efficacious for the renewing of the mind, the directing of affections, and the expressing of our love to Jesus, but it is also profoundly efficacious in that it creates new realities of life and thus it

---

[37] Taylor, *Modern Social Imaginaries*, p. 26.
[38] Taylor, *Modern Social Imaginaries*, p. 25.
[39] James K.A. Smith, *Desiring the Kingdom: Worship, Worldview, and Cultural Formation* (Grand Rapids: Baker Academic Publishing, 2009), p. 25.

invites readers to have new expectations in our engagements with biblical texts.

It is the shaping of affections and attunement to the world that Scott Ellington addresses in his essay on 'History, Story, and Testimony'. In it he argues, 'Through the biblical text, God creates in our imaginations an alternative image of reality, a new vision of how the world could be'.[40] Ellington argues that the Pentecostal worshiping communities' lived-experience is a gauge for testing the stories of the biblical text.[41] He sees this as a necessary factor for fully explicating a Pentecostal hermeneutic.

Secondly, it is my contention that Pentecostal worship begins with lived experiences and goes to texts rather than beginning with texts and moving to lived experience.[42] Rather than propositions and dogmas shaping Pentecostal sensibilities, a preferred way of being for Pentecostals is to allow Pentecostal sensibilities to shape propositions and dogmas and ultimately to shape the reading of the text itself. From the genesis of Pentecostal movements, adherents have favored a plain reading of the text that grew out of their experience with the Spirit and the community's conviction that the Spirit would lead the readers into all truth.[43] I argue that this expectation was fostered in the environment of worship.

I contend that Pentecostal worship allows for the retelling of biblical stories through preaching, testimony, prayers, and songs. It calls Pentecostal adherents into identification and solidarity with the stories being told. This solidarity is forged through the lived experiences of the ones hearing, praying, and singing, cast in the light of the biblical narrative. Pentecostal worshipers often recast themselves as the principle characters in the story in an aforementioned role-play. These unique Pentecostal ways of understanding texts take seriously the mystical, supernatural, and enchanted worldview that people of the Spirit enjoy. In so doing, they are predisposed to reading and understanding the text through hermeneutical lenses that are crafted in seasons of worship.

---

[40] Ellington, 'History, Story, and Testimony', p. 257.

[41] Ellington, 'History, Story, and Testimony', p. 257.

[42] Simon Chan, *Pentecostal Theology and the Christian Spiritual Tradition* (JPTSup 21; Sheffield, UK: Sheffield Academic Press, 2000), p. 20.

[43] Kenneth J. Archer, *A Pentecostal Hermeneutic for the Twenty-First Century: Spirit, Scripture and Community* (JPTSup 28; London: T&T Clark International, 2004), p. 5

Finally, contemporary Pentecostal worship appreciates and inculcates the whole of Spirit-Word-Community paradigm as hermeneutical framework for the creation of meaning. Evangelical, Pentecostal, and Orthodox traditions all emphasize different aspects of centeredness of hermeneutics and meaning. They all seek different sources for couching the authority of their hermeneutical claims. Pentecostals have evolved to become comfortable with an ever-broadening understanding of how meaning is created through an amalgamation of these three norms. Because the nature of Pentecostal life inclines toward a bible centered understanding of the Christian faith, any viable hermeneutical method must uphold the primacy of Scripture within the lives of the faithful. Because of the centrality of worship in the Pentecostal life, hermeneutical methods must be filtered through the worshiping community for shared interpretation and shared meaning.

12

TAKING THE RISK: THE OPENNESS AND ATTENTIVENESS OF LATIN AMERICAN PENTECOSTAL WORSHIP

Wilmer Estrada-Carrasquillo[*]

Sobrellevad los unos las cargas de los otros, y cumplid así la ley de Cristo.[1]

Cuando el extranjero habite con vosotros en vuestra tierra, no lo oprimiréis. Como a uno de vosotros trataréis al extranjero que habite entre vosotros, y lo amarás como a ti mismo, porque extranjeros fuisteis en la tierra de Egipto. Yo, Jehová, vuestro Dios.[2]

The Gift of Translatability

One of the ways in which God expresses his love to all cultures is through the gift of translatability. By translatability I do not simply mean God's openness to communicate with humanity (whatever

---

[*] Wilmer Estrada-Carrasquillo (MDiv, Pentecostal Theological Seminary) is a PhD Candidate in Contextual Theology at Asbury Theological Seminary and Adjunct Professor of Theology for the Center for Latino Studies at the Pentecostal Theological Seminary.

[1] 'Bear one another's burdens, and thereby fulfill the law of Christ' (Gal. 6.2). Unless noted otherwise, all scriptural quotations are from the *New American Standard Bible*.

[2] 'When a stranger resides with you in your land, you shall not do him wrong. The stranger who resides with you shall be to you as the native among you, and you shall love him as yourself, for you were aliens in the land of Egypt; I am the Lord your God' (Lev. 19.33-34).

cultural form it takes) but also God's attentiveness to our *response-ability*.[3] The opening chapters of Genesis serve as a backdrop for such a gift. Once God created Adam and Eve (Gen. 1.27), he translates himself to them (Gen. 1.28). Furthermore, he does not only speak to Adam and Eve, he also is attentive as they reply to him (Gen. 2.10).

Thankfully, this gift of God's translatability is not lost regardless of our fallen state. On the contrary, instead of becoming utterly silent, God kept translating who he is to us. And still today, he keeps translating Himself in order to restore the 'common-unity' that was interrupted. Perhaps there is no greater image of that future hope than what John the apostle 'hears and sees' in Rev. 7.9: 'After these things I looked, and behold, a great multitude which no one could count, from every nation and all tribes and peoples and tongues, standing before the throne and before the Lamb'.[4]

This chapter (and probably this whole book) is the product of the gift of translatability. It is a testimony of God's openness to call us into community and his attentiveness to our response through worship. In particular, I will present a Latin American perspective on Pentecostal worship.[5] The structure of the argument is the following: a brief survey of previous contributions from fellow Latin American Pentecostal theologians,[6] followed by an analysis of two

---

[3] I borrow the term 'translatability' from two theologians who have focused their work on non-Western culture, Lamin Sanneh and Andrew Walls. They both argue that the gospel has an undeniable translatable characteristic that enables it to take root in any culture. See Lamin Sanneh, *Translating the Message: The Missionary Impact on Culture* (Maryknoll, NY: Orbis Books, 1989); Andrew F. Walls, *The Missionary Movement in Christian History: Studies in the Transmission of Faith* (Maryknoll, NY: Orbis Books, 1996).

[4] Regarding this crowd, J.C. Thomas states, 'this crowd shares intimate fellowship with God and the Lamb and stand in very close proximity to them'. Though Thomas approaches his study strictly within the confines of the book itself and at time dialogues with the Johannine community, there is doubt that this 'intimate fellowship' points to God's restoration of what had been lost in Eden. See John Christopher Thomas, *The Apocalypse: A Literary and Theological Commentary* (Cleveland, TN: CPT Press, 2012), p. 269.

[5] By no means do I believe that my perspective is representative of all Latin American Pentecostals. Nevertheless, it is a testimony of how I experienced God in worship in the context of Puerto Rican Pentecostalism. I am especially in debt to my first mentors and pastors, Carmen J. Carrasquillo Rodríguez and Dr. Wilfredo Estrada-Adorno (*mami y papi*).

[6] Though it is a small representation, their contributions are consonant with other resources consulted. For example see Justo L. González and Catherine

practices that have been transformational in my Pentecostal worship experience.

Previous Testimonies from the Latin American Pentecostal Community

It is no secret; orality and praxis have played an important role within Pentecostal spirituality.[7] These two are primordial foundations of Pentecostalism.[8] By primordial I do not mean that Pentecostal spirituality is backward or underdeveloped. Contrary to that, both characteristics are preferable or fundamental ways of embodying our Pentecostal spirituality. And as I will briefly explain in this section, Latin American expressions of Pentecostalism are vivid examples of orality and praxis.

Darío López Rodríguez

In his work '*La fiesta del Espíritu*', López seeks to describe the distinctive character of Latino Pentecostal worship. From the outset, the title of the book immediately describes the context of how López defines the whole event. First, he describes it as a 'festivity' (*fiesta*) or a celebration. According to López, when Latin American

---

Gunsalus González, *The Liberating Pulpit* (Nashville: Abingdon Press, 1994); Eldin Villafañe, *El Espíritu Liberador: Hacia Una Ética Social Pentecostal Hispanoamericana* (Buenos Aires: Nueva Creación, 1996); Juan Sepúlveda *et al.* (eds.), *Voces del pentecostalismo Latinoamericano: identidad, teología, historia. II* (Concepción: Red Latinoamericana de Estudios Pentecostales (RELEP), 2009); Daniel Chiquete *et al.* (eds.), *Voces del Pentecostalismo Latinoamericano: identidad, teología, historia. IV* (Concepción: Red Latinoamericana de Estudios Pentecostales (RELEP), 2011); Eldin Villafañe and AETH, *Introducción Al Pentecostalismo: Manda Fuego Señor* (Nashville, TN: Abingdon Press, 2012); Carmelo Alvarez, *El Ministerio de La Adoración Cristiana: Teología Y Práctica Desde La Óptica Protestante* (Nashville, TN: Abingdon, 2013).

[7] This form of expression and transmission was what they had in hand. Thus, they became the central mediums for transmitting the Gospel. 'Where Pentecostals work in a pre- or post-literary society', comments Hollenweger, 'they do not think along systematic and logical lines, but in parables and associations'. Walter J Hollenweger, *Pentecostalism: Origins and Developments Worldwide* (Peabody, MA: Hendrickson Publishers, 2005), p. 33.

[8] To recognize orality and praxis as two important elements of Pentecostal Spirituality does not mean that Pentecostals reject formal training (the academy), the use of literature (print), and *theoria* (reason). Regarding this tension, Archer states, 'They (Pentecostals) do theology primarily in narrative forms'. However, Archer moves beyond orality and the non-academic and prefers to use pietistic models. Kenneth J. Archer, 'A Pentecostal Way of Doing Theology: Method and Manner', *International Journal of Systematic Theology* 9.3 (July 2007), p. 307.

238 *Toward a Pentecostal Theology of Worship*

Pentecostals join in worship they 'enter into a space where spontaneity, happiness, fellowship, mutual acceptance, free access, and openness to the Word, create a sense of festivity and a unique aroma that only occurs when friends come together'.[9] However, for López, this is not like any other celebration, he qualifies the event as the festivity 'of the Spirit' (*del Espíritu*). It is a divine initiated event. Regarding this López expands, 'the Spirit of God is the one who creates the common ground for such festivity of the Spirit'.[10] These two, according to López, serve as general contours of Latin American Pentecostal worship. Once López establishes the context of *el culto* (the worship service), he then identifies four distinct features that he describes as 'ingredients that mediate a unique flavor to the worship event'.[11] These are prayer, singing, testimony, and preaching. Let me briefly summarize why López understands these four as distinctive features of Latin American worship. First, through the practice of *prayer* the Pentecostal community 'affirms that the God with whom they are dialoguing – whose immediacy they never deny – walks with them constantly'. Thus, prayer becomes a sign of being close to God. Second, the practice of singing 'becomes the vehicle of liberation, whose inexhaustible fountain is the vivifying presence of the Holy Spirit'. In other words, songs (*coritos*) serve as a declaration of the expected future. Third, testimony serves as revelatory experience in which the community, 'narrates a story where the central figure is the God of life, the God who accompanies his people en every step of life'. Through the practice of testimony the Pentecostal community inserts their story into the biblical narrative. Finally, López describes preaching as the moment where the story of the Gospel is woven together with the 'daily events of the community, sharing the good news of salvation and challenging the hearts of the preacher and the hearers'.[12]

---

[9] Darío López Rodríguez, *La fiesta del Espíritu: espiritualidad y celebración pentecostal* (Lima, Perú: Ediciones Puma, 2006), p. 29. My translation.
[10] López Rodríguez, *La fiesta del Espíritu*, p. 26. My translation.
[11] López Rodríguez, *La fiesta del Espíritu*, p. 26. My translation
[12] López Rodríguez, *La fiesta del Espíritu*, pp. 47-55. My translation

Samuel Solivan

In chapter 3 of González's *¡Alabadle! Hispanic Christian Worship*,[13] Samuel Solivan presents a Hispanic Pentecostal worship.[14] Prior to presenting what he understands are distinctive Hispanic Pentecostal features, Solivan preambles his argument by explaining the context and the 'liturgical style' of Hispanic Pentecostal worship. Regarding the context he states, 'The location of Pentecostal churches is not accidental. They are located where the largest portion of the Hispanic community lives.'[15] Furthermore, for Solivan context is more than time and space, he also underscores the importance of the ethnic traits of Hispanics. 'The fact that we are a *mestizo* people (the *mestizaje* varying in its composition in relation to geographical location) is also reflected in our worship, in our songs, music, leadership, and liturgical styles'.[16] Hence, Solivan understands that the distinctiveness of Hispanic Pentecostal worship is intrinsically connected to our cultural and geographical contexts. In addition to the context, Solivan underscores the importance of the 'liturgical style'. Though it may be that a formal 'liturgical style' is absent, Solivan affirms that those who are more familiarized with Pentecostalism can agree that there is a 'discernable liturgy'.[17] This 'informal Pentecostal liturgy' is sustained by three elements that help nurture the contextual approach of Hispanic Pentecostal worship. Solivan describe these as: 'ministry of laity', 'noncreedal stance', and 'nonliturgical tradition'.[18]

---

[13] See Justo L. González (ed.), *Alabadle!: Hispanic Christian Worship* (Nashville, TN: Abingdon Press, 1996).

[14] Though elsewhere I am using the term Latin Americans, in this section I will use Hispanics in order to stay true to Solivan's contribution.

[15] Samuel Solivan, 'Hispanic Pentecostal Worship', in Justo L. González (ed.), *Alabadle!: Hispanic Christian Worship* (Abingdon Press, 1996), p. 46.

[16] Solivan, 'Hispanic Pentecostal Worship', p. 48.

[17] Solivan, 'Hispanic Pentecostal Worship', p. 48.

[18] By ministry of laity, he means the opportunity that laity, youth, and children along with clergy have 'to play a role in the worship of the community'. With regard to 'noncredal', he explains, 'It is not a denial of the content of the confessions and creeds of the church generally recognized by the Reformed Protestant tradition. Rather, it is a relocation of the people's place and function in the life of the community.' By 'nonliturgical' Solivan does not mean that there is no theological reasoning. What he means is, it is 'open to the Holy Spirit'; it is 'expectant to the Holy Spirit'; it is 'open to praise God and God's Word'; and it is 'passionate and participatory'. See Solivan, 'Hispanic Pentecostal Worship', pp. 48-51.

Having stated the context and the 'liturgical style', Solivan identifies five components of Hispanic Pentecostal worship. Similar to López, Solivan recognizes prayer, songs, testimonies, and preaching. Due to the similarities between López and Solivan I will not develop further these four. Yet, Solivan adds a fifth element, which is the reading of both the Old and New Testaments.[19] Two premises undergird Solivan's argument. First, 'Rarely is one Scripture reading given more authority than another'.[20] The second, Latin American Pentecostals hold in high regard the Word of God.[21] Undoubtedly, Latin Americans approach the reading of the Word as a moment where God Himself speaks in our language.

As we have seen, the previous survey underscores the importance of orality and praxis through prayer, songs, testimonies, preaching, and Scripture reading.[22] To a certain extent these practices were common across the various resources consulted. However, if Pentecostalism is a 'dynamic movement', it will be in order to explore other practices that have been part of the Latin American Pentecostal experience. Hence, what follows is a personal testimony of two practices that played a transformative role within my Pentecostal community.

The Openness and Attentiveness of Latin American Pentecostal Worship

Public Spoken Requests (*Peticiones*)

Much of my Pentecostal formation has taken place within the Puerto Rican context. And it did not take me long to learn that there are some practices that may threaten to 'sabotage' (this is how some non-Pentecostal friends have described it) the worship service. One of these risky and messy practices is what we call *peticiones* (public spoken requests). It is no secret that *el culto pentecostal* is highly partic-

---

[19] Solivan, 'Hispanic Pentecostal Worship', p. 51.

[20] It is probable that this was true to Solivan's personal experience. However, this might be changing as of today. Solivan, 'Hispanic Pentecostal Worship', p. 51.

[21] Solivan, 'Hispanic Pentecostal Worship', p. 52.

[22] I understand that these are not exclusive features of Latin American Pentecostals. According to Steven Jack Land, these are also central to Pentecostal Spirituality. See his seminal work, *Pentecostal Spirituality: A Passion for the Kingdom* (Cleveland, TN: CPT Press, 2010).

ipatory. Something interesting about this high participatory nature is that those in the pulpit and those at the pews play an equal role. Participation is not only manifested by spontaneous physical responses and out loud praises, but also through an intentional space that is open for sharing *any* spoken request.

Notice the emphasis that I am placing on 'any'. For someone that has not experienced such a moment, it could be quite unnerving. However, for both the person who is sharing and the community that is listening, it is something normal. One reason why this is a risky moment is due to the transparency that an individual reveals as he/she shares with the community his/her story. For him or for her, the worshiping community is an extension of the family. For Latin Americans, family is more than blood connections; it expands from the nucleus of parents and siblings to the 'extended' family and bonds of friendship.[23] Therefore, there is no sense of inhibitions or secrecy. Regarding this familial image of the worshiping community, Justo González observes that the image of the church as an extended family is one of the contributions that Latin American theology brings to ecclesiology: 'there can be genuine openness to the world and its various realities'.[24]

If such a practice is on the border of being messy, why keep encouraging it? First of all, there are obvious cultural reasons, which some of them have been previously mentioned. Yet, I understand that more than an extension of cultural patterns, there is something transformative that takes place when we are given the opportunity to share our needs publicly. I believe that Leonardo Boff may be helpful. On the one hand, socialization cannot happen in isolation and on the other hand, being is realized as we live in community. Boff adds to this by arguing that each human being, as a creature made in the image and likeness of the Triune God, will always have a need of other humans.[25] Therefore, the human condition presup-

---

[23] See Eldin Villafañe, *The Liberating Spirit: Toward a Hispanic American Pentecostal Social Ethic* (Grand Rapids, MI: Eerdmans, 1993), p. 96.

[24] And even more, this image of extended family is key within Latin American communities that are away from their native land. Justo L. González, 'In Quest of a Protestant Hispanic Ecclesiology', in Jose David Rodriguez and Loida I. Martell-Otero (eds.), *Teologia En Conjunto: A Collaborative Hispanic Protestant Theology* (Louisville, KY: Westminster John Knox Press, 1997), p. 94.

[25] Leonardo Boff, *Trinity and Society* (Eugene, OR: Wipf & Stock, reprint edn, 2005), p. 149.

poses that all human beings are social beings and in need of one another. I would add that this need of the other is not satisfied through a partial presence of the other but through an integral commitment and attentiveness from her/his community.

Many of the individuals that stand up in the midst of the worshiping community may go through the weekly routines unheard. Possibly, their situations consume them to such an extent that their public participation in the midst of the worship service is not only a catharsis, but also a moment of sharing their burdens with the community and voicing to God their feelings. By negating the opportunity for publicly sharing the needs of their brothers and sisters, the community loses much more than what she can gain by not taking the risk. For example, by rejecting the public participation and the sharing of burdens we may be rejecting our brother and sisterhood.

The first quotation in the epigraph above might be helpful in explaining the importance of this practice. Though Paul's command in Gal. 6.1-10 responds to a specific event where an individual is caught in transgression, Paul's call for action is helpful for the present discussion. After calling for the restoration of the individual caught in transgression (v. 1), the apostle Paul follows by commanding his readers to 'bear one another's burdens' (6.2).[26] What I found interesting in this command is how Paul frames his argument. He alludes to their kinship; he refers to them as *adelphoi*. For Paul, the call to bare the burdens of one another is not the responsibility of the non-Christian community. On the contrary, such response is one of many characteristics that we must embody as brothers and sisters. In other words, the inability of sharing the burdens of the other brings into question their fellowship in Christ. Commenting on this passage Dietrich Bonhoeffer states, 'If one does not experience it (bearing one another's burden), the fellowship he [she] belongs to is not Christian. If any member refuses to bear that burden, he [she] denies the law of Christ'.[27] Therefore, by taking the risk of opening such space we are truly embodying a Christ-like community.

---

[26] *Baztazete* is an imperative command of action. There is no room for choosing not to.

[27] Dietrich Bonhoeffer, *Life Together: The Classic Exploration of Faith in Community* (Princeton, NJ: HarperOne, 2009), p. 101.

Welcoming Visitors (*Presentación de Visitas*)

We have already seen how the concept of the Latin American Pentecostal community as an extended family empowers the individual for speaking publicly and calls for the bearing of burdens. In like manner, this family extension has important implications for the practice of welcoming. Hence, if the Latin American Pentecostal community is an extension of our family, how must this affect those who are gracefully driven by God to visit our communities?

Broadly speaking, the practice of welcoming is defined as an act of receiving the other. Unfortunately, this broad definition seems too passive and does not speak of the transformative character of welcoming – especially within the Christian community. According to Christine Pohl, the practice of welcoming is an intentional and dignifying act that transforms both the guest and the host.[28] Reflecting on this, I can recall the importance that my local church and other Pentecostal churches placed upon the practice of welcoming their visitors.

Just as with the spoken request, worship is not stopped to welcome the visitor; actually, welcoming the other is itself an act of worship. It is a time where the visitors are recognized, not as a whole mass of people, but by their names. It is a time of dignifying them as human beings. Simple as it might seem, calling out the names of the visitors brings along with it a sense of recognition and affirmation of their personhood. More than a routine announcement, when we take time to welcome our visitors, it becomes a call of love and a prophetic invitation to be part of the community. Moreover, it is an expression that tells the guest, 'You are home'![29] By calling them by name we are reclaiming them for God (Isa. 43.1). Yet, calling out their names from the pulpit is not all, the community is also encouraged to move out from their comfort zones and walk towards the visitors and greet one another with a holy kiss (1 Cor. 16.20). Interestingly, the greeting is not limited to

---

[28] For a thorough study on the practice of hospitality, see Christine D. Pohl, *Making Room: Recovering Hospitality as a Christian Tradition* (Grand Rapids, MI: Eerdmans, 1999).

[29] Regarding this, Meeks says that home is also a place where you 'can count on being confronted, forgiven, loved, and cared for. Home is where there is always a place for you at the table. And, finally, home is where you can count on sharing what is on the table.' See M. Douglas Meeks, *God the Economist: The Doctrine of God and Political Economy* (Minneapolis, MN: Fortress Press, 1989), p. 36.

those who are visiting, but as you walk by your brothers and sisters, many expressions of love are being shared among the community. Concerning the practice of welcoming, a pastor once told me, that every time they welcome their visitors, they approach it as one of the most profound and impacting ways that the community expresses their love to one another.

The community cannot give what they have not experienced. Thus, if welcoming the other is a way of expressing their love, it means that each individual that forms the community was a recipient of it. The practice of welcoming, 'begins by being the recipient of hospitality, by being the "other", the one being taken care of, helped, loved, and dignified ... Making ourselves vulnerable will teach us a lesson of how important it is to make room for the "other".'[30]

The second quote in the epigraph above speaks directly to this practice of welcoming the other. Verses 33 and 34 of Leviticus 19 are part of a long list of sundry laws that are given to the Israelites. These two verses in particular serve as a reminder of what God had previously commanded.[31] God recalls their experience as foreigners and sojourners in Egypt, and commands them to use that experience as a catalyst for being hospitable to the foreigner. Sometimes it is very easy to 'forget' (or be selective of) what God has done for us in certain times. Interestingly, this was a common pattern as the Israelites sojourned from Egypt to the promise land. For example, after they had been witness of the mighty way God liberated them from the oppressive hand of Pharaoh, they complained to Moses, 'then they said to Moses, Is it because there were no graves in Egypt that you have taken us away to die in the wilderness? Why have you dealt with us in this way, bringing us out of Egypt?' (Exod. 14.11). After this complaint and Moses' conversation with God, a way was made through the Red Sea. Following the powerful manifestation of God and the Israelites' response in worship, the grumbling surfaced once again. This was prompted by the scarcity of

---

[30] Wilmer Estrada-Carrasquillo, 'Reflection on Making Room: Recovering Hospitality as a Christian Tradition', *Journal of Latin American Theology* 8.2 (2013), p. 112.

[31] Exodus 22.21, 'You shall not wrong a stranger or oppress him, for you were strangers in the land of Egypt'. Exodus 23.9, 'You shall not oppress a stranger, since you yourselves know the feelings of a stranger, for you also were strangers in the land of Egypt'.

'drinkable water'. Following the previous pattern, God once again responds to their claims, 'Then they came to Elim where there were twelve springs of water and seventy date palms, and they camped there beside the waters' (Exod. 15.27).[32]

Memories like these were the ones that God was evoking when he commanded the Israelites to be welcoming to the sojourner and the alien. But this command was more than a call to remember; there were other specific requests. First, God requested that His people not use violence or oppress the alien (Lev. 19.33). Thus, it was not only a matter of opening space for them and receiving the other, they were responsible for treating them righteously, equally, as a fellow people. The alien and the sojourner were to be treated as one of them. Following, God makes an even more challenging request. This request is in addition to the texts that are found in Exod. 22.21 and 23.9. God commands, 'you shall love him [her] as yourself, for you were aliens in the land of Egypt; I am the LORD your God' (Lev. 19.34). What I find powerful in this verse is God's restoration of otherness. From alien and sojourner, to a fellow Israelite, to love them as oneself.[33] This transformation did not only affect the space of the alien and the sojourner, but also the space of the Israelites. God's commandment to love the other was a drastic redefinition of who was part of the Israelite household. While the Israelites had a narrowed understanding of whom they loved, God's definition of *oikos* is far more inclusive than what they had in mind.

Conclusion

Pentecostal worship experiences need to take the risk and become both attentive and welcoming. I do not say this because my desire is to make your local community become more Latin American. Contrary to that, I understand that by embodying such practices we be-

---

[32] This pattern is repeated three times. See the narratives of the manna, the meat, and the water from the rock.

[33] Regarding this M. Volf adds, 'However, at the root of Christian self-understanding as aliens and exiles lies not so much the story of Abraham and his posterity as the destiny of Jesus Christ, his mission, and his rejection, which brought him to the cross. "He came to what was his own, and his own people did not accept him" (Jn. 1:11).' See Miroslav Volf, 'Exclusion and Embrace: Theological Reflections in the Wake of "Ethnic Cleansing"', *Communio Viatorum* 35.3 (January 1, 1993), p. 236.

come more like God. God has taken the risk of being attentive and welcoming to all peoples.

In sum, let us never forget that we are aliens and sojourners who were welcomed into the community of the triune God and given the opportunity to 'draw near with confidence to the throne of grace, so that we may receive mercy and find grace to help in time of need' (Heb. 4.16). Therefore, let us take the risk of becoming better listeners and hosts in a world that is hostile and deaf.

13

AN AFRICAN AMERICAN CONTRIBUTION TO THE THEOLOGY OF WORSHIP: CONSIDERING THREE SITUATIONS OF INTEGRATED AFRICAN AMERICAN LED WORSHIP FROM PRE-CIVIL RIGHTS TIMES

Antipas L. Harris[*]

Scholars widely agree that African American worship has been among the significant contributions that the Black Church has made within American Protestantism as well as within the formation of American society and culture. The role that the Black church's worship has played in the healing of race relations in the 20th century remains a terrain for further exploration. Much of the credit for the success of the Civil Rights Movement has been given to a handful of prominent names that have lingered in the forefront of history. While names such as Rosa Parks, Martin Luther King Jr., Thurgood Marshall, Whitney P. Young Jr., and others remain momentous to the Civil Rights Movement, a closer look into the crevices of the 19th and 20th centuries reveals that there were significant grassroots efforts from across the country that nudged forward the healing of race relations prior to the Deep South Civil Rights Movement that officially launched in 1955.

---

[*] Antipas L. Harris (DMin, Boston University) is Associate Professor of Practical Ministry, Regent University, Virginia Beach, VA, USA.

This paper unearths three of the precluded yet key historic pastors, whose legacies reveal that along with the noted speeches, marches, fights for legal rights and opportunities, and non-violent protests, music and worship played a great part in softening racial divisions at the grassroots level: John Jasper, founder of the Sixth Mount Zion Baptist Church of Richmond, VA, founded in 1867, William Seymour and the Azusa Street Mission of Los Angeles, CA in 1906, and William Herbert Brewster, pastor of East Trigg Avenue Baptist Church of South Memphis, TN in the 1930's to 1987. Notably, each of these cases reflects surprising moments of racial integration during a time in history when racial hostility was common in American society. Whites were hanging Blacks, scrubbing their hands after shaking Black people's hands, using separate restrooms marked 'white people only', and more. Blacks were planting their own churches as Whites assembled in their predominately White churches. Church historian Vinson Synan points out that for Blacks and Whites to participate in integrated worship services during the Jim Crow era and with a Black minister in charge, employing traditional Black spirituality in worship was a miracle at the time.[1]

African American Worship

This study focuses on three cases – two of which are located within the context of the Black Baptist tradition, and one is the situation of early 20th century American Pentecostalism. First, this work locates the origins of Black worship as distinctively an emergence from African spirituality with accompanying expressions. The difference between Black worship and White worship seemed clearer until the latter quarter of the 20th century. No definition for Black worship was necessary. However, the multi-racial/cultural impact of both integration and the influx in immigration has redefined worship experiences. Therefore, a cogent explanation for what this work means by Black worship becomes necessary.

This work focuses on traditional Black worship as defined by spirituality that is stirred by rousing sermons, call and response, fervent prayer, soul-stirring music, shouting, dancing, and passionate

---

[1] Antipas L. Harris. Interview with Vinson Synan. Regent University, Virginia Beach, VA, April 3, 2014.

testimony. The Pentecostal worship experience of the early 20th century separated mainline Black churches from the Black Holiness–Pentecostal churches, mainly on the issue of speaking in tongues, holy dancing, and incorporating drums, guitars, and wind instruments as part of the worship experience. Yet most Black churches' commonalities in preaching styles, singing, shouting, prayers, and testimonies were characteristic of Black worship, broadly speaking. Holiness–Pentecostal worship expanded upon Black worship in most Black churches. The common thread was the extension of African spirituality in Christian worship.

Black Christians had to break through the cultural constraints imposed upon them by White religious and cultural domination. From the transport across the Atlantic Ocean, Blacks had been treated as animals in need of White domestication. This included their indigenous worship expressions that accompanied their spirituality in Africa. On occasion and sporadically, in the Jim Crow period, a few African American leaders led grassroots movements that exposed Black worship's capacity to forge unity despite the country's landscape of racial division.

Theologian Frederick L. Ware points out,

> Worship that touches the emotions reaches people where they are, in the realm of qualitative distinctions, the place at which they live out their lives. This realm or place is where people gauge their lives by the barometers of success and failure, joy and sorrow, happiness and frustration, want and need, comfort and pain.[2]

The phenomenon of Black spirituality in worship engages persons on such levels of emotions, helping people to encounter God in a way that 'affects all aspects of the believer's life, his or her intellect is touched by God as well'.[3] Understood in this way, traditional Black worship possessed the gift needed during the Jim Crow era to connect Black and White believers to God's love and compassion. By doing so, Black worship also proved to possess the capacity for lifting Blacks and Whites beyond their civil and political differences

---

[2] Frederick L. Ware, 'The Church of God in Christ and the Azusa Street Revival', in Harold D. Hunter and Cecil M. Robeck Jr. (eds.), *The Azusa Street Revival and Its Legacy* (Eugene, OR: Wipf and Stock, 2009), p. 251.

[3] Ware, 'The Church of God in Christ and the Azusa Street Revival', p. 251.

to connect as human beings, children of the one God. The worship realm or sacred space becomes more than a cultural experience but a theological embodiment of a divine call for human beings to live out the image of God as one Body of Christ.

Black Worship and Racial Unity in the Jim Crow Era

Just two years after the Civil War ended, in the heart of the war-torn capital of the Confederate States of America, Richmond, Virginia, Rev. John Jasper was probably the most prominent former slave preacher who led worship out of the Black Baptist worship tradition and drew Blacks and Whites together in the establishment of the historic Sixth Mount Zion Baptist Church. At the turn of the century, Rev. William Seymour, a son of former slaves, grew up in Centerville, Louisiana, and then by way of Houston, Texas began an itinerant ministry in Los Angeles. Seymour led one of the most prominent Great Awakenings in modern History. That movement continues today, a movement rooted in worship approaches that emerged from a freedom of worship expression that was characteristic of Black worship. At the precipice of the Civil Rights Movement another worship experience cultivated amicable race relations in the heart of the Bible Belt. Rev. Herbert Brewster's Sunday evening radio show in Memphis became the talk of the town. An uncommon worship experience with Black and Whites crowded East Trigg Avenue Baptist Church, a Black church in the heart of the racially segregated city of Memphis, TN.

The above cases provide not only insight into the grassroots role that Black worship played in leading racial healing during Jim Crow, but also at a deeper level, these examples implicate theological values that are intrinsic to free and expressive worship. The expressed freedom of the body, soul, and spirit in traditional Black worship has served as invitation to a divine gravity, which draws together the kaleidoscope of ethnic diversity to a holy unity. As such, they imply a broader theological vision that worship has potential to sustain ethnic integration within an increasingly multicultural world.

Jasper and the Richmond Contribution to African American Theology of Worship

Rev. Jasper was a Baptist preacher; and, as a Baptist, he was not part of a denomination that promoted a doctrine of speaking in tongues like the Pentecostals would after the turn of the century. Moreover, when he was still a slave, Jasper was seeking God for answers and had a spiritual experience that he calls 'a conversion'. Perhaps the experience was comparable to what Wesleyans typically refer to as John Wesley's 'heartwarming experience' at Aldersgate in 1738. Pentecostals sometimes locate Wesley's experience as similar to a Pentecostal experience. In like manner, Jasper describes his 'conversion experience' as deeply spiritual. It bears similarities to a description of Pentecostal worship led by African Americans that would explode around the globe after the turn of the century.

A White scholar, William E. Hatcher, one of Jasper's contemporaries, wrote Jasper's biography. Though Jasper was Baptist, Hatcher's record of the emotional character of his conversion testimony in some ways seems similar to stories from early Black Pentecostals – from a later period. According to Hatcher, Jasper explained his 'conversion' experience in the following way.

> I was seekin' God six long weeks – jes' 'cause I was sich a fool I couldn't see de way De Lord struck me fus' on Cap'tal Squar', an' I left thar badly crippled. One July mornin' somethin' happen'd. I was a tobarker-stemmer – dat is, I took de tobarker leaf, an' tor'd de stem out, an' dey won't no one in dat fac'ry could beat me at dat work. But dat mornin' de stems wouldn't come out to save me, an' I tor'd up tobarker by de poun' an' flung it under de table. Fac' is, bruthr'n, de darkness of death was in my soul dat mornin'. My sins was piled on me like mount'ns; my feet was sinkin' down to de reguns of despar, an' I felt dat of all sinners I was de wust. I tho't dat I would die right den, an' wid what I supposed was my lars breath I flung up to heav'n a cry for mercy. 'Fore I kno'd it, de light broke; I was light as a feather; my feet was on de mount'n; salvation rol'd like a flood thru my soul, an' I felt as if I could 'nock off de fact'ry roof wid my shouts.

'But I sez to mysef, I gwine to hol' still till dinner, an' so I cried, an' laffed, an' tore up de tobarker. Pres'ntly I looked up de table, an' dar was a old man – he luv me, an' tried hard to lead me out de darkness, an' I slip roun' to whar he was, an' I sez in his ear as low as I could: 'Hallelujah; my soul is redeemed!' Den I jump back quick to my work, but after I once open my mouf it was hard to keep it shet any mo'... all I know'd I had raise my fust shout to de glory of my Redeemer.[4]

The uncontrollable worship that is expressed throughout Jasper's conversion testimony epitomizes a spirituality that is best understood through an African religious hermeneutic. Henry H. Mitchell points out that within the Black church tradition, there is an apparent parallel between the human emotive expressions of the anointing of the Holy Spirit in Scripture and the common notion of spirit possession from ancient Africa of being possessed by deity.[5]

After his conversion experience, Jasper grew in popularity as a preacher. He later founded Sixth Mount Zion Baptist Church. In general, the worship experience at the Black Baptist church was very different from the worship experience of most slave owners' churches. Hatcher describes the slave masters' churches as having been integrated. Yet, other sources suggest that the slaves were not able to sit together in an integrated fashion at slave masters' churches. Also, as Hatcher points out,

> The church buildings were always constructed so that the white people and the negroes could worship in the same house. They were baptized by the same minister, they sat down together at the communion table, they heard the same sermons, sang the same songs, were converted at the same meetings, and were baptized at the same time.[6]

Other records confirm Hatcher's historical account of Blacks and Whites in worship together during slavery; yet Hatcher's account does not mention the important caveat that slaves were not integrated into the worship experience as leaders in worship. Many

---

[4] William Eldridge Hatcher, *John Jasper, the Unmatched Negro Philosopher and Preacher* (New York: Fleming H. Revell, 2nd edn, 1908), pp. 24-25.
[5] Henry H. Mitchell, *Black Belief: Folk Beliefs of Blacks in America and West Africa* (New York: Harper and Row, 1975), pp. 136-52.
[6] Hatcher, *John Jasper*, p. 44.

other sources suggest that the slaves participated in the services from the periphery, the balcony, or on the outside. The White slave masters' preachers conducted the services. Slaves learned Scripture from the White slave masters' preacher; yet, they felt spiritually unfulfilled. Hatcher further explains, 'Oft times, and in almost all places, they were allowed to have services by themselves. In this, of course, they enjoyed a larger freedom than when they met in the same house with the white people'.[7] When the White pastors would allow them the space to hold their own services, the Black slaves' indigenous spiritual instincts compelled them to express their worship to God in a way that only the Black slaves could, as Hatcher calls it, 'they enjoyed a larger freedom'. The 'freedom' in worship expresses a theology of African American worship that has survived until today. African American worship is theological, not based on doctrinal statements, nor based on the content of sermons. It is theological because it stirs up spirituality that ushers a supernatural presence in the midst. The divine presence in worship not only affirms the marginalized but also draws people to a common spiritual place. It bears the potential for helping to overcome differences and creating a space of love and unity.

Hatcher describes Jasper's worship leadership in the following manner:

> His prayer had such contagious and irresistible eloquence that whatever the Lord did about it, it surely brought quite a resistless response from the crowd. When the white preacher ended his tame and sapless address, the multitude cried out for Jasper ... Jasper took fire and on eagle wings he mounted into the heavens and gave such a brilliant and captivating address that the vast crowd went wild with joy and enthusiasm.[8]

Noting the impact of the African American worship experience on Jasper's multi-racial/cultural audiences, Hatcher adds,

> He [Jasper] ... drew crowds that could not be accommodated. When it was rumoured that Jasper was to preach ... the Rev. Dr. Keene, of the First Baptist Church, and many other white people attended. They were much concerned lest his coming should

---

[7] Hatcher, *John Jasper*, p. 44.
[8] Hatcher, *John Jasper*, p. 42.

produce a disturbance, and they went with the idea of preventing any undue excitement. Jasper, flaming with fervid zeal and exhilarated with the freedom of the truth, carried everything before him. He had not preached long before the critical white people were stirred to the depths of their souls and their emotion showed in their weeping.[9]

The unexpected emotion that Hatcher explains as part of the White experience in Jasper's services reaches beyond the charisma of the Black preacher. The stirring to the depths of their souls was the Holy Spirit at work amidst a worship context that has been cultivated to welcome the Holy Spirit's presence. So the White people who came as spectators were engulfed by the presence of such spirituality.

Among the White people who attended this Black Baptist preacher's meetings were the Virginia Governor, legislators, and White social elite. Some Whites were highly suspicious of the congregating of Blacks. In 1831, the slave Baptist preacher Nat Turner led a slave revolt, claiming his faith as impetus for it. Undoubtedly, the officials' earnest interest in Jasper's meetings may have been coupled with their keen awareness that since the Nat Turner case in 1831, there were strict laws in Virginia to regulate Black preachers from inciting an uprising.[10] However, the Civil War had ended. A new day was on the horizon; yet, the clutch of the Jim Crow era bore lingering attitudes and suspicions from slavery. One of Jasper's White contemporaries Peter Randolph reports that some of the Whites argued, 'If the Negroes were set free they would murder and kill the white people. But instead of that, they were praising God …'[11] Moreover, contrary to the many White people's suspicions to meet chaos, they had an encounter with God that drew them into the time of worship and adoration to God.

While the assembly of believers is a notable value in all worship experiences, Jasper led worship in the Black tradition that supersed-

---

[9] Hatcher, *John Jasper*, p. 45.

[10] According to June Purcell Guild, *Black Laws of Virginia: A Summary of the Legislative Acts of Virginia Concerning Negroes from Earliest Times to the Present* (Richmond, VA: Whittet & Shepperson, 1936), p. 107, in 1831 the Virginia Legislature passed the following bill: '… It is enacted that no slave, free Negro or mulatto shall preach, or hold any meeting for religious purposes either day or night'.

[11] Peter Randolph, *From Slave Cabin to Pulpit* (ed. Paul D. Sporter; Chester, NY: Anza Publishing, 2004), p. 31.

ed only one quality that is indispensable to the worship gathering. There were multiple facets that impacted the worshiper – from the message of his sermons to his way of preaching to the apparent love that filled the worship space.

Hatcher describes a freedom in worship that was unique to Black worship. More than characteristic of Black culture, that freedom applied in their worship welcomed a divine moment. For example, Hatcher describes a time when Jasper was preaching on the power of God at the crossing of the Red Sea. He depicts Jasper's worshipful animation in this way:

> Jasper himself was leading the host, cheering, shouting to them not to be afraid, and telling them that God would bring them safely through. It looked to me as if half of the women were clapping their hands and dancing, and the other half were rolling off the benches in the excess of the rapture, as the last of the children of Israel cam trudging out upon the banks.[12]

Alongside the Black people, when Jasper preached, White people were 'stirred to the depths of their souls and the emotion showed in their weeping' because his worship fostered a meeting place between the people and God. As diverse ethnic groups open up to the 'larger freedom' that the slaves had discovered, they encountered God together. That spiritual experience in a 'larger freedom' of worship in the African American tradition was more than a vertical encounter with God. It was also equally a horizontal encounter with God in creating space with potential for racial unity.

Furthermore, Jasper's legacy impressed upon the entire religious culture in the Richmond area and beyond. As proof of Jasper's worship influence, historian Vinson Synan says that during his time at the University of Richmond in the early sixties, the White ministry students were called affectionately 'Jaspers'.[13]

---

[12] Hatcher, *John Jasper*, p. 161.
[13] Harris, Interview with Vinson Synan.

Seymour and the Los Angeles Contribution to African American Pentecostal Contribution to African American Theology of Worship

Seymour began his ministry as a Holiness preacher from the Church of God headquartered in Anderson, Indiana. His search for ministry preparation landed him at Charles Parham's classroom door in Houston, Texas in 1905. He could not sit in the classroom with White people because of the Jim Crow segregation laws. There Seymour learned all that he could about the Holy Spirit and the accompanying gift of speaking in tongues. He then journeyed to Los Angeles and launched the Azusa Street Mission in 1906. The one-eyed Black revivalist preached in obscurity until he landed on the front page of the *Los Angeles Times*. On April 18th, 1906, in a scathing article called 'A Weird Babel of Tongues', the journalist mocked what signaled the potential for a great stride in race relations in this way: 'Colored people and a sprinkling of whites compose the congregation, and night is made hideous in the neighborhood by the howlings of the worshippers who spend hours swaying forth and back in a nerve-racking attitude of prayer and supplication'.[14]

With the exception of speaking in tongues, the worship expressions described at the Azusa Street Mission were not new to some of the Black Christians who were accustomed to spending time in their own worship space.[15] In fact, when Charles Parham learned about the outpouring of the Holy Spirit with accompanying tongues at Azusa Street, he was first both flattered and excited that his teaching on speaking in tongues as initial evidence of Spirit Baptism was influential in the newfound outpouring of the gifts of the Spirit.[16] However, when Parham visited Azusa Street, he was shocked with the worship experience. Contrary to the complaints by many

---

[14] Referenced in Vinson Synan, *The Holiness-Pentecostal Tradition: Charismatic Movements in the Twentieth Century* (Grand Rapids, MI: Eerdmans, 1997), p. 85, and in Philip Zaleski and Carol Zaleski, *Prayer: A History* (New York: Houghton Mifflin, 2006), p. 180.

[15] African American freedom in worship that dates back to the slave church experiences that Hatcher references in his discourse on John Jasper and the former slave worship meetings. Many African American historians share a similar description of slave worship.

[16] Later documents reveal, however, that Seymour and Parham disagreed on some doctrinal issues such as Parham's eighth day creation and the annihilation of the wicked.

White bystanders, Parham was less concerned with the integration of Whites and Blacks in worship;[17] but, he favored a calmer environment similar to the ones that he had led from a traditional American church perspective. The integration of African American slave approaches to worship was off-putting to him. Parham commented,

> What makes my soul sick at my stomach is to see white people imitating unintelligent, crude negroisms of the Southland, and laying it on the Holy Spirit.[18]

Stuck in the Jim Crow mindset, Parham wanted the 'conditions' to be controlled by White leadership in a White framework.[19] He could not accept a divinely sanctioned situation wherein what Hatcher calls the African Americans 'larger freedom' of worship would become prominent worship that attracts the full participation of Whites. When Parham saw this, he was convinced that things had gotten out of hand and that God was not in it. Using strongly critical language, Parham in another place reflected on the Azusa Street Revival in this way:

> Men and women, whites and blacks, knelt together or fell across one another; frequently, a white woman, perhaps of wealth and culture, could be seen thrown back in the arms of a buck nigger, and held tightly thus as she shivered and shook in freak imitation of Pentecost. Horrible, awful shame![20]

In a recent article, Eddie Hyatt offers a sympathetic read of Parham's attitude toward race relations.[21] Hyatt continues the James R.

---

[17] Vinson Synan and Charles R. Fox Jr., *William J. Seymour: Pioneer of the Azusa Street Revival* (Alachua, FL: Bridge Logos, 2012), p. 74, note that Parham believed in interracial 'cooperation' as evident in his relationship with Lucy Farrow from Norfolk and Seymour while in Houston.

[18] Charles F. Parham, 'Sermon by Charles F. Parham', *Apostolic Faith* (Baxter Springs, AR) 3 (April 1925), p. 10; quoted in Synan and Fox, *William J. Seymour*, p. 74, and in Robert Mapes Anderson, *Vision of the Disinherited: The Making of American Pentecostalism* (New York: Oxford University Press, 1979), p. 190.

[19] Synan and Fox, *William J. Seymour*, p. 74.

[20] Charles F. Parham, 'Free Love', *Apostolic Faith* (Baxter Springs, AR) 1.10 (December 1912), p. 405, and Synan and Fox, *William J. Seymour*, p. 74.

[21] Eddie Hyatt, 'Across the Lines: Charles Parham's Contribution to the Inter-Racial Character of Early Pentecostalism', *Pneuma Review* 17.4 (Fall 2014). Online: no page numbers. http://pneumareview.com/across-the-lines-charles-parhams-

Goff thought[22] that insists that because Parham befriended Seymour, Farrow, and other Blacks, and risked his religious affiliation with the Black Pentecostals, having them to preach at his meetings, he should not be considered in the category of racists of the early 20th century. Hyatt, argues further that Parham's legacy should be counted among the heroes of race relations among early Pentecostals.[23] Hyatt's point only makes sense through lenses that evade the value that the unique contribution that African American spirituality in worship played in the issue of racial relations. While Parham may have been more sympathetic to Black people than many of his contemporaries, importantly Parham failed to see that it was the 'larger freedom', which is characteristic of traditional African American worship, that opened up the spiritual space in which the Holy Spirit (not Parham) used African American leaders (not Parham) to unify the races in a time when racial unity was not a popular phenomenon in the larger society. On the issue of spirituality, Parham did more to frustrate the Spirit's work in racial unity than to characterize or perpetuate it. In this way, Parham was indeed culturally racist, while he sought to move beyond superficial presentations of racism.

Because Parham's offensive polemics against African American worship could not correct the early move of the Spirit in the midst, the multi-racial/cultural worship experience at the Azusa Street Revival quickly exploded. African American worship pointed toward the capacity of African American spirituality to lead in overcoming Jim Crow's segregated society. Not fully comprehended, it forced a re-segregation among races. As the movement continued toward the 1920s, cultural biases of the Jim Crow era started to seep into the formation of ecclesial bodies that resulted from the Azusa Street Revival. At this point, worship was no longer the main focus. Rather, church development with organizing structures overshadowed the capacity of unity that the worship had established. Most Pentecostal denominations that resulted from the Azusa Street Revival, however, tended to mimic a similar African American 'larger freedom' in worship within their own segregated settings. Stated differ-

---

contribution-to-the-inter-racial-character-of-early-pentecostalism/ Accessed Mar. 7, 2015.

[22] James R. Goff Jr., *Fields White Unto Harvest* (Fayetteville, AR: University of Arkansas Press, 1988), p. 108.

[23] Hyatt, 'Across the Lines'.

ently; the White Pentecostals learned how to express deeper spirituality in worship from early African American Pentecostals. White Pentecostals valued Black spirituality as an asset to anyone's spirituality in worship. Yet, as a whole, until today, White Pentecostals cannot see themselves in submission to African American leadership – another topic for another article.

Brewster and the Memphis Contribution to African American Theology of Worship

Herbert W. Brewster was a well-loved pastor at East Trigg Street Baptist Church in Memphis. Vinson Synan was amidst the young White people from his Pentecostal Holiness Church in Memphis who joined the integrated worship experience. In an interview with Synan, he reports that Whites loved the worship at that Black Church.[24] In addition to the Whites from the Pentecostal Holiness Church on Lamar Avenue, other young Whites attended from the First Assembly of God Church on Mclemore Avenue, among whom was the soon to be famous young Elvis Presley.

It is widely reported that, at the height of his rock and roll career, Presley admitted that the Black church and Gospel music influenced his music. Presley attended the late night musicals at East Trigg Street Baptist Church. Though Synan says that he never met Presley personally, he confirms that each of their church's youth groups attended the same services at East Trigg Baptist Church. Synan explains, 'East Trigg Street Baptist church was where the big crossover was. Every Sunday night at 11 pm, even the bishops of the white churches, church leaders, but mainly the young people, came and just loved the music and the preaching'.[25]

Synan comments that Black worship at East Trigg Baptist Church miraculously drew Blacks and Whites together during his experience of the Jim Crow era in the 1950s similarly to how Black worship was the center of attraction in Jasper's meetings just after the Civil War and in Seymour's meetings just after the turn of the century. Synan recalls the power and influence of Black worship at East Trigg Street Baptist Church in the following manner:

---

[24] Harris, Interview with Vinson Synan.
[25] Harris, Interview with Vinson Synan.

WDIA was a popular radio station in Memphis at the time. WDIA played mainly Black music. All of my friends would listen to that music all day long. One of the places we went to hear gospel music was East Street Baptist Church. They had an 11pm Sunday night broadcast. Rev. Brewster would preach a short 5 or 10 min. sermon. He was a very dynamic preacher and had a great choir. He had great soloists. Queen C. Anderson was one of them. She had a deep heavy bass voice for a lady. People would shout and jump out of their seats when she would sing, 'These are they who have come through the great tribulation'. There was also a blind soloist. His name was Lee Cunningham. He was a great soloist. Then, they had a black lady who I call a shouter. She sat up on the platform. She would shout at different times – stand up and shout. Her stockings would roll down; you knew that you had hit the height of the service when her stockings hit her ankles. That was something that we would remember. Also when the choir was singing people would get happy … Some of the sisters and brothers would get happy and shout. The deacons would form a circle around someone who was shouting and dancing and kind of walk them out to the back some times – for their own protection, afraid they might fall.[26]

As implied here, Synan does not hesitate to admit that the worship at East Trigg Street Baptist Church was the center of the inter-racial draw. As with Jasper and Seymour, the Whites came from various echelons of society and from various theological traditions for the Black worship experience. If the issue were doctrinal, the likelihood for the draw of such diversity would have been less than favorable. However, traditional Black worship has a way of moving beyond the impasses that doctrine, theological traditions, and, importantly, racial faction create. Before they knew it, Whites and Blacks experience a racial unity that only the Holy Spirit brings.

Brewster's case like the other two – in Richmond and in Los Angeles – took place during the Jim Crow era. Synan expresses that while during his time in Memphis, he and his friends loved to listen to the Black music on WDIA, nothing beat the experience of being in worship together with the Blacks on Sunday nights.[27] Although

---

[26] Harris, Interview with Vinson Synan.
[27] Harris, Interview with Vinson Synan.

Presley pursued a career in Rock and Roll, he chose to stir up the Spirit on one of his records by recording 'I've Got Confidence', a song written by Andraé Crouch, a young Black Pentecostal contemporary of Presley. Presley and others not only loved the songs that they sang, they were drawn to the 'larger freedom' in African American worship that stirred a deep spirituality in the human soul.

Further, Synan explains that there was an obvious decrease in the worship integration that the Whites and Blacks in Memphis had enjoyed just after the Civil Rights Movement. Similarly to the climate just after the Civil War mentioned above, Whites were afraid that Blacks would reject them and even become hostile as a result of a culture of White oppression under the Jim Crow era. One wonders if the American Church has struggled to return to the leading role that African Americans once played in a theology of worship, creating space for racial integration.

Conclusion

Jasper, Seymour, and Brewster have two main attributes in common. They were African Americans, and they were preachers. The common thread stringing through these commonalities is that they poured deep spirituality with accompanying expressions from their former African history into their Christian experience. The mingling of indigenous expressions with Christian spirituality proved subversive to a culture of racial division between Whites and Blacks. These African American preachers' worship spaces drew together Whites and Blacks when it was unpopular to do so.

Glimpses into these historical episodes suggest that during the Jim Crow era, African Americans displayed an aptitude for drawing upon their historical cultural resources to create a deeply spiritual worship context for racial reconciliation within a Christian context. They draw attention not only to African American worship but also to African American leadership. Before the Civil War, a young slave Richard Allen led a group of African Americans out of a White slave master's Methodist church to start their own church after being denied communion at the altar. It was 1794. The slaves were tired of a culture of worship oppression. They learned about God from the slave owners, but their worship was uniquely their own, and they needed full freedom to worship God. White oppression over Black slaves was in full fling. Blacks could not sit together with the Whites nor could they worship at the altar with Whites. The potential for worship as racial reconciler was squandered, leaving the slaves with nothing better than to start their own church – the African Methodist Episcopal Church.

A little less than a century later, in Richmond, Jasper, the former slave, pastored a church wherein he welcomed the interested White people to be part of the worship experience. More than mere interest drew White people to worship together with Black people. It was the premium placed on a 'larger freedom' in Spirit-filled worship formed by African American Spirituality. Seymour often explained the worship experience at the Azusa Street Revival as one that frees the heart to love God and others. Whether Jasper's 'shout to de glory of [the] Redeemer'[28] or 'unintelligent, crude negroism of the Southland'[29] expressed at the Azusa Street Revival, African American worship opens up the human soul to a common spiritual experience whether White, Black, or others.

African American spirituality was born out of thousands of years that nurtured their ancestors' indigenous spirituality in Africa. African American Christians transferred that spiritual heritage on to their newly found religion, Christianity. It is that dynamic spirituality – which William Hatcher describes as 'a larger freedom in worship'[30] – that opened up the windows of heaven. The gravity of a unified human dignity was formed under that heavenly worship experience. Anyone who was amidst that spiritual experience in worship not only experienced God but also experienced the capacity of human persons to move beyond the evils of humanity to love and cherish one another – a distinctive spirituality in worship that was neither commonplace among slave masters' churches nor White churches during the Jim Crow era.

Tying love in unity with the worship experience at Azusa Street, Seymour explained, 'Divine love ... is the real biblical evidence'[31] that the worship expressions of rousing sermons, call and response, fervent prayer, soul-stirring music, and passionate testimony were

---

[28] Hatcher, *John Jasper*, p. 25.

[29] Parham, 'Sermon by Charles F. Parham,' p. 10.

[30] Hatcher, *John Jasper*, p. 44.

[31] William J. Seymour, 'Questions Answered', *Apostolic Faith* 1.11 (October to January 1908), p. 2; cited in Synan and Fox, *William J. Seymour*, p. 78.

authentic. Synan agrees that in Memphis, Brewster's services were all the more beautiful because the intensity of worship moved beyond racial and denominational boundaries and caused a 'miracle' in Memphis in the 1950s. Each of these cases imply a broader theological potential for traditional African American 'larger freedom' in worship to create continued spaces for love and to foster unity.

14

BETWIXT AND BETWEEN THE CROSS AND THE ESCHATON: PENTECOSTAL WORSHIP IN THE CONTEXT OF RITUAL PLAY

Peter Althouse[*]

Worship in a Pentecostal setting is a narrowly defined term that refers to the segment of the liturgy that occurs primarily in the first half of the service and is accompanied by music and congregational singing. Simply called praise and worship, this segment incorporates variations of music, singing, kinesthetic expressions such as standing, swaying, clapping, vocal and sacred utterances, testimonies, charismatic rites such as glossolalia, signs and wonders, prophecy, falling (or fainting) under the power of the Spirit, and so on. However, worship in a more general sense designates the totality of Pentecostal liturgical practices such as preaching, prayers, speech acts, transitions, processions, and recessions. At a macro-level, Pentecostal liturgies may include evangelistic services, revival meetings, healing services, musicals of one kind or another, as well as various kinds of age specific services such as youth or children's services, para-church organizations, education, and fellowship events. Pentecostal worship in the general sense constitutes the ritual practices

[*] Peter Althouse (PhD, University of St. Michael's College and Toronto School of Theology [at the University of Toronto]) is Professor of Religion and Theology at Southeastern University, Lakeland, FL, USA.

that form the symbolic meanings of the Pentecostal worldview and sanction ways of feeling, behaving, and believing.[1]

Is the language of ritual or the more theological term of liturgy not counterintuitive when discussing Pentecostal worship? Pentecostals have traditionally rejected ritual and liturgy as dead and meaningless, preferring instead the spontaneity of the Spirit and fresh spiritual experiences. Daniel Albrecht is correct to insist however that Pentecostals misunderstand ritual and in fact engage in ritual settings, but describe it as spiritual practices, distinctives, or worship. Albrecht then defines ritual as acts, actions, dramas, and performances created by the sacred community that recognizes and sanctions modes of behavior, attitudes, sensibilities, values and beliefs. Rites are particular phases in the liturgy that designate specific actions that are recognized by Pentecostals as legitimate in the overall corporate ritual. By way of illustration, a revival or healing service are ritual events, while glossolalia and anointing with oil are liturgical rites.[2] Albrecht draws on the metaphor of ritual performance in his delineation of Pentecostal–charismatic spirituality, but fails to capture the metaphor of play in his analysis. Ritual play is a lens through which an understanding of the varieties of Pentecostal worship is particularly salient for understanding Pentecostal ritual in a way that bridges both scientific and theological analyses.

In this chapter I shall argue that Pentecostal styles of worship can be understood through the analysis of ritual studies. Specifically, in Pentecostal worship participants enter a liminal phase in which various types of ritual play are engaged. Liminality is connected to ritual play in that liminal play employs the subjunctive ('as if') mood rather than the indicative ('as is') mood. Understanding worship as space for liminal play also has implications for theological notions

---

[1] See Daniel E. Albrecht, *Rites in the Spirit: A Ritual Approach to Pentecostal/Charismatic Spirituality* (JPTSup 17; Sheffield: Sheffield Academic Press, 1999), pp. 252-59; also see Joel Robbins, 'Pentecostal Networks and the Spirit of Globalization: On the Social Productivity of Ritual Forms', in B. Kapferer *et al.* (eds.), *Contemporary Religiosities: Emergent Socialities and the Post-Nation-State* (New York: Berghahn Books, 2009), pp. 55-66. For a general discussion on ritual see Catherine Bell, *Ritual: Perspectives and Dimensions* (New York: Oxford University Press, 1997), and R. Grimes, *Beginnings in Ritual Studies* (Lanham, MD: University Press of America, 1982).

[2] Albrecht, *Rites in the Spirit*, pp. 21-22. Although Albrecht is more careful of differentiating ritual from rite, I am more comfortable with using rite and rituals synonymously.

of the pneumatological and eschatological imagination. In other words, in the context of Pentecostal worship the subjunctive is engaged in which the community of faith remembers the redemptive life and work of Christ 'as if' it is tangible reality in the present and hopes for the coming eschatological day 'as if' the Spirit is already making its dawning a reality. The subjunctive spurs the coming of faith to imagine its possibilities and potentialities in hope. In order to accomplish this task I shall first discuss the theoretical orientations of liminality and ritual play that comes out of the social sciences. Secondly, I shall propose a typology of ritual play in which I will place various kinds of Pentecostal worship and spirituality along a continuum of types. Pentecostalism is a vastly differentiated movement in which no one style of Pentecostal worship takes precedence. It makes more sense to speak of Pentecostal styles of worship than Pentecostal worship as a tightly defined category without variation. Finally, I will suggest some theological implications of liminality and ritual play. Engaging Jean Jacque Suurmond and Wolfgang Vondey in particular, I shall argue that in the interplay between the rules and boundaries of ritual play (Word) and the unlimited and open possibilities of the kingdom coming (Spirit), the imagination is inspired to glimpse and grasp the realities of the future kingdom.

Liminality and Ritual Play

The transformative role of religious ritual in the life of the faith community is a subject taken up by cultural anthropologist Victor Turner. Drawing on E. Durkheim's symbolic interactionism and E. van Gennep's theories of rites of passage, Turner addresses the symbolic significance of ritual in providing liminal space for creativity and imagination. In the ritual setting, participants pass through pre-liminal, liminal, and post-liminal phases in which they step out of the expectation and structures of society into a 'betwixt and between' phase of possibilities and potentialities. Liminality (literally 'threshold') is, according to Turner, a kind of anti-structure in which profane social relations are set aside, rights and obligations are suspended, and the participants engage the sacred in complex episodes of sacred space-time through subversive, playful events. This anti-structure is capable of storing alternative models of reality that can influence mainstream social structure and therefore direct social change.[3] In ritual, people 'play' with familiar social elements or symbols in unfamiliar ways through which novelty emerges. Liminality takes on playful characteristics in which anti-structure provides potential alternatives and innovation to the structures of the social systems. Games, fiestas, festivals, and costuming become ritual disorders and rites of reversal that provide cultural creativity and potentiality for change.[4] An important aspect of ritual for Turner is the ludic or playful quality.

The playful quality of ritual has been a subject of interest for some time. Johan Huizinga[5] and Roger Caillois[6] were interested in understanding the role of play in culture. Huizinga describes the human as '*homo ludens*' (man the player) because he thought the categories of '*homo sapein*' (man the knower) and '*homo faber*' (man the maker) were insufficient for understanding the human species.[7] Although too broad in his assessment, Huizinga saw play as the basis for the developments in civilization. For Huizinga, play was first of all free without the coercion of biological determinist elements or moral duty. Second, play was disinterested in satisfying needs such as food or shelter or maximizing life interests such as economic or political advances. Third, play is distinct from ordinary life in that it creates its own time and space, direction and meaning. Finally, play creates its own order in the limitation of time and space. Play is subjunctive and embraces the quality of imagination where ritual action can glimpse possibilities through the rearrangement of cultural elements and hope for potential outcomes. In the betwixt and between of the liminality of ritual play, people can imagine through their thoughts, sentiments and actions a potential reality as if that reality exists now.

---

[3] Victor Turner, *From Ritual to Theatre: The Human Seriousness of Play* (New York: Performing Arts Journal Publications, 1982), p. 33. Turner differentiates between liminal, as ritual practices from tribal cultures, and liminoid as ritual practices in the modern societies. For simplicity, I prefer to use liminal to describe the phases of ritual in all situations (p. 28).

[4] Turner, *From Ritual to Theatre*, pp. 24-28.

[5] J. Huizinga, *Homo Ludens: A Study of the Play-Element in Culture* (Boston: Beacon Press, 1950).

[6] Roger Caillois, *Man, Play and Games* (trans. Meyer Barash; Chicago: University of Chicago Press, 1961).

[7] Huizinga, *Homo Ludens*, pp. ix-x.; see James H. Evans, Jr., *Playing* (Minneapolis: Fortress Press, 2010), pp. 4-5.

Caillois develops Huizinga's work but criticizes it as too idealistic. Specifically, Caillois suggests that play is subversive and revolutionary and occurs in particular settings in time and space. Moreover, although subversive to ordinary or mundane structures, play, while free and undetermined, occurs in structures with rules and boundaries. In other words, play occurs in the context of the game that provides the boundaries for the free innovation of play.[8] Caillois also categorizes play into four categories: competition, chance, simulation, and vertigo – a topic we will pick up below.[9]

Rituals of play are a theme picked up by social scientists and theologians and applied to the understanding of Pentecostalism. André Droogers uses the lens of play to analyze Brazilian and Chilean Pentecostalism. On the one hand, Droogers argues that understanding the role of religion is facilitated by the subjunctive of play. Through the subjunctive, humans become aware of other possible dimensions of reality and are able to transpose between the different dimensions. According to Droogers,

> The capacity to deal at the same time with two or more ways of classifying reality makes use of symbolic means to introduce the idea of an extra dimension of reality. From the double perspective revealed in the ability to play, people consider themselves simultaneously autonomous and dependent, unique and part of the universe ... It facilitates a possible distinction between a natural and a supernatural dimension.[10]

In the play of religious ritual, humans can intuit another reality, one that Pentecostals identify as the supernatural, the presence of the Spirit, or as the foretaste of the coming kingdom. On the other hand, Droogers also proposes methodological ludism as a non-reductionistic approach to the study of religion. Specifically, Droogers employs methodological play as a way in which ethnographers can step inside the worldview of the persons under study. The subjunctive mode allows the participant observer to embrace the other's worldview 'as if' it is one's own, while simultaneously

---

[8] Caillois, *Man, Play and Games*, pp. 9-10; Evans, *Playing*, pp. 6-7.

[9] Caillois, *Man, Play and Games*, pp. 14-26, 81-128.

[10] André F. Droogers, 'The Third Bank of the River: Play, Methodological Ludism and the Definition of Religion', in Anton van Harskamp *et al.* (eds.), *Playful Religion: Challenges for the Study of Religion* (The Netherlands: Eburon Academic Publishers, 2006), p. 88.

embracing the rational objectives of research. Thus ludic analysis has implications for understanding the participants under observation, as well as the observer who participates in the religious world.[11]

Margaret Poloma devotes several chapters in her book *Main Street Mystics* to the investigation of charismatic worship in the charismatic revival known as the Toronto Blessing and now known as Catch the Fire. The analysis of contemporary worship music, altered states of consciousness, emotional arousal, kinesthetic and bodily behavior, fits, visions, and trances are interpreted through the lens of ritual play. The extended time of ecstatic expression is a liminal state in which participants are betwixt and between the mundane and sacred. The most controversial behaviors in the worship style of the charismatic revival – uncontrollable animal noises and behavior, falling to the ground and apparent inebriation known as being drunk in the Spirit – is explained as prophetic mime.[12] John Arnott, the pastor of the Toronto church, calls these manifestations symbolic prophecy. While most prophecy is expressed verbally, Arnott sees the ecstatic behaviors as figurative expressions.[13] Michael Wilkinson and I have recently conducted a study on Catch the Fire and likewise see the worship rituals through the lens of liminal play. In the betwixt and between of worship, participants play in the 'Father's love' in which they express themselves emotionally and bodily as they experience the presence of God. Specifically, pilgrimage to Toronto, playful worship where bodily behavior and charismatic expressions are prominent, holistic healing through forgiveness, and impartation or transference of the Spirit through touch are important play rituals enacted in liminal states.[14]

---

[11] Especially, Droogers, 'The Third Bank of the River', pp. 75-96.

[12] See chapters 2 and 3 of Margaret M. Poloma, *Main Street Mystics: The Toronto Blessing and Reviving Pentecostalism* (Walnut Creek, CA: AltaMira Press, 2003), pp. 68-75.

[13] John Arnott, *Manifestations & Prophetic Symbolism: In a Move of the Spirit* (West Sussex, UK: New Wine Press, 2008), pp. 50-51.

[14] Michael Wilkinson and Peter Althouse, *Catch the Fire: Soaking Prayer and Charismatic Renewal* (DeKalb, IL: Northern Illinois University Press, 2014), especially chapter 2. Also see Peter Althouse and Michael Wilkinson, 'Playing in the Father's Love: The Eschatological Implications of Charismatic Ritual and the Kingdom of God in Catch the Fire', *ARC: The Journal for the Faculty of Religious Studies, McGill University* 39 (2012), pp. 93-116.

Types of Pentecostal Worship

As mentioned earlier, Caillois proposes a categorization of play that Seligman, Weller, Puett, and Simon arrange in a typology. This typology is helpful for classifying and understanding different Pentecostal ritual practices. If one divides four types of ritual play into quadrants, the left side of the quadrant consists of agôn (competition) and mimicry (simulation). These two types allow the players to retain their self-control. The right side of the quadrant consists of alea (chance) and ilinx (vertigo) in which the players surrender self-control. The top tier of the quadrant affirms players' roles while the bottom tier subverts players' roles. Agôn or competitive play brings out innate skills in the player, while alea places the player at the whims of external forces that are beyond one's control. Mimicry allows the player to assume alternative identities and worldviews, while ilinx creates a sense of panic or intoxication as players give in to the forces around them.

Agôn values ritualized competition in which the external conditions are equalized so that the innate skills and qualities of the player are revealed. It sets one player or group of players against another in order to assess who is better. The competition reveals the player(s) identity – aggressive, defensive, strategist, opportunist, winner, or loser. Mundane examples include games such as chess or football, while a sacred example would be formal liturgical practices where religious participants are able to demonstrate competencies in reciting the creeds and prayers, memorizing scripture, or mastery of doctrinal explications.

Alea (literally dice) values chance, randomness, or gambling. Divinization and votive rituals are prominent in this type. Victory or defeat is not based on the player's skills, but is determined by external causes over which the player has little or no control. While players' identities are revealed in a way similar to agôn – one can be aggressive or strategize when rolling dice or playing poker – they lack control over the outcome. Alea rituals tend to be less repetitive than other types and can slip out of the subjunctive into the indicative more easily. Pleas for healing can just as easily result in a cure as not, depending on whether the gods or saints grant the request or refuse it. Seligman *et al.* place the charismatic movement in this type where votive rituals beseech the divine for help and favor thereby affirming the participant's role in the group, but in a way that one must surrender one's fate to the divine. For charismatics this means that believers surrender control to the charismatic leader (in the Weberian sense).[15]

Mimicry accepts to some extent an imaginary universe, whether children pretending to be animals or a performance in the theatre. In this kind of play, the ending is known, whether in the conclusion of a play or drama. The content of the play matters and the stage orients one to a cosmic worldview. Roles are clearly defined, but different players can assume different roles, and there is always the possibility that the player(s) self can dissolve sufficiently so that anything is possible. Everyone knows that even though donning a mask at Carnival, we revert to our mundane roles in the morning; but there is a possibility that the subverted roles will result in riot and carnage instead of good fun. People will say and do things in the betwixt and between that they would never say or do in the mundane world. Thus festivals and carnivals are secular examples of this type of ritual play. In a sacred setting, Good Friday always ends in Easter Sunday, or a preacher adopts a specific role in the performance of his or her sermon, but the role itself can take over so that the preacher's identity merges with the role being assumed.

Ilinx is a type of vertigo or panic that overtakes a person in ritual play. For children, spinning in circles or tickling connotes this type of play. Examples for adults is skiing, white-water rafting, or roller-coasters. Ilinx is giddy, ecstatic, rapturous in which all is surrendered and anything is possible. The threat of chaos is a double-edged sword that can be horrifying or exciting. It is inherently unstable and quickly routinized and institutionalized by those who fear it. Ilinx play usually ends in collapse from exhaustion, a dizzying fall, or giggling immobility. This type of ritual play can involve innovations and experimentations that can be either be reinstitutionalized or collapse into chaos. The great mystics must be incorporated into the traditions of the church, but if they are too far removed from institutional boundaries their mystical insights dissipate into the shrouds of history or transformed into a new religious

---

[15] Adam B. Seligman *et al.*, *Ritual and its Consequences: An Essay on the Limits of Sincerity* (New York: Oxford University Press, 2008), p. 80.

movement. Both mimicry and ilinx exist on the periphery of society while agôn and alea are dominant within the center of society.

Figure 1: Types of Ritual Play[16]

	Self Retains Control	Self Gives Up Control
Affirm Roles	Agôn (competition) • innate skills • competitive • ritualized battles/ games • purification • magic • sacrifice • e.g. formalized liturgies	Alea (chance) • external causes • lack control • divinization • votive ritual • follows charismatic leader • e.g. roulette, lotteries
Subvert Roles	Mimicry (simulation) • imaginary universe • rites of reversal • ritual drama • sacrifice • e.g. pretending to be lions	Ilinx (vertigo) • panic • spirit possession • intoxication • communitas • e.g. spinning, tickling

This typology is helpful for identifying and classifying all sorts of ritual interaction whether religious or secular, but for our purposes I shall limit my comments to variations in Pentecostal ritual. Of necessity, the following is a brief sketch of different forms of Pentecostal ritual as they are placed within the typology and not intended to be a thorough examination.

While Seligman *et al.*, place the charismatic movement in alea, I would suggest that there are two ways in which Pentecostal rituals fit into all four types. In one sense, specific rituals that span across the spectrum of Pentecostal-charismatic styles of worship can be role affirming or role subverting, and retains control or surrenders control. For instance, alea allows the player to play the part of a god and retains a certain amount of control, whereas ilinx differs in that the player gives up control and is possessed by the god.[17] To illustrate in the context of Pentecostalism, uttering prophecy or words

---

[16] Seligman *et al.*, *Ritual and its Consequences*, p. 78.
[17] Seligman *et al.*, *Ritual and its Consequences*, p. 78.

of wisdom, a favored Pentecostal ritual in which the speaker utters something like 'I say unto you my children', or 'thus saith the Lord', takes on the divine perspective as a type of mimicry. The speaker clearly maintains a modicum of control but assumes a subversive stance within the subjunctive. Conversely, when a person voices glossolalic utterance from within an ecstatic state, the person has surrendered control and assumes a subversive role. Glossolalic utterance can shift back into mimicry, however, when the utterance occurs in a more subdued state and sounds similar to the vocalizations uttered in earlier ritual settings by different people. In other words, the sounds of glossolalia uttered by different people are phonetically similar suggesting a learned quality. This is not intended to invalidate the rituals, but an observation of how the ritual functions in a particular community.

In a second sense, different Pentecostal–charismatic groups adopt rituals that lean to one or another quadrant depending on the group's emphases. For instance, African and Asian Pentecostal groups as well as different charismatic communities engage in deliverance ministries. The powers of darkness are believed to be the cause of sickness, poverty, and other sorts of social ills; and healing and exorcism rituals are employed to realize human wholeness and restored relations.[18] In the United States, Christian Healing Ministries is a charismatic organization that engages in prayer rituals for healing that include inner healing of emotional turmoil and deliverance from evil spirits. This type of charismatic worship is alea in the sense that one surrenders control within the dualistic worldview of good and evil spirits, but adopts a role of a petitioner.

Alternatively, in a charismatic ministry such as Catch the Fire (commonly known as the Toronto Blessing) with its festival or carnivalesque worship that includes resting in the Spirit or slain in the Spirit (when a person falls as if fainting), bodily jerks and animal noises fits into the ilinx type. If one falls to the ground spontaneously as the charismatic leader prays (referred to as under the anointing or impartations), one surrenders to those giddy forces and vertigo ensues. However, imitating the lion of Judah or an eagle is a

---

[18] See Martin Lindhardt, 'Introduction', in Martin Lindhardt (ed.), *Practicing the Faith: The Ritual Life of Pentecostal-Charismatic Christians* (New York: Berghahn Books, 2011), pp. 15-18; also Amos Yong, *In the Days of Caesar: Pentecostalism and Political Theology* (Grand Rapids, MI: Eerdmans, 2010), pp. 122-24.

kind of dramatic performance (and therefore the retention of a modicum of control but a form of imagination that subverts the performers' mundane roles, e.g., salesperson or electrician). What one does in a charismatic ritual context would not normally be replicated in the secular, though at times there may be slippage between the sacred and the secular.

Although Pentecostals in the general sense value spontaneity in their worship, sectors in some denominations have incorporated a more formal liturgical style by adopting a generic evangelicalism and therefore fit more easily into agôn. For instance, Margaret Poloma and John Green have developed a typology of Pentecostal churches from their fieldwork on the Assemblies of God (AG).[19] They identify four types of church: evangelical, traditional, charismatic, and alternative. With the adopting of evangelical modes of worship, some AG churches have developed formal liturgies, albeit with the incorporation of mass media technologies that routinize worship. While some may see this as a betrayal of the movement, other kinds of agôn rituals can be found in Pentecostal worship from its inception in the memorizing of Scripture (often done in Sunday school) or the subsuming of particular doctrines. The point is that while agôn rituals may seem counterintuitive to Pentecostal worship, they have been part of its ritual practices from the beginning.

Although brief, differentiating the kinds of Pentecostal rituals and classifying them in a typology of play helps to shore up our understanding of Pentecostal worship. Ritual play adds to Albrecht's investigation of Pentecostal ritual as performance in order to expand our knowledge of Pentecostal worship as an engagement of different types of play. I would like to shift to a theological perspective in order to suggest how ritual play can contribute to a theological discourses that value the creative and imaginative qualities of Pentecostal worship.

---

[19] Margaret M. Poloma and John C. Green, *The Assemblies of God: Godly Love and the Revitalization of American Pentecostalism* (New York: New York University Press, 2010), pp. 23-44; Adam Stewart, *The New Canadian Pentecostals* (Waterloo, Ontario: Wilfrid Laurier University Press, 2015), has traced the shift to generic evangelicalism in the Pentecostal Assemblies of Canada.

Theological Implications of Ritual Play

Play rituals are not only taken up by social scientists in their study of Pentecostalism, but have been a subject of interest to theologians as well. Jürgen Moltmann, who sees play as a revolutionary force that frees people to envision alternative futures,[20] and Harvey Cox, who wants to re-incorporate liturgical play in the religious life,[21] are two of the more prominent theologians who have discussed a theology of play. James Evans Jr. has taken up the theme of play to argue that it is a powerful ritual that subverts the inhumane and destructive powers (especially in the context of American slavery) and thereby breaks the chains of oppression.[22]

There are a few who have taken up the discussion of ritual play in their interpretation and construction of Pentecostal theology. Jean Jacques Suurmond takes ludic thought and applies it to an understanding of the divine. He argues, 'A prominent characteristic of play is its uselessness. It serves no purpose, but is an end in itself. This attitude of play seems to be the only right attitude to God, to our fellow human beings and to creation itself'. Suurmond goes on to say,

> Anyone who tries to prove God's existence by demonstrating the need for God makes the same mistake as those who claim that in our modern secularized society God no longer has any function and has thus become superfluous. Both begin from the usefulness of God. But God is useless.[23]

Using the Sabbath rest as an appropriate symbol for playful celebration in God, Suurmond claims that creation is not the product of some intelligent designer, but the manifestation of the free play between Word (the logos that sets the structure and rules) and Spirit (the free, spontaneous and innovative expression of the divine) in the game of divine Wisdom. Therefore worship is 'useless' (mean-

---

[20] Jürgen Moltmann, *Theology of Play* (trans. Reinhard Ulrich; New York: Harper & Row Publishers, 1972), p. 12. The one caveat Moltmann makes is that the crucifixion cannot and should not be viewed as a moment of play. In the cross play ceases.

[21] Harvey Cox, *Feast of Fools: A Theological Essay on Festivity and Fantasy* (New York: Harper & Row Publishers, 1969), pp. 10-14.

[22] Evans, *Playing*, pp. 21-35.

[23] Jean Jacques Suurmond, *Word and Spirit at Play: Towards a Charismatic Theology* (Grand Rapids, MI: Eerdmans, 1994), p. 29.

ing non-utility) because humans place themselves in the position of an unpretentious child who recognizes the gratuitousness of their existence and through worship enter into the non-coercive and vulnerable game of creation in their participation or play with Word and Spirit.[24] Suurmond's proposal critiques modern atheist strategies that have infiltrated contemporary theology and liturgy as well as the pragmatic underpinnings that contribute to the secularization of Christianity in the West.

Wolfgang Vondey picks up on Suurmond's work and attempts to expand it. Vondey proposes play as an interpretive key to understand the characteristics of global Pentecostalism and as a paradigm shift that has the potential to revitalize the ecumenical crisis of theology, because it creates new theological insights and trajectories. Theology under the grip of modernity has truncated the liminal with its accent in utilitarian usefulness, performance, competition, rationalism, and functionality. In particular, the root metaphor of 'performance' privileges usefulness, purposefulness, productivity, and orderliness over human existence. It gives priority to cognition without an adequate representation of other elements of human life. Conversely, the spontaneity and improvisation of play embodies the gospel in the freedom of the Spirit and full participation of God's people. In worship, Pentecostals engage in discernment with the Spirit in free, unexpected, and transformative ways. Thus play rather than performance is a better metaphor for grounding global theology because it invites all to participate fully rather than to sit passively under the performance of professionals. However, the distinction Vondey makes between performance and play is not as contradictory as he suggests given the use of performance in mimicry noted above.

Moreover, Vondey is interested in rehabilitating the role of the imagination in global theological discourses and believes that Pentecostal liturgies are able to help him in this task. He employs the notion of the pneumatological imagination as an organizing principle in the theology. Taking Amos Yong's work in *Spirit-Word-Community* as his cue,[25] Vondey argues that theological reflection is inspired by the enduring but unfinished dynamic of the pneumatological imagi-

---

[24] Suurmond, *Word and Spirit at Play*, pp. 34-35.

[25] See Amos Yong, *Spirit-Word-Community: Theological Hermeneutics in Trinitarian Perspective* (Eugene, OR: Wipf and Stock, 2002), pp. 119-217.

nation as it points one toward the divine encounter. The unfinished and unlimited capacity of ritual play ignites the pneumatological imagination. This imagination values theological improvisation with the divine, biblical improvisation with Scripture, and ecclesial improvisation in the church.[26] Put another way, in the context of Pentecostal worship, the liminality of playful rituals transform the roles and identities of participants as they anticipate divine encounters in hope for the coming kingdom, the imagination is inspired as if God is reality present and the kingdom is really here. This alternate becomes a hoped for reality that urges Pentecostals to seek and work for the kingdom. For Vondey, ritual play is an invitation to a global theology where everyone has a voice in the global construction of theology.

My choice of the title 'betwixt and between the cross and the eschaton' is deliberate in order to capture the theological range of Pentecostal worship. 'Betwixt and between' is an expression coined by Victor Turner to highlight the liminality of ritual interaction. Crossing the liminal threshold places one in an alternate, subjunctive reality that plays with cultural elements symbols in order to intuit or imagine possible futures. 'Between the cross and the eschaton' is an effort on my part to note the backward looking, historical anchor of Pentecostal spirituality in the life and work of Jesus Christ in the power of the Spirit of Pentecost and the forward looking, eschatological hope of the dawning of the kingdom that one may glimpse in the present in the act of worship. The juxtaposition of 'ritual play' is also deliberate in order to capture the range of sacred time and space. Rituals end. But they also create worlds of unending truth that have no end. Play is unrepeatable with an unknown ending that only ends when the play stops. Ritual incorporates the past and makes the past present. Play defers the present into the future at which point the ending will become clear. Ritual is centripetal and brings people together in the cohesion of social bonds thus forming the sacred community, or to put it in theological language – the church. Play cuts across social bonds and instills newness. Ritual defines boundaries in order to posit wholeness. Ritual opens up to the limitlessness of possibilities that rewrites the

---

[26] Wolfgang Vondey, *Beyond Pentecostalism: The Crisis of Global Christianity and the Renewal of the Theological Agenda* (Grand Rapids: Eerdmans, 2010), pp. 40-44.

boundaries.[27] Ritual play is an eschatological mode that, with and in the Spirit, hopes for things not yet seen.

Conclusion

The goal of this chapter has been twofold. On the one hand, I have drawn upon the insights of ritual studies in the social sciences in order to explicate the role of ritual play in Pentecostal worship. Ritual is a liminal phase that allows participants to explore alternate roles, identities, and realities. By employing a typology of ritual play, various kinds of Pentecostal rituals and rites can be classified and used to understand Pentecostal liturgy as well as its social and theological implications. On the other hand, I have taken the insights from ritual studies to suggest some theological implications of Pentecostal worship. Ritual play offers the believer the opportunity to live, explore, and be influenced by a theological continuum that ranges from the life and work of the crucified one and the early apostles who proclaimed and acted on Christ's initiative, through the present life in the church where the people of God remember and reenact the past in the present, to the future life in the kingdom that is merely glimpsed as a possibility in the present and grasped in hope for its future reality.

---

[27] Seligman *et al.*, *Ritual and its Consequences*, pp. 74-76.

15

FROM 'HALLELUJAH!' TO 'WE BELIEVE' AND BACK: INTERRELATING PENTECOSTAL WORSHIP AND DOCTRINE

Daniel Castelo*

Pentecostals have often self-identified (and perhaps even taken a certain pride with the gesture) as being a people of the Spirit, a group of Jesus-followers who are intent on living out their commitments rather than being wedded to a formalism or rationalism that can represent the height of religious hypocrisy. Pentecostals traditionally have not been about 'man-made creeds' or excessively religious corruption and lethargy; rather, they have been about the kind of 'heart religion' that would prioritize the authority of Scripture and the leading of the Spirit.

These ways of living into the Christian faith are compelling on their particular terms. Pentecostals have always prioritized experiences of the Spirit, ones that were understood to involve changed and transformed lives. This last claim in itself is quite radical for many to accept, and it is in tension with a host of plausibility structures. But such tension is what partly makes the point compelling: There is something to be said for the Christian gospel to be characterized as something dramatic, unexpected, and surprising.

---

* Daniel Castelo (PhD, Duke University) is Professor of Dogmatic and Constructive Theology at Seattle Pacific University and Seminary in Seattle, WA, USA.

At the same time, when one considers the above claims rhetorically, they are potentially misleading. After all, Pentecostals have always been keen to relate their experiences and to situate them within broader theological schematizations. In other words, perhaps despite themselves, Pentecostals have always found it important to engage in the orderly (one could even say systematic) presentation and communication of their experiences all the while denouncing such forms in theory. Put quaintly, early Pentecostals often complained about theologizing and made it a point to characterize theologizing as something 'un-Pentecostal' to do, yet they expressed these warnings and concerns by ... theologizing. Their sense of their role in salvation history, their accounts of what God was doing in the 'latter days', their vision of God's call and the required responses to it – these were all theologically framed through and through. And when disagreements inevitably ensued regarding such narrations, theological disputes emerged. When observers note the reality on the ground, it chastens the rhetoric quite definitively: Pentecostalism in the American context splintered quickly after its founding revivals, and the splintering usually was in terms of theological disputes and contentions. Initial evidence logic, the nature of sanctification in the Christian life, and the viability of trinitarian framings for God-talk – these are indisputably theological concerns. For all the talk that Pentecostals have sustained about themselves regarding how they resist the encroachments of overly systematizing their faith, they have in fact been exemplary purveyors of this tendency.[1]

This tension, detectable in the movement from its very beginnings, points to the spirituality-theology or worship-doctrine interface. How do these two dynamics play out conceptually, and what can their interactions suggest for the ongoing work of Pentecostal theological endeavoring? By way of suggesting answers to such queries, in the following I will raise one example of Pentecostalism's 'anti-formalism' and work through its claims so as to see what is at stake with such concerns. I will subsequently offer some constructive reflections on the spirituality-theology interface so as to freight

---

[1] A significant work that undercuts this rhetoric is Douglas Jacobsen, *Thinking in the Spirit: Theologies of the Early Pentecostal Movement* (Bloomington: Indiana University Press, 2003).

and privilege the term 'worship' as an existential modality out of which Pentecostal theology is expressed and so pursued.

A Test-Case

Richard G. Spurling is one of the early figures of the American Pentecostal movement. He and his family were some of the pioneers of what would become the Church of God (Cleveland, TN) and its denominational progeny. By all appearances, he was a man of deep commitment who longed for God and God's reign in his own day. That longing is articulated in a little pamphlet titled *The Lost Link*.[2] In it, Spurling speaks of his desire to see the church be renewed so that it could reclaim its first love. Part of this call can be substantiated from details of his life: Spurling was a maverick of sorts who ran into some trouble with Baptist life in Appalachia when he began to resist conformity to some of his denomination's beliefs. He was a licensed minister, but he was asked to give up his credentials. Ultimately, he was a man searching for greater depth-dimensions in the Christian life, a process that began in earnest in 1884. By 1886, Spurling and others were making their concerns known, and they were met with resistance and scorn. Interestingly, they saw a need for a greater reform than the Protestant Reformers ushered since the latter failed to 'reform from creeds, they adopted the law of faith when they should have adopted the law of love; and third, they failed to reserve a right of way for the leadership of the Holy Ghost and conscience'.[3] As the figurehead of a new movement emerging in 1886, Spurling's desire was that primitive Christianity be restored and a union of all denominations be established. His call to an assembly on 19 August 1886 – one that could be considered the official beginnings of the Church of God – included the following:

> As many Christians as are here present that are desirous to be free from all man-made creeds and traditions, and are willing to take the New Testament, or law of Christ, for your only rule of faith and practice; give each other equal rights and privilege to

---

[2] R.G. Spurling, *The Lost Link* (Turtletown, TN, n.p., 1920); subsequently republished by White Wing Publishing House.

[3] L. Howard Juillerat, *Book of Minutes* (Cleveland, TN: Church of God Publishing House, 1922), pp. 7-8, as quoted in Charles W. Conn, *Like a Mighty Army* (Cleveland, TN: Pathway Press, 1977), pp. 6-7.

read and interpret for yourselves as your conscience may dictate, and are willing to sit together as the Church of God to transact business as the same, come forward.[4]

The Lost Link helps substantiate these claims a bit more. Straightaway, Spurling remarks that what follows in this pamphlet's pages has doctrinal implications and on occasion has been shaped doxologically: 'I have prayed, studied and preached on the doctrines which I do here set forth in the following pages by songs and short lecture, all pointing to a needed reformation among God's people'.[5] On the basis of this quote, one would think that Spurling is not against doctrines per se, for he admitted that he himself was offering some in his pamphlet. But in the bulk of what follows in this work Spurling makes a case for a distinction between the law of Christ and man-made laws. As noted above, the law of Christ is the law of love, the law of unity, and the law of liberty. All are to follow the prompting of the Spirit to read the New Testament as the Spirit guides them with the aim of fulfilling the great love commandments. Naturally, these are not negative claims in the least. But the pronounced focus of the pamphlet is on the insufficiency and idolatry of what are termed 'man-made creeds'. *The Lost Link* is best understood as a critique of denominationalism, and it is to this feature of the work we now turn for its implications for the task of doctrinal formulation.

No doubt speaking out of his own experience, Spurling finds that denominationalism breeds a kind of conformity that goes against the working of the Spirit. Notice how potentially autobiographical is the following: 'The commandment of God has been so abused that no sect of earth is willing to let their brother read, believe and practice for themselves. Read it like we see it and do as our doctrine says or we will exclude you from our church'.[6] In this case, 'doctrine' seems to be those belief-structures that denominations artificially develop to create boundaries between themselves and others. Doctrines function, in other words, as barriers to Christian unity. Interestingly, Spurling makes the case for his tendency by drawing on no less of an event than the Council of Nicaea. Spurling

---

[4] Juillerat, *Book of Minutes*, p. 8, as quoted in Conn, *Like a Mighty Army*, p. 8.
[5] Spurling, *The Lost Link*, p. 7.
[6] Spurling, *The Lost Link*, p. 14.

cites some of the historical and theological happenings surrounding the Arian challenge and goes on to say,

> Constantine caused [the Council] to make the Nicaean creed by which Arius was condemned as a heretic, and expelled him and his followers from their fellowship and communion *regardless of their love for God and one another.* One party became the Catholic church and the other the Arian church, each following their creed instead of God's law. This change gave birth to creeds and every creed has made a sect or denomination.[7]

Again, one can guess that Spurling's sympathetic reading of the Arians is driven in part by his own experience; Arius, like himself, should have been first and foremost considered in terms of how he lived out the 'lost link' rather than how well he fit into a doctrinal apparatus.

Spurling has a very difficult time admitting the value of creeds and articles of faith. He says that these are necessarily fallible, and on that basis they are unreliable since they would not be in conformity to God's word.[8] He makes this broad assessment of ecclesiastical history:

> For centuries we have been under creeds or doctrines and instead of unity it makes division; instead of peace they make strife; instead of unity they bring discord; instead of love they bring hatred … So on goes all the creed systems, the blind leading the blind and falling into the ditch of the apostasy.[9]

Earlier he levels the following indictment: 'It is impossible to teach the doctrines and commandments of men and not insult the Holy Ghost'.[10]

What are we to make of Spurling's claims? On the one hand, it is difficult to deny that he has a point. In his own life and in the case of many others, people have been excluded from denominational fellowships for simply not falling in line with the status quo, one that is often driven (as Spurling sensed) by power arrangements that betray an agenda of godlessness and so infidelity and idolatry. Spurl-

---

[7] Spurling, *The Lost Link*, p. 23 (emphasis added).
[8] Spurling, *The Lost Link*, p. 19.
[9] Spurling, *The Lost Link*, p. 26.
[10] Spurling, *The Lost Link*, p. 25.

ing warns, 'If you want to see a church scattered, just pull the string of church doctrines and you can destroy more good than the greatest revivalist can do'.[11] Apparently, Spurling's alternative is to allow a certain open-endedness to the dynamic of what people would come to believe on the basis of God's Word. This liberty, of course, is within a pneumatological dynamic, as he remarks,

> Dear reader, ask the Lord to help you to know the truth and to obey it. If we have right to anything in the world, it is to read God's Word. He has promised to give His Spirit to His people and what he wants is perfect love to God and each other and perfect liberty. As Archard says in his history, Liberty of the soul is the breath and element of that religion inculcated in the New Testament.[12]

If doctrines function regulatively, they could take the place of a dynamism that should exist between the Bible, the Spirit, and the believer. Without this dynamism, we are back to the formalism of religious hypocrisy, the kind so blatantly and repeatedly decried by the Scriptures themselves. All in all, one comes away from reading *The Lost Link* with the impression that doctrines, creeds, and articles of religion are fallible, humanly contrived, artificial, divisive, and so unnecessary to the life of faith. This kind of sensibility secured through these rhetorical forms, I would guess, is not limited to Spurling but very much a part of the ethos of early Pentecostal life. I would imagine that the classical Pentecostal denominations, to the degree that they continue to be in continuity with their originating conditions, are still haunted by such rhetorical framings and evaluations, even despite developing 'declarations' or 'statements' of their beliefs with the passing of time.

One of the main difficulties with Spurling's proposals has to do with an early remark that was quoted above. Spurling is willing to grant that what he has on offer in *The Lost Link* is a set of 'doctrines' even as he goes on to denounce 'man-made' doctrines and creeds. In other words, Spurling grants for himself a certain privilege that is difficult to sustain on its own terms: Churchly doctrines are man-made fallible constructs that are all the negative things said above, but such a charge does not apply to the doctrines he himself

---

[11] Spurling, *The Lost Link*, p. 37.
[12] Spurling, *The Lost Link*, p. 42.

is espousing in *The Lost Link*. Has Spurling inevitably indicted himself? If his claims are true, should they not be applied to himself and all that he says in *The Lost Link* as well? And if not, what legitimates this place of privilege in Spurling's case?

My goal through this explored example is not to draw away from Spurling, either in terms of his own integrity or the importance of his contribution as summarized in *The Lost Link*. But I do wish to show that the general impression of doctrines which is communicated in this document is insufficiently developed. Doctrines can function in the way Spurling describes – as tools for conformity that work against spiritual vitality – but they need not operate in such a way (as the very existence of *The Lost Link* assumes). What Spurling is essentially doing is calling into question a certain way of framing doctrines *through his own doctrinal proposal*, one that from its beginning proclaims, 'But before the reader can feel the need of a reformation from the laws of men to the laws of Christ he should have the law of God put in his heart and written in his mind'.[13] The underdevelopment of *The Lost Link* leads us back to the spirituality-theology interface. What roles do doctrines play in the embodiment, pursuit, and perpetuation of Christian spirituality?

The Spirituality-Theology Dynamic

In my proposal on Pentecostal ethics, I have sought to develop the social – particularly ecclesial – dimensions of the practice of Pentecostal spirituality.[14] I chose this approach in part because I wished to honor how I have typically understood Pentecostal spirituality to be from the beginnings of its classical forms: Usually, the context of Pentecostal revivalism and the fostering of Pentecostal spirituality had deeply embedded communal dimensions. The idea that the movement simply 'fell out of heaven' falls short on the basis of historical, social, cultural, and theological narratives; and the notion that this spirituality came to be and took off because of a kind of unmediated individual encounter with God repeated in sundry cases does not usually hold up to 'thick descriptions' of happenings as they unfolded. I agree with Spurling in the quote above: I believe

---

[13] Spurling, *The Lost Link*, p. 7.
[14] Daniel Castelo, *Revisioning Pentecostal Ethics – The Epicletic Community* (Cleveland, TN: CPT Press, 2012).

readers of his pamphlet as well as other theological materials should have the law of God put in their hearts and written in their minds. The all-important question for me is, And *how* does this process take effect? To say simply one needs a 'God-encounter' is insufficient to me, for how one describes such an encounter, what one comes to expect of such an encounter, and the effects that in turn become registered from such an encounter are all deeply constituted by wider commitments shaped within the conditions of 'ordinary time'. As favorable as the imagery of the Day of Pentecost happenings documented in Acts 2 is for Pentecostals – one that speaks of a mighty rushing wind suddenly coming and anointing those gathered with tongues as of fire – other features of the happenings are equally important to note, including the waiting and organizational actions depicted in Acts 1, as well as the communal experiments of holding all things in common toward the latter part of Acts 2.

Why are these details worth noting? Because running in the early Pentecostal literature (and this would apply to other Pietist traditions as well) is a focus on the affective dimensions of Christian existence.[15] It is the affective register that can account for such things as the need for the law of God to be put in a person's heart and mind. In other words, Pentecostal spirituality is characterized, enlivened, and perpetuated all with a vital sense that it is affectively grounded through and through. And yet, that this point can be registered in a medium like this one (a book chapter) suggests that the affective can traffic in some conceptual or linguistic sense, not so that (to use tropes that may be misleading but necessary for the sake of clarification) the 'textual' takes the place of the 'existential' but that the 'textual' and the 'existential' demonstrate themselves to be much more closely aligned than some narrations would have it. To use the language another way, 'texts' can create 'experiences' and 'experiences' can create 'texts'. Put a third way, one may have some kind of affective development that one comes to label 'an encounter with God', or one may read about such experiences and go on to seek and experience them at some point in the future.

It is this kind of dynamic that precisely makes the spirituality-theology divide much more complicated than many would have it.

---

[15] I am using 'Pietist' in the way it is registered by Jason Vickers, 'Holiness and Mediation: Pneumatology in Pietist Perspective', *International Journal of Systematic Theology* 16.2 (2014), pp. 192-206.

It is certainly more involving than simply a narration that would label the dimension of spirituality 'primary' and the theological as 'secondary' so that the latter is always a byproduct or elaboration of the former. Notice the implications of Rom. 10.17, which would be that faith comes through hearing the word of Christ. If one grants that 'the word of Christ' can take any number of possible forms and is ultimately driven by the Spirit's work through persons, places, and things, then the idea of 'primary' and 'secondary' forms of privilege within the spirituality-theology interface – forms that are so prevalent in Pietist traditions and even at work in Spurling's *The Lost Link* – just does not account for the complexity involved. Of course, no one wishes to dispute the importance of such long-standing claims within the Christian consciousness such as 'faith seeking understanding' or 'I believe in order to understand'; the question to be pressed, however, is if the binary is sustainable, if faith/belief does not carry with it some assumed sense of (possibly renewed) understanding in order for it to be faith/belief in the first place. Rather than a blind leap into the unknown, is not faith best understood as a form of trust predicated upon some kind of disclosure and so understanding of the One in whom one believes/trusts? Again, what is being problematized here is the strong disjunction often at work in discussions related to the spirituality-theology interface, which can also be understood in terms of other contrastives (including 'God's work' and 'human work'). Contrary to Spurling and others, I tend to believe the interface to be quite convoluted and messy, and rather than unfortunate characteristics, I wish to suggest that such qualities of indeterminacy and complexity precisely constitute the life of the disciple as *pneumatikos* to its core in a generative and enlivening way.

Worship as Life and Doctrines as Worship

In the aforementioned work on ethics, I speak of the existential modality of worship. I need to clarify here that for me 'worship' is not simply an activity one does on Sunday mornings as part of 'having church'. For my constructive proposals, 'worship' suggests a way of being. It points to a 'master modality' so to speak in that it captures a working sense of human meaningfulness so beautifully captured by the Westminster Catechism: 'What is the chief end of [humanity]? To glorify God, and to enjoy [God] forever'. In this sense, there is no distinction between 'ordinary' and 'sacred' time, for all time is 'sacred' in that it takes place before and alongside the God of Christian confession. As humans, we are nothing more and nothing less than worshipers, and in fallen and broken conditions, we are called to nothing more and nothing less than to be worshipers of the living God. If such claims do not seem compelling or adequate, it may be that an impoverished or reductive account of worship is at play. Again, for me, 'worship' is not simply what one does at choice moments but part of the narrative Christians use for describing who they are and how they live and participate in the world. 'Worship' points to the conditions and possibilities for the God-honoring and God-enjoying form of life.

If one can think and speak of 'worship' in such a way, the 'textual' and the 'existential' can play roles in this dynamic. This can be so because at the heart of a vision of life as worship is a prevalent, thoroughgoing account of the presence and work of the Spirit in and alongside all things. That humans are fundamentally called to be worshipers is predicated upon the call for them to be Spirit-bearers. To live, move, and have one's being in the Spirit means to speak, think, and act in the Spirit. Within this economy, the work of God (in which the law of God is put in hearts and minds) and the work of God-fearers and God-lovers (who bear witness to that which they have seen, heard, and felt concerning the Word of Life) need not be pitted against one another. Certainly, humans can sin against the Spirit and frustrate, quench, and blaspheme the Spirit. Doctrines can be put to use in such dynamics. But humans, by the grace of God, can worship God, bless God, and confess God. In this sense, they can be conduits of the Spirit's work on earth, signs and first-fruits of an eschatologically framed reign. Doctrines can be put to use within this dynamic and toward these alternative ends, too, as indicators and gestures by which the church comes to confess God, stay faithful to God, and render its account of who God is and what God has done and is doing.

One of the most distinguishable and important contributions Pietist traditions such as Pentecostalism make to the whole of the Christian *oikoumene* is the valuation that the point of Christian existence is for the human to render praise. The most fundamental thing a Christian in Christian community can do is to render one lifelong, heartfelt 'Hallelujah!' to the God who is the source and end of all things, including the works of creation, salvation, and healing. Spurling intuitively knew this; one could even say that this is very much at the heart of what he sees as 'the lost link'. The privileging of the laws of Christ, 'the great law of love', 'fellowshipping each other by the law of love' – Spurling uses a variety of expressions to account for this fundamental commitment of Pietist faith. Since this lifelong, heartfelt 'Hallelujah!' involves the embodiment and performance of a human life, then all dimensions of that life can be located within this one goal. One such dimension can be doctrinal formulation. When operating optimally, doctrines are not ideological touchpoints that beckon outward conformity for ultimately human-driven ends. On the contrary, they can and often do function in a God-honoring way by being expressions of a worshipful community that help it stay faithful to its calling to abide in God as God abides in it. The Spirit can bring about doctrines, work through doctrines, and change and even overturn doctrines as necessary as God-seeking communities strive after God in the dynamics of quotidian existence. How the Spirit does so (and how one would know if such is the case) is obviously a discernment issue, which is another longstanding challenge of any people who long to live into their calling to be Spirit-bearers. If we may put that matter to the side, however, the point being registered here is that doctrines can be conduits of the Spirit's presence and work. To use the Wesleyan language, they can be 'means of grace' that the Spirit employs to sanctify and heal a people, and as such, their use and appropriation can be but one other expression of the church's collective 'Hallelujah!' here on earth.

'Man-Made' Denominations and God-Ordained Uses

When classical Pentecostalism transitioned to denominational forms, significant transitions took place. In the case of Spurling's progeny, a number of groups emerged, including the Church of God (Cleveland, TN). Part of American denominational life is the formulization of 'creedal-like' statements of belief. In the case of the Church of God, it now has a 'Declaration of Faith' of fourteen points, and simply on first blush one cannot help but wonder if the document represents something like a 'man-made' creed of the type

Spurling so vehemently denounced. For those who find the association more than appropriate, a 'fall narrative' is tempting, one that involves the desire for the Church of God to be like other evangelical denominations on the American landscape, as demonstrated in its formal inclusion into the National Association of Evangelicals (NAE) in the 1940s and the formulation of its 'Declaration of Faith' in that very same decade. When the Church of God succumbed to these pressures – so the narrative goes – it betrayed an important feature of its heritage. From the other side of the spectrum, some could argue that formulizing a statement of beliefs is practically necessary for a group of the size and complexity like the Church of God was becoming. Various forms of ministry, sundry engagements with the wider world, increasing members at the lay and clergy levels – these are all important factors that necessarily contribute pressure to the devising of such a document.

Whichever account is appealing to students of this history, the persistent question to be raised in relation to documents like the Church of God's 'Declaration of Faith' has to do with the establishment of identity. Spurling's *The Lost Link* raises the question of identity within the following binary: Is a document like this infallible or fallible? Obviously, he would go on to say, it has to be fallible since only one infallible standard of truth exists, namely the Bible. The problem with Spurling's framing, of course, is the strong differentiation between Scripture and all else in terms of available ecclesial authorities. Although I cannot consider the matter extensively here,[16] the framing is problematic on both scores. The valuation of Scripture as infallible in the way Spurling seems to suggest pictures it as a kind of epistemological foundation that potentially takes away from its role as a sanctified and sanctifying text. And, on the other hand, God can and does use 'man-made' things to bring glory to God, be they church structures, anointing oil, musical instruments, and – most pressingly for Pentecostals – other human bodies in terms of tongues, laying on of hands, shouting, singing, and so on. Doctrines would fit into such possibilities as well.

The question to be posed to Pentecostals as they consider the task of doctrine-making is: What role do doctrines (as displayed in

---

[16] For my take on these matters see my *Pneumatology: A Guide for the Perplexed* (London: Bloomsbury T&T Clark, 2015), particularly chapter 5.

'declarations' or 'statements' of faith) play in denominational life? The question here is ultimately one of *function* or *use*. To understand what doctrines are (the identity question) in a particular context requires an answer related to the way they are used. This kind of inquiry would involve pragmatic and teleological concerns: How are these documents used, and what are they used for? If the answer is that statements of faith are primarily used to regulate who is in and who is out of a particular denomination, it is hard to envision escaping from features of Spurling's impassioned analysis. We would be back to the problem he worried about over a century ago. If the answer would be otherwise, however, a different tack would be possible.

What if such statements could point to the 'holy mysteries' of faith, not strictly in terms of defining them for the sake of memory and rehearsal but as invitational prompts to 'taste and see that the LORD is good' (Ps. 34.8)? In other words, what would 'denominational life' look like if Pentecostal groups would actively seek to 'indoctrinate' in such a way so that a claim about the resurrection or the authority of Scripture or the nature of the sanctified and Spirit-baptized life has in turn some level of experiential concretization in the worshipful life of the people of God? The links would have to be intentionally made and pronounced, which is no small task since it would require the kind of disciplining of church life in a way that what is said about itself and its beliefs is actually available and performed in communal life. For instance, I can only imagine how difficult it would be to confess 'divine healing in the atonement' if one has never experienced or seen a miracle take place. Or I can only fathom what people may come to associate with the claim 'holiness is God's standard' when holiness language is considered either archaic or synonymous with legalism. And, obviously (and to some degree shamefully), there is the challenge of 'seeing' and witnessing the prompts for the second coming of Christ, which were so key for past generations of Pentecostals and yet so ignored and unavailable today.

Perhaps specific denominations and churches already engage in such a process to some degree. Again, though, I am not suggesting that the question of use and function is settled via the rehearsal of these documents periodically in worship settings or their memorization by new converts. Those uses are helpful to some degree, but they would not be in themselves full expressions of the role *sacra doctrina* is to play in the church's life. To return to Spurling's original call: Unquestionably, we all need the law of God put in our hearts and written in our minds. This process can be understood to take place when the Spirit emboldens a people to take the following charge: That their speech and common life are increasingly aligned in a way that one reflects and mutually reinforces the other with the end that the God who is the beginning and end of all life is rightfully, fittingly, and lovingly praised.

Index of Biblical (and Other Ancient) References

Index of Names

34492647R00176

Made in the USA
San Bernardino, CA
30 May 2016